"Ian Waddell was a parliam[...] effective, always thoughtful [...] Canada's national interest."

　　– Brian Mulroney, former prime minister of Canada

"The best damn Liberal in the NDP. Always a fighter for the little guy, and he was nice to his mother too!"

　　– Sheila Copps, former MP and cabinet minister

"Readers are in for a treat as Ian Waddell pulls back the curtain on some of Canada's biggest political and parliamentary events. What shines through is a consistent commitment to justice, particularly through the Berger Inquiry and the evolution of legally recognized Indigenous rights."

　　– Elizabeth May, leader of the Green Party of Canada

"Ian Waddell has been a champion for water security and water justice long before most Canadians knew our water was vulnerable to corporate and foreign control. He knows the threat to our water is greater than ever as the planet and our continent are facing a water crisis. Read his book and take up the torch for water."

　　– Maude Barlow, Council of Canadians

"Ian Waddell rewrote our constitution, laid the foundation for Canada's thriving film industry, broke down cultural barriers and inspired a generation of young people to engage in politics. A gifted lawyer, MP and film producer, Ian's boundless energy, enthusiasm and zest for life inspires those who are lucky to know him."

　　– Dylan Playfair, actor

TAKE THE TORCH:
A Political Memoir

IAN WADDELL

Take the Torch

A Political Memoir

NIGHTWOOD EDITIONS

2018

Nightwood Editions
P.O. Box 1779
Gibsons, BC VON 1VO
Canada
www.nightwoodeditions.com

COVER DESIGN & TYPOGRAPHY: Carleton Wilson
COVER PHOTOGRAPH: Joshua Berson
All interior photographs are from the author's own collection.

Nightwood Editions acknowledges the support of the Canada Council for the Arts,
which last year invested $153 million to bring the arts to Canadians throughout the
country. We also gratefully acknowledge financial support from the Government of
Canada and from the Province of British Columbia through the BC Arts Council
and the Book Publishing Tax Credit.

This book has been produced on 100% post-consumer recycled,
ancient-forest-free paper, processed chlorine-free
and printed with vegetable-based dyes.

Printed and bound in Canada.

CIP data available from Library and Archives Canada.

ISBN 978-0-88971-347-5

to Isabel and Frankie

CONTENTS

Prologue

Harry Chingee, chief of the Sekani people, was showing me how to cast a fly rod. My friend Jack Woodward was wading in the middle of the fast-flowing river. We were near the town of Mackenzie, in the middle of British Columbia, though it seemed like the North to me. Sitting on the grassy riverbank below Harry's log house, I was far from my birthplace of Glasgow and even from Vancouver, where I had "emigrated" via Toronto and set up a law practice. Jack and I were representing the Sekani for a Royal Commission hearing whose purpose I have long since forgotten. What I haven't forgotten is the story of how these people, Harry's people, were displaced from their homes ten years earlier by the flooding that created Williston Lake when the W.A.C. Bennett hydroelectric dam was built on the Peace River in 1968.

Later that week Jack and I, along with a probation officer named Jim Fulton, flew in a small plane over the vast reservoir behind the Bennett dam. We heard that many of the trees had been left standing in the river valley before the flooding. Hydro had said there was no market for the wood, and besides, they were in a hurry! But now those trees would sometimes rise up from the floor of Williston Lake, shooting to the surface like ballistic missiles. Occasionally they hit Sekani canoes, holing or capsizing them. Other times the canoes would get caught in a tangle of debris. People had died in both types of incident.

As our catch sizzled in butter in a small pan by the water's edge, a couple of big logging trucks thundered along the road past Harry's house. "Are they your trucks?" I asked Harry.

"Are you kidding?" he replied. "They belong to the logging company, and they come and go as they please."

"But what of your rights, Harry?" I asked in my earnest-young-lawyer voice.

I thought I was familiar with Aboriginal rights in Canada. I had read the 1973 Calder case, a foundational case in Aboriginal law, in which Canada's Supreme Court acknowledged that Aboriginal title to land existed before colonization. And I had spent three years with Tom Berger, the lawyer who argued the Calder case, as his assistant on the historic pipeline inquiry in the Northwest Territories. But I was discovering that I still had a lot to learn.

Later as we relaxed by a crackling fire in Harry's home, I pressed him again. Harry is a quiet man. But after a long pause he replied, "Ian, I can't stop those damn trucks. I don't have that kind of power." I inquired what he would ask for if he were to have some say over the loggers. He told me his people just wanted to be recognized and included, to have a "piece of the action," by which he meant having a say in the place and pace of development around them. Then and there I decided that I wanted to be part of making Harry's wish happen.

Before we left the town of Mackenzie, Harry Chingee took Jack Woodward, Jim Fulton, Liz Fulton and me up a bumpy logging road to the top of Morfee Mountain, a small mountain near town. At the summit, a small group of Sekani were having a late-afternoon picnic. I recognized some of them from the hearings. One in particular, a good friend of Harry's, seemed like a sort of spiritual leader. As we watched the sun set, we did a little dance, holding hands (it was the 1970s after all). Jim and I had just confessed that we were going to try to win the federal NDP nominations in Skeena (for Jim) and Vancouver Kingsway (for me). Both would be tough nomination fights, and we knew it would be even tougher to knock off the incumbents in the general election, which would have to be called sometime in 1979. Harry's friend told Jim and me that we were both going to win. Everyone cheered. I thought we all must be stoned!

I have always had a revolutionary idea about law: that it is about justice and that it can be used to make change in society. That's why I started as a criminal lawyer, and why I went on to be a storefront lawyer, assistant to Tom Berger, and then a member of both the federal parliament and the BC legislative assembly. What I love about Canada is that we are still a young country and still a place where you can make change happen. In this book I describe some of those changes—many of them are big changes, historic events for our country and our people; others are tiny incidents that helped only one person or a small group, but they're still important. Often I played a minor role, but my part was big enough to give me an inside look at how change happens. I try to write in plain English, which can be difficult for a lawyer. And I tell a lot of stories, probably too many stories—about the fights we won and lost, the actions we took, and the lessons we learned—served up with a touch of humour because, from time immemorial, people have remembered, enjoyed and learned from stories. I wanted to create a kind of road map, landing somewhere between the practical and the visionary, that shows how it is possible to make social change.

I start with the first consumer class-action lawsuit in Canada. Then I describe the historic Berger Inquiry into the Mackenzie Valley Pipeline, where the modern environmental and Indigenous rights movements started to come of age, and my election to the Canadian parliament,

With Pierre Elliott Trudeau.

where I was thrown into the fire as a young NDP energy critic when Prime Minister Trudeau (Pierre, not Justin) brought in the National Energy Program, pitting the West against the East. These issues of law, rights, environment and energy are just as relevant today. I continue with the repatriation of our constitution from Britain in 1982, and the drafting of Section 35, the Aboriginal rights amendment that finally gave Chief Chingee and his people some real power over their land and their future. Now they could stop the logging trucks if they wanted. And pipelines too.

After that I show how an ordinary member of parliament, with some luck and commitment, can help shape international policy—in this case the creation of the International Criminal Court. Then I go from the federal House of Commons to the provincial legislature of British Columbia (though not willingly). I try to show the difference between the two jurisdictions, describing my role as a provincial minister in Vancouver/Whistler's successful Olympic bid and the expansion of the film industry into Hollywood North.

When I left politics—or was fired by my constituents—I was at loose ends for a few years, practising law and doing a fair amount of travelling. I realized people didn't know how politics work on the ground, so I thought I'd produce a little documentary showing the inside workings of an election campaign: how phone banks work to raise money and get out the vote; the role of the campaign manager, the candidate, the volunteers; how platforms are developed, and speeches and ads written. But as the movie developed, it turned into a film about young people voting, or not voting. In the process of producing that movie, I rediscovered my own journey, using law and politics to tackle the big issues of my time. I also saw how this new generation could do the same.

So in this book I try to pass on some of the lessons I learned about setting goals for social change and the methods to use to get there. You might find some of my "methods" strange. They go from debating, protesting and marching, to "biting dogs" at press conferences (following the old adage "dog bites man is not a story; man bites dog is a headline"), writing op-ed pieces for newspapers, getting elected, taking on prime ministers, dictators and kings, grabbing maces, lobbying diplomats in the lobby of the United Nations and bucking your own party. Even writing novels.

We may be in the midst of a technological revolution, but we don't have to reinvent the wheel. Old lessons can be applied to new challenges. My recent work with young people in the film industry has shown me youth today are smart, as committed as my generation and looking for ways to make social change. I do hope people of my generation, through this book, can relive some of their history—maybe with a few fresh insights. I hope a new generation of political activists will find they can use some of these techniques to "bite their own dogs," as they will inevitably need to do to make Canada and the world better places. But above all I wanted to tell my story of how we got to where we are today. Commentator Bruce Anderson, on a CBC-TV panel, lamented the fact that unlike their American counterparts, most Canadian politicians go to their graves with secrets and inside stories of Canadian history. Well, not this one!

Ian Waddell
Vancouver, BC

CHAPTER I

Community Law

Class Action

Every time I look at the stone lions in front of the Vancouver Art Gallery, I think of our justice system. You see, the gallery used to be the main Vancouver courthouse. And as a cathedral puts people in awe of God, the size and scale of this courthouse, with its porticos, inner rotunda and columns, were meant to put people in awe of authority and the law. Well, it is awesome, but it didn't provoke fear in everyone. Not in Karen Chastain.

In 1972 I was director of the Vancouver Community Legal Assistance Society (VCLAS) when Karen, a mature student at Simon Fraser University, came into our small storefront office on East 11th Avenue, then a poorer part of Vancouver's East Side. She was there to complain that she had been required to pay a security deposit before her hydro was hooked up. She had lived in Hope, BC and had not been asked for a deposit. She had paid her bills regularly. Why did Hydro need a security deposit now?

It turned out that Karen Chastain was not alone. David Mossop, my assistant counsel at VCLAS, soon discovered that BC Hydro was demanding security deposits from students, unemployed people, artists and generally anybody it thought might not pay their bills. (We found out later that Hydro had not a bit of evidence to back up this assumption.) The deposits ranged from fifty to seventy dollars (and remember, this is in 1970 dollars when the *Globe* newspaper cost fifteen cents) and the demands were accompanied by a threat that if the deposit was not paid, power and gas would be cut off. When the customers closed their accounts and the deposits were returned, Hydro didn't even pay interest on the money it had collected from these, its poorest customers.

David Mossop is a rumpled figure, slow speaking but with a scorching sense of humour and a good legal mind. With a little research he was able to find old legal cases I had never heard of. He found one case where a utility, a government monopoly in Ontario, had charged one company one rate and another company another rate. The court held that the monopoly could not randomly discriminate against customers. Armed with this we wrote to Hydro, asking on what legal authority it was charging these people for security deposits. The utility's response was basically "We are BC Hydro and we can do what we want." (Later when we were in court, Hydro lawyer R.D. Strilive argued that Hydro was not a public utility but a superpower authority created by statute for a specific purpose. Just to give some context for younger readers, in those days W.A.C. "Wacky" Bennett was premier of British Columbia and the most powerful guy in the province, and Hydro was his baby. This may have been how it came to have super powers!)

Shortly before Karen Chastain came into our office, I had been in Washington, DC for a conference of community lawyers. US president Lyndon Johnson, in his "War on Poverty," had established many community programs including one that placed legal offices, staffed by young lawyers, in poorer areas of the country. These lawyers gave the community programs legal advice, just as corporate lawyers advised big corporations that hired them. Subsequently, President Richard Nixon and his successors trimmed or eliminated nearly all of the local anti-poverty programs except the law offices. Lawyers are, after all, hard to kill. Ask Shakespeare. The offices still exist today. Recently a certain community lawyer by the name of Obama did well in US politics—he had worked for three years as director of the Developing Communities Project (DCP) in Chicago.

But back then in the early 1970s, at the Washington community law office in a ghetto within sight of the magnificent US Capitol, I learned about a new American concept, the "class-action lawsuit," in which you sued on behalf of a number of people suffering from the same illegal action. This is in contrast to the usual lawsuit, in which one person sues another person, business or government. Mossop and I decided to frame our Hydro action using this new class-action concept. We got a young law student by the name of Philip Rankin, as well as my brother Al Waddell, to add their names to the action so it read "Karen Chastain, Philip Rankin, Alistair Waddell, suing on behalf of themselves and suing on behalf of all other individual persons in residential premises being required to pay security deposits or who have paid security deposits to the British Columbia Hydro and Power Authority for the supply of gas and electrical power, plaintiffs, versus British Columbia Hydro and Power Authority, defendant."

As we worked on the lawsuit, we also had to worry about costs, which you have to pay to the other side if you lose the case. Dorothy Jacques, an older lawyer at VCLAS, who had more common sense than David and I did, suggested we put the matter before our board of directors. Our directors had been concerned that the board did not represent a broad enough political spectrum, so we had gone to the big Vancouver law firm of Ladner, Downs and recruited a big-C Conservative lawyer, John Fraser. At the meeting of the board where I advanced the case against Hydro for court action over security deposits, John Fraser spoke first, saying that justice demanded we do the case, and to hell with the risk of lost costs! (This is the same John Fraser who later, as a Conservative MP and Speaker of the Canadian House of Commons, had to discipline me when I grabbed the parliamentary mace. More on that later.)

So it was on a cloudy October day that David and I, in our legal gowns, joined by Karen, Phil and Al, waited nervously under the moulded plastic rosettes and cartouches of the courthouse's great rotunda for a courtroom and a judge. It helps to have a good judge. In those days the chance of getting a progressive judge was like playing Russian roulette with six bullets in the chamber. The legendary Fred Messenger, who had already been working at the court for nearly twenty years, was in charge of allocating the cases to the various courtrooms. Our case was sent to a certain courtroom but we were second on the list. That meant we had to wait until the first case finished and then face a judge who, to put it politely, was very "old school" and probably would have summarily thrown our case out.

After a short wait, though, Fred came to get us. He had found an empty courtroom and a judge, Mr. Justice William McIntyre, who had been on the bench about five years, which made him comparatively new and fresh in relation to the other judges. When he entered at the highest point of the wood-panelled courtroom, we all obediently stood up. The hierarchy in front of, and lower than, the judge's bench started with the clerks, then the lawyers and their clients, and ended with the public rows. Witnesses sat just below the judge, the theory being if you sit next to God, you'd better tell the truth.

Justice McIntyre was mostly silent during the five-day trial. A good listener, he only corrected Mossop and me when we called Hydro "extortionists." He smiled slightly when in response to Hydro counsel's offer to open Hydro's books, I agreed, saying, "That would achieve what every opposition politician has asked for since Hydro was created." McIntyre ruled the offer irrelevant. I had little experience in civil law cases. In fact, this was my first one. My time as a city prosecutor, where I would deal with up to five cases a day, gave me the confidence I needed (that, and being twenty-nine years old!).

On October 31, when both sides finished presenting their arguments, the judge reserved his decision. A week later, at the swearing-in of a new judge, Nancy Morrison, who had been a city prosecutor with me and was a Saskatchewan friend of Judge McIntyre, Mossop and I saw our judge. He told us to expect a decision before the end of the year. Mossop thought he was smiling. The decision did "come down," as lawyers say:

> The mere fact that the defendant (Hydro) is not subject to the provisions of the *Public Utilities Act* does not alter its essential character. It partakes so much of the nature of a public utility that it must be amenable to the law governing public utilities. For the great majority of the people of British Columbia and for all the plaintiffs joined or represented in this action, the defendant has a monopoly on the supply of gas and electricity.

So, Judge McIntyre continued, as a public utility and a monopoly, it can't discriminate amongst its customers. A security deposit required of some customers but not others was discrimination. Thus he allowed an injunction banning Hydro from collecting or keeping deposits. We won!

Hydro was ordered to repay $350,000 to 12,500 people—and, to rub it in, the new Minister of Natural Resources, NDP MLA Bob Williams, ordered them to pay 6 percent interest. Our clients were pictured on the front pages of the local newspapers. About a week after the decision I got a phone call from John Farris QC, probably the top civil lawyer in the province, senior partner in Farris and Company, and later chief justice of BC. He said, "Mr. Waddell, I have been instructed by the BC Government to appeal Justice McIntyre's decision. We can agree, I assume, that the injunction will not take effect if at all until after the appeal."

My reply: "Thank you, Mr. Farris, but I wouldn't make that assumption." In other words, pay the money back now. Mossop, eyebrows raised, said, "You said what?!"

A few days later I got another phone call from John Farris. This time he said, "I have been instructed by the new premier [Dave Barrett of the

Being sworn in to the House of Commons.

NDP] to abandon the appeal." And to his credit he added, "Congratulations, Ian." Forty years later, Mossop wryly told the Community Legal Assistance Society's anniversary gathering that we had arranged to win the 1972 provincial election to prevent an appeal. That drew a big laugh.

Oddly, there was not much discussion in the actual judgment or elsewhere on the class action itself. Unlike other huge changes in the law, our case was never litigated at the Appeal Court or Supreme Court of Canada. Gradually the written or "statute" law changed. In 1978 the province of Quebec brought in a law to certify class actions. Ontario followed in 1991 and British Columbia in 1993. But I believe our case was the first consumer class action lawsuit in Canada. Now class actions are huge, and lawyers have done very well by them. The Government of Canada in 2005 paid 79,000 survivors of the First Nations residential schools almost $5 billion in damages. Because our case never went to appeal, it seems to have been lost in the mists of past cases, but I do believe a determined Ms. Chastain made legal history.

Community Law

Our storefront Vancouver Community Legal Assistance Society law office was the brainchild of a cheerful young lawyer who called himself "the grey-flannel guerrilla." His name was Michael Harcourt, just "Mike" to everybody. He wanted VCLAS lawyers to represent community groups, take some test cases and supervise evening legal-aid clinics where UBC law students gave advice to people who had been charged with crimes, or who believed they had a case against government or business. The student clinics gave a lot of ordinary people access to the law. The VCLAS office was modelled on other Canadian community law offices, like ones in Point St. Charles (Montreal), Parkdale (Toronto), Halifax and Saskatoon.

In many ways, Mike was more an organizer than a trial lawyer. When he was twenty-nine, he, Darlene Marzari, Margaret Mitchell, Joe Wai and Shirley Chan had been part of a citizen's coalition that stopped a Seattle-like freeway being ploughed through Vancouver, saving Strathcona, Chinatown and Yaletown. After a couple of years setting up VCLAS, he moved on to politics, running for Vancouver city council (Marzari went with him to city council and then provincial politics, while Mitchell became MP for Vancouver East, and Chan continued to work tirelessly in the community). Although nicknamed "Ho Chi Harcourt" after Vietnam's communist leader Ho Chi Minh, Harcourt was not really that much of a radical. He was more a practical guy who liked to get things done. And Mike didn't do too badly in politics—councillor, mayor, MLA and premier. He was and is much loved, especially in Vancouver.

I'm not sure why he chose me to succeed him as VCLAS director. I had come to British Columbia from Etobicoke, a suburb of Toronto. After my call to the bar at the Vancouver courthouse in 1969, I would have gone back east to work for John Munro, a Liberal cabinet minister, except the job fell through at the last minute. Instead I was hired by Stewart McMorran, the tough, conservative Vancouver city prosecutor. Suddenly I was in the swirl of traffic, family and criminal courts, learning trial law under pressure as counsel for the Crown, dealing with five cases each day and dealing with tough defence counsel like the legendary Harry Rankin.

McMorran sent me out to family court after a year in the prosecutor's office. Mistakenly, I thought that was a demotion. Later I learned it was a promotion; if McMorran sent you out of his immediate reach, it meant he trusted you. Not understanding this, I quit the prosecutor's office and joined defence counsel "Slippery" Sid Simons in his office at the corner of Hastings and Main, across from the provincial courts. There we defended alleged drug addicts and hippie marijuana dealers, among others. I learned about a slice of life totally different from my suburban upbringing in Etobicoke. In court, Sid used every trick in the book in favour of his clients. I was amazed that he always believed them; I suppose that is the mark of a good defence counsel. Outside the courtroom, Sid was a cultured, cool guy. He introduced me to author George Ryga, British Columbia's greatest playwright, whose play *The Ecstasy of Rita Joe* drew from a transcript of one of Sid's cases.

Mike Harcourt came into Simons' office one day and offered me the job of legal director of VCLAS. The proposal seemed to come out of the blue, but looking back, I realized we had done some cases together in family court when I was a prosecutor. I had also visited the VCLAS office, one of many community groups in what is now the Vancouver East Cultural Centre, "The Cultch." Also Mike and I got to know each other socially when he and his wife Becky, along with Dr. Peter Hupfau, Don Rosenbloom, Tony Dransfield, Frank and Frieda Kaplan, D'Arcy and Nancy Thorpe, and others shared a ski cabin together in the Emerald Estates area of Whistler. To be young at the beginning of the growth of Whistler was to be in heaven. And to succeed Mike at VCLAS was a great gift.

Our budget was $112,000 for myself (my salary was $17,000), the office and a staff of five, all of whom went on to successful legal careers. One, Harvey Field, became a judge. A lot of today's senior BC lawyers like Tom Roper QC started as law students at the free clinics we supervised. VCLAS used "test cases" like the Chastain case to advance social justice and law reform, but we also used other means to tackle social issues. For example, each year four or five old men would die in hotel fires on the Downtown Eastside. These weren't hotels where tourists stayed. They were what are known as SRO hotels—single room occupancy, which means they rented rooms to individuals as permanent residences, not for one or two nights. In those days the old hotels had no sprinklers.

One of our young lawyers, Alan MacLean, had been working with a woman who photographed conditions in these SRO hotels. Alan called a press conference to show the pictures. As the new VCLAS director, I presided at the press conference, my first of many. After one such fire that resulted in another death, I phoned the coroner, whom I had known since my prosecutor days, and asked if I could make a submission at the inquest. "Why don't you come on the coroner's jury?" he asked.

I had assumed that lawyers couldn't serve on juries, which is true, but only for criminal and civil cases. So unlike many lawyers, I got the experience of serving on a jury and observing its inner workings. When MacLean showed the photos to the jury, the jury recommended that sprinklers be installed in the Downtown Eastside hotels. Within a short time, a city bylaw made sprinklers mandatory in the hotels. Old guys don't die in those kinds of fires anymore. Those photos were worth more than a thousand words and helped make changes to the law.

VCLAS lawyers weren't the only ones working for social change. This was the era of Vancouver mayor Tom Campbell and his wars against the "hippies" and the drug dealers, which culminated in the "Gastown Riot" of August 1971. Vancouver police, including four on horseback, attacked a group of protesters who were peacefully demonstrating against the use of undercover cops and for the legalization of marijuana around the statue of "Gassy Jack" in the heart of Gastown in Vancouver. One eyewitness told the press that the police behaved with "almost satanic arrogance." Another recalls "the spark of the horses' hooves" against the cobblestones. When demonstrators fought back, they were arrested. Many were clubbed by police wielding nightsticks. (There is a huge photo re-creation of the scene, *Abbott & Cordova, 7 August 1971*, by artist Stan Douglas in the Woodward's Building in downtown Vancouver.) After the riot, a group of defence lawyers calling themselves the East End Bar (in contrast to their brethren who worked for the big, downtown, largely conservative law firms) got together to defend those charged, pro bono (without fee). VCLAS allowed me to join this group of progressive lawyers.

My client was an Indigenous guy, Patrick Natrall, who simply got out of a bar that night, picked up a rock and threw it. He was arrested, charged and convicted, but was too poor to pay his fine so he went to jail in default of payment. I took his case after the conviction and sentence and appealed the sentence, arguing that sentencing a person convicted of a crime to incarceration because he could not afford to pay a fine created "one law for the rich and one law for the poor," and was therefore "unconstitutional." Canada didn't have a Charter of Rights in those days (that came later, in the 1980s), though it did have the Bill of Rights John Diefenbaker introduced in 1960. But the BC Court of Appeal disagreed with me.

The case generated an article in the *Vancouver Province* under the headline "Indian Jailed for Poverty," which revealed that almost one quarter of all offenders in provincial jails were serving time because they couldn't pay a fine, and many of them were Indigenous people. Sounded like *Les Miserables*! I also got the Canadian Bar Association, essentially the lawyers union, to pass a resolution calling for clarifying legislation. I did that so I could argue it wasn't only little VCLAS but also "the lawyers of Canada" that wanted the law changed. This and the other publicity resulting from the trial did produce results. In 1974 the BC government introduced the *Summary Convictions Act*, which states, "No person shall be imprisoned only by reason that he defaults in paying a fine." This is an example of how you can change the law even if you lose a case.

One of the most valuable lessons in how to conduct ourselves as "progressive lawyers" came from my mother. The evening of the day I was called to the bar, we celebrated in a rental house on Point Grey Road. Today it's the site of the Lululemon mansion, but in those days before the "1 percent," students actually rented the old houses in that neighbourhood. My mum Isabel was in town and she loved dancing, so she came to the party with me. She looked at the dance floor, where most people were in jeans and T-shirts, then turned to me and asked, "Why didn't you invite some lawyers?"

"Mum," I replied, "there are twenty lawyers in this room."

"Well, they don't look like lawyers," she said.

Listening to her, a former waitress and factory worker, made me realize how important appearance was. When I became VCLAS director, I required our staff to wear dress shirts and, for the men, ties. Jeans underneath were okay, as they were young, but I wanted poor people to see them as lawyers. And I wanted to ensure community law was not seen as second-class law. I had only one suit to my name, tailored in Vancouver but with material I got from Savile Row in London. I always wore it in court.

A Death in Burns Lake

Josephine Alec, an Indigenous woman from Burns Lake, one thousand kilometres north of Vancouver, came to one of our law clinics in

Vancouver. She had been charged with the murder of her husband; she claimed he had beaten her, and she killed him in self-defence. I believed her and thought it was important to make people aware of the issue of violence against women. I also wanted to keep my hand in criminal law, so I agreed to defend Ms. Alec. The preliminary hearing was in Burns Lake, and the trial took two days in Prince Rupert (imagine—a murder trial in two days!).

I was able to find a witness, a teenage girl who testified she had seen violent acts committed by the husband. She also said that he had had vision problems. The stabbing had happened outside a party house in the rain. I remember a very honest Mountie, in full red serge, testified that he asked Ms. Alec, who was muddy and in a state of shock, how she had held the knife, giving her a ruler to illustrate. He demonstrated what she showed him, so we knew the angle of the thrust. I thought I had no defence until the Crown's forensic expert, whose report I had not seen (in those days they didn't have long, drawn-out "discoveries"), testified the fatal wound went "up and back."

That enabled me to put two possible defences to the jury. Either the victim had rushed into her and onto the knife, or he was on top of her and she thrust the knife up into him. The former was accident; the latter was self-defence. I asked the jury to choose. When the jury went out to deliberate, the Crown counsel and I went to the judge's chambers. The judge asked me to bring a bottle of whisky, and the three of us settled down together to drink it. Since this was my first murder trial, I'd assumed this was the common practice. Mistake.

The jury soon came back for directions. Their question: if my client intended to hurt her husband but not kill him, could she be guilty of murder or anything at all. The judge said no. He asked counsel for comments. Something in my clouded mind said maybe the judge should say something to the jury about manslaughter, a lesser crime, but I chose to shut up. Soon after that, the jury came back. They found Ms. Alec not guilty. As we left the court, I heard a couple of sheriffs say the group of First Nations who had come to support Ms. Alec still had time to go to the bar before closing. In fact, they all went back to Burns Lake cold sober. It was the judge who invited me for a nightcap.

The Crown had thirty days to appeal. Sure enough, on day twenty-nine I got their notice. The appeal took place in the old law courts in Vancouver. I lost, two judges to one. The dissenting judge, as fate would have it, was Chief Justice John Farris. His dissent allowed me to appeal to the Supreme Court of Canada. While I was arguing there, I produced the murder weapon and moved the knife the same way the Mountie had done at the trial. The Court was not amused and went after me, especially Justice Louis-Philippe Pigeon in his high-pitched, squeaky voice. I began to lose the line of my argument. At that point, Bora Laskin, Chief Justice of Canada and my old law professor, intervened. "Forgive me, brother Judge Pigeon, but I think counsel was referring to page eight of his factum." I fumbled, quickly turning to page eight. "You were referring to the second last paragraph, were you not, counsel?"

"Yes, of course, my Lord," I replied. Then I read out the paragraph. The court reserved its decision, and when I was leaving I was handed a note by Laskin's clerk. The Chief Justice welcomed my first appearance but wondered when I had become Queen's Counsel. In fact, I didn't become a QC until 2013, forty years later. But QCs at the Supreme Court were allowed to stand closer to the bench. I had seen the government lawyer, a distinguished QC, do just that, and since I didn't think the presentation of my client's case should be handicapped in any way—and was also concerned that some of the old judges might be a bit hard of hearing—I did the same. Always a rebel! Perhaps it worked. A few months later the Supreme Court ruled in our favour.

CHAPTER 2

The Immigrant

Like Sir John A. Macdonald, another Scottish Canadian politician, I came to Canada from Scotland. My family emigrated from "dirty old Glasgow," as my dad used to call our birthplace, when I was five. Dad came first with his pal Jack Harris. My dad was a licensed electrician. He had worked with Harris during the war in the Clydebank shipyards. Later I would ask him why he was not a veteran. That was why—he did his war work in the shipyards, building and repairing battleships. The Luftwaffe, the Nazi air force, carried out major bombing raids on Clydebank. Family lore says that, as a baby, I was taken into an air raid shelter during the bombing. So I guess I am a true veteran of the Second World War!

My mum and I came to Canada with my "Aunt" Jesse, Jack's wife, about a month after the guys. Later she and Jack had two boys of their own, Ross and Colin. My brother Al was born a couple years after we arrived. I remember nothing of Scotland, though apparently I was beginning to read, and I've been told my parents feared I might turn out to be "deaf and dumb," as they said in those days, like my dad's grandparents. My parents needn't have feared, as I uttered my first words from a carriage outside our house in Scotland: not "Dad" or "Mum" but a full sentence, "Motor car go by." Unfortunately, as some of my friends might say, I haven't stopped talking since then!

Why do people immigrate? I am sure a lot of new Canadians have asked the same question of their parents. My parents never really told me. I recently saw in London an exhibition on the life of David Bowie where I saw his parents' food ration books, and I understood better why my parents left. Post-war Britain was pretty drab.

Ian in kilt arrives in Canada with dad Jack and mum Isabel.

I never did see three of my grandparents again but I did get a beautiful country, great schooling and a prosperous, booming, post-war economy. My first memory in life is of looking out on islands in the St. Lawrence River during the Trans-Canada Airlines flight from Scotland. We had come overnight from Prestwick, Scotland, to Gander, Newfoundland, which was not yet a part of Canada. C.D. Howe, the powerful Canadian Minister of Reconstruction, was said to be a fellow passenger. The flight was rough, we were sick and the British stewardesses on the first leg of our journey were not very nice. But in the morning the sun was bouncing off the runway in Montreal when we landed. The big change my mum noticed was how friendly the Canadian stewardesses were after the snotty Brits. It was a beautiful day, November 15, 1947.

We went on from Montreal to the Toronto airport, at Malton. It was evening now, and it was snowing. I remember being bewildered and exhausted after the long journey, but I felt better as soon as I saw my dad. After an emotional reunion, Mum, Dad and I crowded into the backseat of Jack Harris's car. I looked out the car window at the darkness and the faint lights of a big city as we drove to our new home. Like so many immigrants before and after us, we made our way to Scarborough, an eastern suburb of Toronto, to a basement apartment. On November 21 I celebrated my fifth birthday in my new country and enjoyed Eaton's Santa Claus parade in my new city. I even got a birthday card from the airline stewardess.

Someone took a picture of my dad greeting us at Toronto's Malton airport. It shows a little boy in a kilt with his parents. Later, as an elected member of the Canadian parliament, I would send greetings to my constituents who had just become citizens. At the top of my letter, on one side, I would have a picture of me getting sworn into the House of Commons; on the other side, the picture of the little immigrant in the kilt arriving in his new country, Canada.

We soon moved to a brand-new, small bungalow on Gamma Street in Alderwood, the southern and poorer part of Etobicoke, a western suburb of Toronto. We often went to movie shows and bowling in neighbouring Long Branch, and lacrosse games and dances at the Sons of Scotland hall in Mimico where my mum worked as a waitress until my brother Al was born. Old Grandma Dickie and my Uncle Bob came from Scotland to live with us.

Having skipped a few grades, I found myself a little boy of twelve in grade nine at a brand-new high school, Alderwood Collegiate institute. There we had the benefit of post-war prosperity with really good teachers. I joined every school club imaginable, but it was Mr. Taylor, our library teacher, who influenced me most with his down-to-earth personality and his clear love of books. Outside school, another librarian, Ruth Kennedy, hired me to be a "page" in the local library. They were the ones who encouraged me to go to university. No one in my family had ever done that. My parents had to quit school at fifteen, as was the custom in Scotland.

But probably what changed my life was winning the school's public-speaking contest when I was in grade eleven. As the winner I got to go to the regional finals, held one evening at the Lions Club on the Queensway, just north of where we lived. The four speakers delivered their set speeches. They were all formal, memorized and boring to the guys in the audience. Then we had to do a three-minute impromptu speech. In my formal speech I solemnly quoted Lester B. Pearson: "The price of peace is not freedom from war; it is ——." I sounded just like the others. But in the impromptu I was given the topic "Is Canadian hockey too violent?" I knew and loved hockey, being a goalie in a local league with my next-door neighbour Ken Hodge, who went on to play for the Boston Bruins in the NHL. Suddenly I became a mini-Don Cherry with even some humour. The Lions guys loved it and it carried me to victory. In the City of Toronto final, the next step, I stood no chance against some pretty smart speakers from big schools. Some of the smartest were Jewish kids and I made a point of hanging around with some of them when I got to university.

Young Liberal

I remember going to the Canadian National Exhibition on my own at age fifteen to catch a glimpse of the new prime minister, John George

Diefenbaker. Who knows where my interest in history and politics came from? My father was shy, mechanical, a bagpiper and opera singer. I remember him singing "La donna è mobile" from *Rigoletto*. I inherited none of his talents. All I can think is that my mother encouraged me to read a lot.

At university I again joined just about every club imaginable, including the Liberal Club—to my father's horror, he being a strong socialist from the "red Clyde" in Glasgow. I thought at the time the Liberals, led by Lester B. Pearson, were the best party for bringing together English and French Canada, which my study of Canadian history told me was crucial for the survival of Canada. We campus Liberals won the parliamentary election at the University of Toronto and I became minister of labour, sitting in the model parliament at the Ontario Legislature. In my speech I criticized the president of the university, Claude Bissell, for some speech he had made—such criticism by students was unheard of at the time. Mine was the only speech that got in the newspapers.

The next summer two of my high-school friends, Richard Elphick and Lorenzo Duso, started a small restaurant at Wasaga Beach, north of Toronto, and hired me as a waiter/dishwasher. I took a few days off during the election campaign of 1962 to drive around some Liberals, including Pearson's press secretary Dick O'Hagan. I was like a sponge listening to those pros. A few weeks later, Gerry Godsoe, the Liberal Club leader, called me urgently. He had been hired for a job in Banff, so he wouldn't be able to drive Lester Pearson and Walter Gordon, an accountant and businessman who was running in a Toronto riding, around southwestern Ontario as he had promised. Could I do it?

Pearson had been a student at Victoria College at the University of Toronto, as was I. In fact, I had written an article about Pearson entitled "Pearson the Lesser" (he had an older brother, which is why he was given that nickname) for *Acta Victoriana*, the college's student literary magazine. Pearson had been Canada's foreign minister when Louis St. Laurent was prime minister, and he had won the Nobel Peace Prize in 1957 for helping to resolve the Suez Crisis by inventing the concept of peacekeeping. Now here I was, nineteen years old and sitting next

Ian and Mum in his "Red Shark" car.

to Pearson, chauffeuring him in a new yellow 1962 Cadillac with big tail fins.

Pearson was a reluctant campaigner. When the local candidate got out of the car and left us alone, Pearson looked relieved. As we drove up to Georgian Bay we talked about schooling, as I was interested in graduate work in Canadian Studies. He encouraged me and appeared very relaxed when he didn't have to campaign. Remember, he was a Nobel Prize winner and had been a cabinet minister and now leader of the Opposition for four years; I was a nineteen-year-old history student who in those days couldn't legally drink or vote, but he treated me as an equal. When we reached Windsor, Paul Martin Sr.'s political machine took over and I didn't see Pearson again on that trip. However, he left me a handwritten note that said, "I have an extra special reason for being grateful to you." The Liberals did not win that 1962 election, but they reduced Diefenbaker's Conservatives to a minority government.

I did see Pearson again outside Maple Leaf Gardens after he gave an election speech in the 1963 campaign. As his security people whisked him out a side door, he passed where I was standing with some friends. He suddenly stopped, turned back to me, and asked how my studies were going—that's the kind of man he was. Pearson went on to win a minority government in 1963, and Gordon became his finance minister. I believe Pearson has been underestimated as a prime minister.

He brought in federal medicare and the Canada Pension Plan, unified Canada's defence forces and introduced the country's new maple leaf flag.

Changing Times

I grew up in a less complicated Canada. Here's an example. As a member of the U of T Liberal club, I went to Ottawa for a meeting. I recall our carpool arriving in snowy downtown Ottawa in 1962. As we rounded a corner I saw the Parliament Buildings for the first time. I was in awe. During our conference we debated whether Quebec should be considered a "nation." The motion didn't pass; a young Quebecer, Marcel Prud'homme, spoke against it. (He became a Liberal MP in 1964.)

After the meeting, I wanted to see the residence of the prime minister, so I walked in the snow to 24 Sussex Drive. There was no security. Instead, a group of journalists was staked out at the front door. The rumour was that Prime Minister Diefenbaker was going to resign, as his minority government was falling apart. It was bitterly cold, and the journalists had been waiting for a long time. Some of them decided to go get a coffee. One of them, Val Sears of the *Toronto Star* (his son Robin later became a friend), saw me shivering there. I was nineteen years old but weighed about 120 pounds then and looked about sixteen. Val motioned for me to get in the car with the seasoned journalists, and we went off to get a hot cup of coffee. On our return it was apparent that Dief, as they called him, had given us the slip and gone across the road to see the Governor General. Our car raced over to Rideau Hall. Again, no security. We waited. Finally Dief came out. I remember he wore a large black homburg hat. The journalists peppered him with questions. I was right in the middle of my first scrum. He hadn't resigned but he did take questions, and I watched in awe.

The year I graduated with a degree in history, there was a need for teachers. I was able to take a summer teaching course at the Ontario College of Education and got a teaching job in the fall at Western Tech, a high school in Toronto. Bless full employment! A fellow teacher, Bob

Richardson, drove me from home to school each day so I could save enough to go to law school. Early in the term I was teaching Canadian history to a raucous group of tech boys and they tried to find out which party I voted for. It was fun, but I held out and refused to answer. Of course, I was too young to vote!

Once I started at law school, I used to drive every day from southern Etobicoke to the U of T campus near Queen's Park in downtown Toronto in my car, a 1959 Chevy that used to belong to my dad. I can still see those fins. The drive took me past a small factory on Queen Elizabeth Way with a sign that said, *G.H. Woods, Sanitation for the Nation.* I could only guess what they made (turns out it was cleaning products). What was most visible was their big flagpole, which all my life had flown the red ensign. This was the unofficial flag of Canada, with the British Union Jack at the upper left and the Canadian coat of arms to the right on a red background. One clear, windy morning in 1965, I passed the Woods factory and saw a different flag on the flagpole. It was the new maple leaf flag, just approved after a long debate by Parliament. I was only twenty-two years old, but I knew right then that my country had changed. We were into the modern era. I did feel proud.

Law School

Law school was at first a big challenge for me. There were a lot of students whose fathers and grandfathers were lawyers. Meanwhile, I had never been in a law office. I hung out with the smart guys and gradually my marks improved.

As an undergrad at the University of Toronto, I again got involved in debating at the Hart House student activity centre. Hart House debates were held once a month during the school year and featured four students and a well-known guest (Senator John F. Kennedy was one, but before my time there). They were based on the Oxford debating model; that is, lots of wit as well as serious debating. At first I was terrified when I "spoke from the floor" in an Oxford-style debate. I remember one night, three of us students, all seventeen years old, were told by a professor who came to the debates that in our lifetime we would see a cashless society. There were no credit cards then. We would see computers, he said. What were computers? And we would change our jobs about three or four times, unlike our fathers. The professor, Arthur Porter, hung around with a group that followed my English professor, a fellow called Marshall McLuhan, who said we now lived in a "global village."

In my second year of law school I became secretary of the Hart House Debates Committee, succeeding Michael Levine (who went on to become a noted entertainment lawyer). The committee that planned the debates included John Bosley (later Speaker of the House of Commons), Frank Felkai, Levine, Paul Moore, Ed Bridge, R.H Thompson, Michael Ignatieff and David Mossop (later my assistant at VCLAS). I set up a debate on the usefulness of the United Nations with special guest Ambassador George Ignatieff. I got his soft-spoken son Michael to oppose him. To debate in support of the ambassador's side, I chose a young kid with big eyeglasses and a keen sense of humour, Bob Rae. Both Bob and Michael were only seventeen at the time, but I thought they might become promising debaters.

We were proud of the fact that we'd had every prime minister since the founding of Hart House in the 1920s as a guest—all except one. John George Diefenbaker, the fiery Saskatchewan lawyer turned leader of the Progressive Conservative party, and prime minister of Canada from 1957 to 1963, had not yet taken part. When I became secretary, I was given the job of going to Ottawa to persuade "Dief the Chief," as he was known, to come to Hart House as our guest debater.

Canada, the second-largest country in the world in land mass, is in many ways a small country—small in terms of how relatively easy it is to have contact with our leaders. I met Diefenbaker in his parliamentary office about an hour before the afternoon question period. He was then leader of the Opposition, which meant he would lead off the QP. You wouldn't have known that from visiting his office, because in contrast to the always-busy Liberal offices that I had been in that morning, Dief's was completely silent. Dief was alone. When he talked, his jaw dropped, his eyes sparkled, his words rumbled out and his jowls shook. "Oh, [pause] what are you studying, Mr. Waddell?"

"Law, sir."

"Oh, [pause] the Queen's justice. [shake] Good." Then he told me a story of the first overseas trip he made as prime minister. He was visiting India, and when in New Delhi the Indian officials asked him if he wanted to see anything special. He replied that he wanted to go to the Indian Supreme Court to see how it functioned. Reluctantly they agreed. When Diefenbaker arrived, lawyers were arguing a case in front of the court. The chief justice of India, seeing a Canadian prime minister in the gallery, immediately stopped the case, recognizing him and suggesting the case at bar be adjourned. No, said Diefenbaker, the case should go on. The chief justice agreed, and the case continued.

After a few minutes of legal argument, the chief justice asked one of the lawyers if he could give the court some "authority" for his argument. In legal parlance that means he was asking the lawyer to refer to a case that was similar to the one being argued, that had similar facts or similar law applied. Diefenbaker looked me straight in the eye and said, "That lawyer cited a case from the Supreme Court of Canada. I was never so proud [pause, jowls shake]. I had argued that case in our Supreme Court." At that point a lone aide came into the office with a single piece of paper. Dief put on his glasses and read it. "So they have appointed Keith Davey as the new head of the Canadian Football League. We'll see!" Davey was a big Liberal insider. Diefenbaker would often use the term "they" to refer to a mysterious group, blame for whose actions he would lay at the feet of the government of the day.

For example, during a speech he gave on a sweltering summer night in the prairies, he thundered, "It was on a night like this that THEY sent Lucien Rivard out to flood the rink." Rivard being a crook who escaped prison in the course of flooding the prison ice rink late the previous winter when the temperature was slightly above freezing! His escape caused a scandal that brought the downfall of one Liberal MP. When Pearson was asked what his most difficult political moment was, he referred to the Rivard incident saying that he was relieved when Rivard was captured in the Laurentians and extradited to an American prison. With a laugh he added, "Rivard even sent me a Christmas card." (Dief never had that kind of self-deprecation.) The day I visited him, Diefenbaker went to the House of Commons and had the Pearson government reeling with question after question about the Davey appointment. Oh, and he did agree to come to Hart House.

Later I was elected to the 31st Parliament along with 283 others including the member for Prince Albert, John George Diefenbaker. Unfortunately he died before the House met, but I did go on the Diefenbaker funeral train. As it snaked across the prairies, passing small towns and farms, people stood and watched respectfully, the men taking off their hats and RCMP officers saluting. It had taken him a number of elections to get to parliament; Dief, the prairie radical and criminal lawyer, would have liked the way he left it.

Becoming a Lawyer

An English poet once wrote that if the Scots ever met God, they would "argue their creator dumb." One day in our living room my dad was arguing some legal point with his bricklayer and plumber friends. One of them turned suddenly to me and said, "Jack, ask your son. He's almost a lawyer." To my surprise I answered that one couldn't give a quick answer. Research was needed, and there might not be a simple answer. On the one hand, the answer could be this; on the other hand, it could be that. Calvin Coolidge, a US president, once protested, "Give me a one-handed lawyer." I knew I was becoming a lawyer!

In 1963, Pearson had appointed a Royal Commission on Bilingualism and Biculturalism. This was a serious topic concerning the relationship between French and English in Canada, and possibly the future of the country, and the commissioners were heavyweights in Canadian affairs. One of my fellow law students, the ever-energetic David Peterson, got a few of us together, organized a couple of meetings after lectures at lunch and drew up a brief that talked about reforming the senate. Sound familiar? Dave somehow fit it into bilingualism and biculturalism by suggesting the provincial premiers either join, or somehow have a role in, the senate. We of course had no idea then that Peterson, "Boot" as we nicknamed him, would become a premier himself one day in Ontario.

To our surprise, the commissioners asked us to appear before them at the Park Plaza Hotel in Toronto. Doug McTavish, John Yates, Gord Michener, David Peterson and I dutifully appeared before this august group. Peterson spoke for us. After our brief, the great poet/professor Frank R. Scott, arguably Canada's greatest constitutional lawyer and teacher, asked us a question. Peterson didn't miss a beat. Fearlessly he replied, "Mr. Waddell will answer that." I can't remember a word I said.

Village Bar

During my time at law school, an intense fellow classmate approached me about joining the "Village Bar." Clayton Ruby had worked with Aboriginal people in Saskatchewan and with the Student Nonviolent Coordinating Committee (SNCC), one of the main civil rights groups in the US South. Ruby had noticed that the Yorkville area, just a few blocks north of our law school, was full of young hippies who were being hassled by the police. With the assistance of a couple of young lawyers, Vince Kelly and Paul Copeland, and fellow law students like Pam Thompson (later a judge), David Peterson, Rob Martin and me, Ruby set up a table and two chairs in front of a Yorkville variety store named the Grab Bag. Thus started the first on-street law office in North America.

The Law Society of Upper Canada, the body that controlled the legal profession in Ontario, was not happy. Ruby and Copeland were called before the powerful G. Arthur Martin, a great criminal lawyer and a bencher of the Law Society. He ordered them not to use the name "Village Bar," since the student lawyers were not yet members of the bar. They didn't like our table, either, or the fact we didn't tell the kids which of us were lawyers and which were students. We changed our name to the "Justice Division" of a local youth aid group called the Trailer. And we continued with the table, though later we rented an actual Yorkville basement suite.

This led to my and Ruby's first case. Twenty young hippies were arrested for squatting in a vacant house on Avenue Road. Well, to be accurate, nineteen young people and one very old man. Trials in those days were held quickly, at a courtroom right in the police station of 22 Division. The charge was Vagrancy A, known as Vag A, section 164 (1) of the Canadian Criminal Code, which said that having no apparent means of support and being found wandering abroad or trespassing, or otherwise being poor, made you a criminal.

At the hearing the old man was questioned and said he loved "crashing" with the young people, who gave him food and "smokes." He agreed he didn't have much means of support other than this. As he was about to leave the witness stand, he paused and added, "Well, I do get the old age pension as well, and I give some to the kids." This, of course, was a complete defence to the charge. The Crown prosecutor threw up his hands and promptly dropped the charges against the other nineteen as well. The trial had become a farce. Twenty-two people took a group photo in front of the police station that day: nineteen young hippies, one old hippy and two happy young law students, Ruby and Waddell, who had won their very first case.

Ruby and Copeland later formed the Law Union, a progressive group of lawyers. They were hauled up before the Law Society and G. Arthur Martin again when they publicly opposed Prime Minister Pierre Trudeau's invocation of the *War Measures Act* in 1970. They went on to become two of Canada's top lawyers and members of the Order of Canada. They were even elected as benchers to the Law Society of Upper Canada. Recently a smiling Paul Copeland, casually dressed and sitting in a plain chair in his office in modern Yorkville, directed my gaze to his bookshelf and the G. Arthur Martin Criminal Justice Medal. He even has a security clearance. But to this day, in spite of all these honours, both Copeland and Ruby continue to defend the poor and outcast of society.

The Law Society of Upper Canada also attempted to censor the law school's student newspaper when we wrote an inoffensive piece about the kind of charity work prominent lawyers did in their spare time. This influenced my decision to come to British Columbia, whose bar I found to be a lot less stuffy and more progressive.

Go West, Young Man… or East

After I graduated from law school in June 1967, I set out with Ian Pit-field, a fellow student, in his old car. Horace Greely once said, "Go west, young man," though he stayed east and made his fortune. "Pit" and I did go west. I had never been west of Windsor, Ontario so when we crossed each provincial boundary, Pit and I shook hands. Problem was, his summer job was in Golden, BC. From there I had to take the bus. It seemed like mountains forever. Once I got to Vancouver, I stayed on the couch of another classmate, Bob Murdoch, who had a place on Robson Street.

I recall going to Stanley Park on a clear June day, looking up at the snow-capped coastal mountains, and reading a chapter from *In Cold Blood* by Truman Capote before falling asleep on the green grass. It was instant love. I had a beer with some recent U of T grads in Vancouver. Given my criticism of the Ontario law society, they urged me to try to get an articling position in Vancouver. So I nervously approached the front desk of the large law firm of Ladner, Downs. When I asked a young secretary about articling, she said that the lawyer in charge of students was away that day. For some reason, probably nerves, I stammered, "I'm interested in labour law."

"Oh, I think Mr. Vickers is in." With that she sent me down to a warm welcome from David Vickers, who asked me what kind of labour law I wanted to practise. I told him my dad was a strong unionist. Vickers patiently explained that he represented business, and then he phoned Ted McTaggart, who was often his opponent in court. David explained how to get to McTaggart, Ellis and Company and gave me a cup of coffee. What a difference from Ontario, and what luck. Ted McTaggart later offered me an articling position and even postponed it for a year when I won a scholarship (from the International Order of the Daughters of the Empire—I kid you not) to the London School of Economics.

Being a student at the LSE in the 1960s was like being in student heaven. Not many classes, lots of theatre and the British Museum, and tuition of £50. The LSE changed that mid-year to £250. I appealed to our student advisor and we were grandfathered at fifty. I suppose that was my second legal victory.

Students had to report to an assigned "tutor" once a month to discuss our progress, a tradition based on the Oxford model. Apparently during my time at LSE one student, a bloke called Mick Jagger, went to his tutor to ask permission to drop out with the option of coming back if necessary. He wanted to promote his new band. The tutor gave Mick permission but added, "Those bands don't go anywhere."

One morning in my small room in the Cartwright Gardens student residence, I heard the BBC report that James Earl Ray, the accused assassin of Martin Luther King, had been arrested in London and would be arraigned at Bow Street Magistrates' Court for an extradition hearing. I hurried down there only to see what the English call a queue of people. Being a pushy North American, I went to the front to speak to the lone policeman at precisely the moment the door opened and the guard let a dozen people into the public gallery, including me. The first cases were charges of petty theft and public drunkenness, but then important Queen's Counsel lawyers appeared, and the case of the United States of America vs. James Earl Ray was called. Ray was dressed in drab street clothes, not too tall and very ordinary looking. He merely acknowledged his name, was denied bail, and the case was put over for two weeks, but I felt like I had been involved in a very sad bit of history.

A Change in Politics

After my year in London I returned to Vancouver and found a one-room apartment at the Barr residence at 1936 McNicoll Avenue on Kits Point. Free at last! I could study (and party) in my new hometown. The world seemed to be my oyster—and it was. As an articling student, I had to take night classes. Mike Harcourt (who later invited me to be director of VCLAS) and I took one course from Gary Lauk. Within a decade, Lauk was a provincial cabinet minister, Harcourt was mayor of Vancouver and I was a member of parliament.

Harcourt got me to canvas for NDP candidates Norm Levi and John Laxton in the 1969 provincial election campaign. I found the British Columbia Liberal party quite conservative, and my readings at the LSE had convinced me intellectually that social democracy was the fairest and best political system humankind had yet invented. Since I lived in the dual riding of Burrard, I voted for NDPers Tom Berger and Dr. Ray Parkinson who were head-and-shoulders smarter than the Social Credit candidates. They lost. Berger, the provincial NDP leader, had been "ready to govern" with a great team. Instead, Premier W.A.C. Bennett was returned to office for the seventh time. Welcome to BC politics.

Three years later the new NDP leader, "fat little Dave" Barrett, as he called himself, ran a campaign with the unofficial slogan, "Just give us a few more seats to keep them honest." He won the government! The new

With Judge Thomas R. Berger in Inuvik.

NDP attorney general, Alex McDonald, asked me if I knew of a good candidate from the law profession to be his deputy. I suggested David Vickers. What goes around comes around.

Norm Levi, now a minister in the Barrett government, appointed me to an alcohol and drug commission led by Peter Stein. Stein had been a commissioner on the federal LeDain Commission. I believe our annual report in 1974 was a roadmap for a sensible provincial policy in this crucial area. We dealt with preventative programs for young people, a detoxification system for the whole province, special counselling services for Indigenous people, the first clinical treatment and training centre, and the organization of impaired drivers courses. Too bad the subsequent Social Credit government, which took power in 1975, didn't follow our path here.

One idea that did survive came from a Nanaimo businessman, Joseph McCarthy, who was a volunteer coordinator for the Nanaimo impaired drivers program. He and I prepared a short report, *The Counterattack on Drinking Drivers*, which I took to the commission. Later, private groups used the same phrase. This is an example of what a local volunteer with passion can contribute, not to mention proof of the power of words. Joe's "counterattack" outlasted our commission.

Only a few people know that on October 8, 1974, Commissioner Ted Milligan prepared a confidential report on legalized heroin at the request of Minister Levi. The report summarized the issues brilliantly and suggested a trial study. It never happened, but had the Barrett NDP government been re-elected, who knows what it would have done. In their book *The Art of the Impossible: Dave Barrett and the NDP in Power 1972–1975*, Geoff Meggs and Rod Mickleburgh say Barrett's government passed more substantial legislation in its three-year term than any administration before or since. Originally from England, as a social worker Norm Levi got a number of prisoners in the BC Pen transferred to England for heroin maintenance. He was a gutsy guy. Had the Barrett government been re-elected, I believe it would have tried a legal heroin maintenance. Instead, even today we leave addicts—sick people—to break into people's homes and cars to deal with their addictions. Surely a missed opportunity!

Meeting "The Judge"

Of course, politics and even the alcohol and drug commission were not my full-time work. I was still director of VCLAS. One day my job was to travel to Victoria with the first group of Indigenous court workers to explain to them how the provincial legislature worked. We were passing the premier's office when, a bit cheekily, I marched the group inside and asked to meet the premier. The secretary said no. But Dave Barrett, jacket off and shirt sleeves rolled up, saw us and came out to say hello. It was Barrett at his best.

Before I left town, I went over to the Victoria courthouse. I looked at the docket and saw that Judge Thomas Berger was presiding in one courtroom that day. Lawyer Don Rosenbloom tells how a few years earlier, he, Berger and a third lawyer, Doug Sanders, were in the lobby of the Royal York Hotel in Toronto, about to go to Ottawa to argue the historic Calder case in the Supreme Court of Canada. They were discussing their opponents in the Justice Department when Berger was paged for a phone call. When he came back, he told the others that the caller was John Turner, Canada's justice minister, offering Berger an appointment to the Supreme Court of British Columbia. Berger was only thirty-eight years old at the time, pretty young for a judge. But already he had been an MP in Ottawa, and an MLA and NDP party leader in British Columbia, only to be clobbered in the 1969 election by W.A.C. Bennett. After returning to British Columbia and thinking about it, Berger accepted. When the appointments of Berger, Richard Anderson and Harry McKay were announced, the *Province* headline was "Tom, Dick and Harry Appointed to Bench"!

Again rather brazenly, I asked to see him at the Victoria courthouse, and he invited me into his chambers for a coffee. In addition to his court duties, Berger had been appointed by the Barrett government to head a royal commission on family law. I asked him about the work of the commission and we hit it off immediately. I think I was sort of like Berger's loyal friend Rosenbloom, energetic and pretty talkative. As a result of our chance meeting in Victoria, Berger asked me to chair a working group for his royal commission that was studying the concept of a unified family court (that is, one court that would deal with issues of divorce, custody, access, adoption and other family issues).

I was leading a working meeting of that group at the commission's Pacific Centre offices when I was called to the phone in an adjoining room. The other members of the group heard my *whoop*. The call was from the clerk of the Supreme Court of Canada, who informed me that we had won the appeal on the Josephine Alec murder case 8–0. Having taken my first and only murder case from Burns Lake to Prince Rupert, Vancouver and Ottawa, I decided to quit while I was ahead. When I finished my report on the unified family court, I resigned from VCLAS after an eventful two years and returned to Toronto. I needed a break, as we all do from time to time, and I needed to think about my future.

Marty Friedland, dean of law at U of T law school, gave me an office to use. My only commitment was to give advice to students who might want to article in British Columbia. The first student I saw was an arrogant know-it-all, a precursor of some neoconservatives I was to meet later in life. The second was a cheerful, intelligent young man from St. Catharines, Ontario named Murray Rankin. I told him not to go to Vancouver because people would always be asking him if he were related to the great lawyer and city councillor Harry Rankin. Instead, Murray went to Victoria and became a great environmental lawyer, a Queen's Counsel, a member of parliament and my lifelong friend.

While I was in Toronto, I got together with one of my fellow law students, Frank Felkai. He had come from Hungary after the revolution of 1956 and was part of a group of students who shared a summer cottage. (That group included another law student, Steve Goudge.) Felkai had contacts in the governing Liberal party, and in our conversation he spoke generally about some pipeline and a proposal to take gas from Alaska and Canada to the United States. The government was going to appoint an inquiry into the proposal. Since Confederation, a number of Canadian governments, both federal and provincial, have appointed over 350 commissions of inquiry under the *Inquiries Act*. Some of these were called royal commissions, and I've already mentioned a few in this book. These inquiries would provide government advice on significant policy questions like federal-provincial relations and the establishment of the Bank of Canada, inquiries on health, bilingualism, Aboriginal peoples and the status of women. Felkai may also have mentioned that David Lewis and the NDP held the balance of power in the Trudeau minority government. But at the time I didn't think any of this had much to do with me.

A month or so later, intellectually refreshed, I returned to Vancouver. Shortly after that, Berger called me to come to his office on the tenth floor of Pacific Centre. I thought he wanted me to do more work on the unified family court. As I entered the office, I looked down across Howe Street onto the square of the old courthouse-cum-art gallery below. A gentle rain was falling. Then I looked over at a large pile of reports that nearly towered over me. They hadn't been there the last time I was in the office. Berger came out of his office and walked to the pile. Leaning over it, he said to me, "The prime minister has just appointed me to do an inquiry into the proposed Mackenzie gas pipeline. I want you to work with me."

I wasn't sure what to say, but eventually stammered, "Tom, I don't know anything about the North."

Berger smiled and looking at the vast pile of documents, said, "We'll learn."

"Okay Judge, when do I start?"

"Tomorrow you go to Yellowknife."

CHAPTER 3

The Berger Inquiry

Old Crow

The jet helicopter touched down on the dirt runway. Although it was long past midnight, the sun shone brightly. We had been travelling all day. From Yellowknife, we flew north by commercial jet to Inuvik in the delta of the Mackenzie River. There we switched over to the helicopter. "We" were Whit Fraser of CBC North, young lawyer Ron Veale with the Council of Yukon Indians, me and of course "the Judge," Mr. Justice Thomas Berger of the Supreme Court of British Columbia.

From Inuvik we flew over the myriad small lakes that make up the Mackenzie Delta, landing at Demarcation Point, an old Distant Early Warning (DEW) line site, to refuel. This relic of the Cold War is right on the border between the Northwest Territories and the Yukon. The fuel drums lay a few metres from the Beaufort Sea. On that warm June day in 1974, the Judge and I could look out and see the greyish ice of the Arctic ice pack; today in June, it is open water. The helicopter took us north, at times low enough to see seals diving into their holes in the ice as we roared past. We came down on a small outpost of land called Herschel Island. A grizzled trapper came out of his wooden cabin. Once he got over his amazement, he invited us into his cabin for coffee. This was the North, after all.

After a short visit we headed west, right along a flat strip of land between the ocean and the British Mountains that run parallel to the coast. Below we saw several wolves, three grizzly bears and migrating caribou but no humans. No one spoke. Having crossed the mountains, we flew over a land of small lakes and rivers called the Crow Flats, which was never covered by glaciers. This is where the people of Old Crow, the most northerly village in the Yukon, go to hunt muskrat. Finally we saw the outline of a small village—rows of wooden cabins and a few bigger buildings like the schoolhouse and the general store—on the banks of the Peel River. There are no outside roads to this village, even today.

"Welcome to Old Crow, Judge," said John Joe Kaye, the chief of Old Crow. His band manager Alfred North was just behind him. At that moment an RCMP truck arrived, having taken the short road from the village to the airstrip. Clouds of dirt billowed up in its wake. The young Mountie offered the Judge a ride to town but Berger, the son of an RCMP officer, politely declined. Later we learned that government officials were notorious for being whisked into these northern villages, doing their business and leaving, usually on the same day. Not Berger.

We all began to walk toward the village. The Judge had told me just before we landed that he was having a slight stomach problem and would like me to find him a comfortable bed so he could have a good sleep. Now the chief said his wife had made a special caribou supper and invited the Judge. I started to intervene but Tom waved me off. "I would be pleased to join you," he said. We continued walking in silence in the post-midnight glow. Berger told the chief that the Government of Canada had asked him to inquire into what social, economic and environmental impacts a proposed construction project might have on the land, the animals and the people of the North.

Arctic Gas, a consortium of the world's big oil companies, wanted to build a natural gas pipeline from Prudhoe Bay, Alaska across the northern slope of the Yukon (near Old Crow) to the Mackenzie Delta, then south along the valley of the Mackenzie River and through Alberta to the United States. It would be the longest pipeline ever built and the most expensive private construction project in the world. The chief asked whether the Judge's inquiry would come to Old Crow and if so, how long it would stay. Berger replied that yes, the inquiry would come to Old Crow, as it would to all the villages affected by the proposed pipeline. He would listen to all the people and stay as long as it took. I would hear that line over and over again as Berger patiently explained his mandate in hearings across northern Canada and in our major southern cities.

Berger did finally get to bed after the dinner with the chief and his family. I even found him a cabin with good curtains to keep out the midnight sun. Next morning I went to wake the Judge. He seemed a bit dazed. "You know, Ian," he said. "Do you realize the magnificence of what we saw yesterday? It's the last of North America, the eighth wonder of the world." In the spring of 1977, in his report to the Honourable Warren Allmand, Minister of Indian Affairs and Northern Development, Berger described the North as Canada's last frontier. "It is a frontier that all of us have read about but few of us have seen. Profound issues, touching our deepest concerns as a nation, await us there." The same could be said today. Later in his report, he had this to say:

> The northern Yukon is an arctic and sub-arctic wilderness of incredible beauty, a rich and varied ecosystem inhabited by thriving populations of wildlife. The Porcupine caribou herd, comprising 111,000 animals or more, ranges throughout the northern Yukon and into Alaska. It is one of the greatest caribou herds in North America. The Yukon coastal plain and the Old Crow Flats provide essential habitat for thousands of migratory waterfowl each summer and fall. This unique ecosystem—the caribou, the birds, other wildlife, and the wilderness itself— has survived until now because of the inaccessibility of the area. But it is vulnerable to the kind of disturbance that industrial development would bring.

We left Old Crow with a promise to return to see the muskratting in the Crow Flats and eventually for a hearing. As our small airplane crossed the border into Alaska, it was struck by lightning! Then we flew along the route of the Alyeska oil pipeline, from the Arctic coast to the port of Valdez on the Pacific coast. It was like we were in a different world, an industrial world.

An Inquiry of a Different Sort

The Berger Inquiry was officially launched by an order-in-council of the federal government on March 21, 1974. Berger lost no time setting up preliminary hearings in April and May 1974. This was a smart move on his part: it allowed him to feel out the players, particularly the interested parties other than the pipeline companies. It also allowed him, with input from the parties, to define and even expand his mandate, his "terms of reference."

After Judge Berger hired me, I immediately left Vancouver on a rainy spring day, caught a connecting flight in gloomy Edmonton, and arrived in Yellowknife to find brilliant sunshine and cold crisp air. This was my first time in Canada's Northwest Territories. I stayed not in the fancy Explorer Hotel but in a somewhat shabby place, the Gold Range, called "the Grange" or sometimes "the Strange" by the locals. When I went out the next morning for a walk on the crunchy snow, I noticed some huge chattering black crows around the Grange and followed them for a few blocks to a somewhat lonely two-storey wooden building with a basement and some big front steps. This became our inquiry headquarters. We also had a small Ottawa office in the Department of Indian Affairs and Northern Development (DIAND) building. Eyebrows were raised in Ottawa when I ordered letterhead saying, *Head Office Yellowknife/Branch Office Ottawa.*

We got our money from Ottawa, though, so the Judge and I had to pay our respects and visit the minister of DIAND, a young Quebec MP named Jean Chrétien. When the Judge and I returned from our morning meeting with Minister Chrétien, we met with the Pipeline Application Assessment Group for the first time. This was a group of experts from different departments of the civil service that Chrétien had assembled after announcing the inquiry. It was under the direction of Dr. John Fyles of the Geological Survey of Canada. Initially this group was to assess the Arctic Gas application and make a report. Berger later convinced the next DIAND minister, Judd Buchanan, to second the Fyles group to the inquiry as our brain trust. If the Canadian civil service can produce more people like the tall, silver-haired, quietly competent Dr. Fyles, we will be well served.

After introducing himself in a friendly manner, Berger told the group of civil servants about our meeting with the minister in detail. You could see the surprise on their faces. This openness was not how Ottawa usually did things. Half the group was uncomfortable and later drifted back to their departments; the other half was ecstatic and gave the inquiry an almost superhuman commitment. We also used outside consultants, people like Don Gamble, Hugh Brody, Ted Chamberlin and Ray Haynes to do additional research. Their loyalty to Berger was amazing and went well beyond the norm.

Before the inquiry began, the pipeline companies had spent over $50 million on engineering and socio-economic studies conducted over five years; the government had spent about $15 million on studies. Berger ordered that all relevant information would be available to all parties and to the inquiry. All parties, including Arctic Gas, had to provide a list of the studies and reports in their possession relating to the inquiry, and everyone else would have access to all the material. We backed this order with Berger's power of subpoena, though we never had to use that.

There were a number of identifiable interest groups like First Nations, environmentalists, local businesses and mental health advocates who wanted to participate. This would be an expensive proposition since we were working in the North, and the inquiry was expected to extend over a couple of years, so at the meeting with Chrétien, Berger raised the issue of intervener funding, especially for legal counsel. Chrétien's deputy minister, A. Digby Hunt, was a very formal guy with a posh British accent. He told the minister, correctly, that there was no precedent for funding lawyers other than government lawyers.

At this point, Hunt's assistant deputy minister Barry Yates, another Englishman, interrupted and said that if you looked at the legal system in England, they had a divided bar—i.e. barristers who argued in court and solicitors who did the background research. Maybe we could fund the lawyers for "research." Hunt was about to reply when Chrétien stopped him and said, "Okay Tom, call it research but don't give them too much." Thus was born the concept of government funding for interveners in inquiries in Canada. When I watched the BBC-TV program *Yes, Minister* many years later, it reminded me of this historic meeting!

Berger fashioned a standard for determining whether interveners were to be funded—they had to have a clear, separate interest that ought to be represented at the inquiry, a record of concern in that interest, inadequate resources to represent that interest, and a plan as to how they would use the funds and account for them. My job was to police the process.

Edward Knowles and I published a summary of the preliminary hearings held in a few communities and in Yellowknife. The cover showed Judge Berger conducting a hearing outdoors. At the conclusion of those hearings, Berger issued two rulings. The first was on intervener funding and full disclosure of scientific studies, mentioned above. The other ruling, which was perhaps even more important, postponed the actual hearings of the inquiry for a year—until March 1975. This gave all participants time to prepare. If you want to prepare properly, especially when you want to be on nearly equal terms with a big proponent like an oil, gas or pipeline company, you need this time. Ottawa was not too happy but being a judge, Berger was independent. He was also determined to do this inquiry fairly.

In those days the Ministry of the Environment was in its infancy, but Canadian Arctic Resources Committee (CARC), a non-governmental organization (NGO) led by UBC law professor Dr. Andrew Thompson, had formed in response to the pipeline proposal and was gathering research on potential environmental impacts. Berger asked Thompson to round up other interested groups and work with them so CARC could represent environmental researchers and activists on one budget. This idea of gathering several smaller groups together and giving them one professional, well-organized voice was another first, and something the plethora of environmental groups today might learn from.

Berger had initially wanted the northern Indigenous groups to have the best lawyers in Canada—experienced counsel from Toronto, perhaps, or the country's finest litigators. The Indigenous groups would have none of that. They didn't want big-name lawyers from "southern

Canada"; they wanted to choose their own. They did and were well served by lawyers Glen Bell, John Bayley and Ron Veale.

But what of lawyers for the inquiry itself? At first I thought maybe I could fulfill that role, but then I got real. No, Berger said, we needed counsel from central Canada. He could also have said we needed someone with more experience, but the Judge was always polite. Also, unlike me in those early days (I was all of thirty-one years old), Berger understood that political and media power resided in Toronto and Montreal. I told him I had a friend from university, Steve Goudge, who worked for Cameron, Brewin and Scott, a small but respected law firm in Toronto. Cameron had been a Liberal MP, Brewin an NDP MP, and Ian Scott was the youngish lawyer who ran the firm and hired a number of hotshots. Besides, and I knew this would influence Berger, they practised mainly labour law and litigation. The Judge and I had dinner with Ian and Steve in Toronto, and it went well. After we got back to Vancouver, Berger decided to hire the two of them as Commission Counsel. "Fly them out to Vancouver," he said.

I replied, "Okay, will do. And I will arrange a meeting this afternoon with Ian and Steve in your office." Berger nodded and returned to a book he was reading. It was then I understood I had found my real role as the Judge's assistant. Tom didn't seem to realize that the early afternoon meeting meant the two lawyers were already in the airplane on their way to Vancouver, hired a little earlier. But the Judge and I were on the same wavelength.

It turned out Ian Scott, who had a tongue on him that could clip a hedge, was a superb commission counsel. He shuttled between Yellowknife and Toronto with his assistants Goudge, Ian Roland and Alick Ryder. Scott was always energetic, always funny, seemingly disorganized, but surgical in his questioning of witnesses. He and Goudge managed to keep the pipeline companies from filing and winning procedural motions against the way Berger proposed to run the commission. He and Berger hit it off from day one. Scott was the best lawyer in the room. Well, except for maybe the Judge.

The inquiry team was having lunch one day in a crowded Yellowknife restaurant when Scott offered a legal opinion, something about how far a government authority could legally go to exert its power. Berger, who had been typically silent as we all chattered away, finally spoke up and said, "No, I think they can go a little further. I believe in the late nineteenth century the matter was settled legally." He paused, thought for a moment, and then concluded, "I think the case was reported in the All England Reports of 1892." Another pause. "Volume 2, I believe. The English Court of Appeal." Have you ever seen four lawyers and a communications officer speechless? We were, if only for a moment.

Media Outreach

At the University of Toronto, in my freshman year, I used to sneak over to St. Michael's College to attend lectures on English by an oddly speaking professor named Marshall McLuhan. He talked about the world as a "global village" and told us that "the medium is the message." Berger was well aware of McLuhan's thoughts and the communications theories of Harold Innis before him. Berger had been in politics, unlike most judges, and he had a good relationship with many journalists. It was no surprise, then, that he had a media strategy from the outset of the inquiry. In his preliminary rulings, Judge Berger said that he wanted to "make this an inquiry without walls." I must confess that although I was involved, I didn't understand this at first. However, some of it must have rubbed off on me, for later when I was in the House of Commons, I was called "a media-savvy MP."

Before the formal inquiry, Berger and I went to Washington. While we were there, Berger arranged for us to have lunch with Frank Rutter, the *Vancouver Sun*'s Washington correspondent. (Yes, in those days the *Sun* could afford a correspondent there.) In the cab Berger cautioned me, telling me that Rutter was a good guy but was a professional journalist; as such, he could accurately quote everything I said in his article, even if he didn't write anything down while I was saying it. I was unusually quiet at that lunch.

Berger wanted to hire a media officer. I mentioned that I knew a smart researcher/reporter, Diana Crosbie, who was working for *Time* magazine and had access to journalists across Canada. I'd known her brother Allan when he was a student at Oxford and I was at the London School of Economics. One winter Allan and I drove up to Scotland to ski. My Scottish aunt loved Allan, but there was no snow so we drove non-stop to Kitzbühel, Austria. There was snow there but we couldn't find a place to stay. Allan finally got one kind landlady to take us in by passing ourselves off as players on the Canadian hockey team. Allan told me later that it wasn't really an untruth as he played for the Oxford *Canadian* ice hockey team (which beat Cambridge that year). We're not sure the landlady heard "Oxford."

Diana was just as smart as her brother and an amazingly hard worker. Berger hired her to carry out media relations with journalists across southern Canada and in the North. We typical lawyers were puzzled. Why did he need her when we were there to answer the media's questions? While Scott briefed editorial boards at meetings set up by Diana, she continuously contacted radio, television and print media outlets to keep them up to date on the inquiry's process. One key journalist was Martin O'Malley of the Toronto *Globe and Mail*. Diana persuaded the *Globe* to send Martin north and that set the precedent for media across the country.

The community hearings were unique and became the trademark of the inquiry. With the help of Michael, Berger took the inquiry to every town, village and settlement in the Mackenzie Valley and Delta, and in the Yukon—thirty-five in all. As Steve Goudge has written, this left an indelible mark on the Canadian North, and on the rest of Canada as well. Thanks to Diana's work getting the message out, Canadians became enraptured by the hearings, for the first time seeing Indigenous people speaking their own languages in their own backyard. Berger always knew Diana's value, but it took a while for us lawyers to understand what a valuable and indispensable member of our team she was. Without her, I don't think we would have gotten our message out to southern Canada.

Berger also had the idea that the CBC Northern Service should cover the hearings, not just occasionally but each evening. Remember, this was before the time of CBC News Network, CTV News Channel and

CNN. In November 1974, before the inquiry hearings began, we met with Andrew Cowan, the head of the CBC Northern Service. The experienced broadcaster listened to us quietly. Our plan was to have me sit in at the formal hearings and then summarize the evidence, and Indigenous journalists would translate and broadcast my summaries. Cowan asked why we didn't trust the Indigenous reporters to deal with technical and legal issues. Berger and I were speechless as we realized he was right. So it came to pass that the CBC Northern Service provided an hour of nightly primetime coverage throughout the vast Mackenzie Valley in English and for the first time ever, in the Indigenous languages of the Arctic. Coverage in English and French was broadcast to the rest of Canada.

I recall seeing Lloyd Roberson, then anchor of CBC-TV's *The National*, doing a stand-up in the snow outside the Explorer Hotel in Yellowknife on the opening day of the inquiry. But my most cherished memories are seeing almost every day that team of irrepressible Indigenous reporters at their table, dressed in their red vests. There was smallish Louis Blondin on his crutches, broadcasting in Slavey and Hareskin; soft-spoken Joe Tobie broadcasting in Dogrib; Jim Sittichinli, the Reverend Jim, in

Abe Okpik broadcasts from Reindeer Station.

Loucheux; Joachim Bonnetrouge in Chipewyan; and the rotund Abe Okpik broadcasting in western Inuktitut dialect for Inuvialuit communities in the Mackenzie Delta and in eastern dialect for eastern Arctic communities—now Nunavut. Whit Fraser, a veteran CBC journalist and a lover of northern Canada, broadcast in English and coached the team. Ironically this was the first time TV was produced in the North. Before that they watched Vancouver news and weather if they watched at all.

Always important in any communities, in the North radio was almost a lifeline. The first Indigenous radio show going across the country was produced, really pioneered, by Bernelda Wheeler from Winnipeg. The show "Our Native Land" sent Drew Ann Wake north first to interview me and then to do a weekly report on the Inquiry. Decades later Drew Ann would still take Inquiry materials across the North and Canada to teach a new generation.

But during the inquiry hearings in Inuvik, Abe Okpik was listening to technical evidence when a so-called geotech expert witness was describing the winter snow depth on a certain river. Abe loudly corrected the expert's evidence. He told me later he knew because he was born in an ice house (igloo) near the spot and had travelled many times over that river by dogsled. One night over dinner I asked Abe if he had ever killed a polar bear on a hunt. "Only two," he smiled. Very Abe. He used to pull out a Canadian two-dollar bill with a scene of Inuit hunting and a ten-dollar bill with a scene of the gas plants at Sarnia. Abe would say with a big smile, "The North, before and after." He told me the Inuit laughed at the two-dollar bill. We southerners saw it as an idyllic Arctic scene. Abe said that Eskimos (as the Inuit were called at that time) saw a guy bending over a seal with his rear in the air. When Abe and other northerners attended the hearing in Toronto, they couldn't get over the fact that their hotel floors were heated. Did they think that the northern way of life was to be put at risk by oil and gas development, and the resultant pipelines, to heat hotel-room floors?

One of our first community hearings in the spring of 1975 was held in the community of Aklavik, not far west of Inuvik. The Judge, jacket off, was filmed listening to Indigenous people telling their stories in their own languages as Sittichinli translated. At the time there was pressure in Ottawa to curtail the inquiry. Not because we were over budget or behind schedule, but because thanks to Diana and others, the media had noticed the inquiry, and previously unheard-from northern Indigenous peoples were clamouring to speak to Judge Berger. No matter who is in power, Ottawa likes to control things, so the budget for the rest of the inquiry was being held up.

After the hearing that night, the Judge asked me to fly back to Inuvik to check on our office there (the ice road to Inuvik was too dangerous to travel). I was puzzled by the instruction. Why did the office need checking? "And by the way," the Judge said, "take Whit's CBC tape. And if the CBC in Inuvik doesn't have staff to do it, send this addressed tape by cab to the airport in time for the daily flight south." Two nights later, a lot of Canadians watched *The National* on CBC and saw a picture of a North as they had never seen it before. They loved it. And amazingly, the inquiry budget sailed through.

Community Hearings

Judge Berger said, "I want the people who live in the North, who make the North their home, to tell me in their own language and in their own way what they would say to the Government of Canada, if they could do that, about the gas pipeline and the development that it will inevitably bring in its wake." He wanted the people living in the communities to "speak in their own language, in their own way," and not be subject to lawyers' cross-examination.

The idea of visiting and listening to people in the communities affected by the pipeline was Berger's, and was a brilliant one. The person who really pulled it off, though, was Michael Jackson—or Professor Jackson as we called him. He was a professor at the UBC law school, but he sure didn't look like one. He was slight, had long black hair and an English accent, and dressed a bit like a hippie. He wasn't a practising lawyer, though he had articled at a stodgy English law firm made up mainly of solicitors—that is, the guys who don't go to court. Jackson was given some family law cases to do. One day a client of his came into the firm's office and eyes began to pop. It was John Lennon.

Jackson believed the northern communities, which were mainly Indigenous, needed some preparation before the Judge came to town. He took his family north and stayed for days in a number of communities. Today we might call this capacity-building, and it worked. Jackson's goal was to create an environment in which Indigenous people would be comfortable. He succeeded.

My job was to organize our southern hearings, but I had to understand what was going on at the community hearings in the North, so I went back to Old Crow. I will never forget the experience. Here's what I wrote about it at the time:

> The hands of the clock are coming to midnight, but the sun is still shining brightly. Tom Berger, Mr. Justice Thomas R. Berger of the Supreme Court of British Columbia, is sitting at the corner of a small schoolroom behind a simple desk in the Chief Zzeh Gittlit School in the Village of Old Crow. This is the Yukon Territory, in the far northwestern corner of Canada. Behind the Judge is a map entitled "Loucheux Map of the Old Crow Country." The Loucheux are the native people in the area. The map is marked with lakes, rivers, hills and mountains, all the land used for many years by these people. At the Judge's side is another map showing the route of a proposed natural gas pipeline to bring Alaskan and Canadian gas to southern markets. The map reflects the same country but indicates totally different uses.
>
> At a table at the right of the Judge is a crew of reporters from the Canadian Broadcasting Corporation, four Indians, an Eskimo and a white person. They're doing a summary of the hearing, which they will broadcast the next day in seven languages throughout the North. A cameraman is on the Judge's left to take the scene via the national TV news to the Canadian people. Near the

camera are two court reporters recording the evidence for the inquiry and later sending this written word as far away as Ottawa and Washington.

The clock goes past midnight making Saturday now Sunday morning, July 13, 1975. Peter Lord, a janitor at the village school and the local philosopher, is telling the Judge how the people live off the land, muskratting for fur in the spring, fishing in the summer, hunting the caribou in the fall and trapping in the winter. "There is plenty of fish and caribou. This is the reason why we would like to keep our country like this." He is a gentle man and seems incapable of speaking sharply. "We don't like to cut our friend's throats way down south and make them sad, we don't make them happy because we don't like the pipelines near Old Crow. We don't want to have people have hard feelings against us because we only want the right to protect ourselves and our children in this country."

The Chief of Old Crow, John Joe Kaye, and his band manager, Alfred North, are sitting close to the interpreter and the witness. Behind them are the old people of the village and behind them, in turn at the back of the classroom and packed into the room, are the young people. The old people tell the story of the past and always add that they would like the young people to come forward and speak. The chief and his councillors, usually middle-aged and the most active men in the village, deal with life as it is now. The young people finally come forward and give their views of the future. There is a certain rhythm to this hearing, a certain natural organization. It started with a blessing.

Edith Josie has been writing a famous column for the *Whitehorse Star* since 1962. It begins "Here are the news" and tells about life in Old Crow, a village of 250 people living in log cabins on the bank of the Porcupine River. There is one road in the village, no cars, no roads to the outside world, no TV, some radio. In some ways, the way of life is virtually unchanged in thirty thousand years. In other ways the influence of the white man is apparent. There is an RCMP detachment, the Anglican Church, a nursing station and a school. The people have seen many scientists and oilmen, especially in recent years. There is a new airstrip. The pipeline could result in a camp of eight hundred workers eight miles from the village.

Now Mrs. Josie is serious and worried. She worries about the dangers of the pipeline as it crosses rivers, about young people being influenced by the construction workers and about alcohol coming with its inevitable family problems.

An old lady in her eighties, frail and bundled, comes forward and faces Judge Berger. She tells how her family has lived off the caribou and the land for as long as any of them can remember. She describes life long ago before guns and how the people caught caribou migrating down from the Arctic Coast by means of caribou fences or corrals made of logs six feet high and the centre with wings up to three miles in length to lead the animals into them. The Judge remembers that these were probably the biggest things yet constructed in the North. Like most of the witnesses, the old lady speaks in the Loucheux language. Jim Sittichinli interprets it into English. He's a man in his sixties and speaks English in Churchillian tones, learned as an Anglican minister. He called the square dance last night and tomorrow will preach the sermon.

The hearing goes on, but the Judge says there is no hurry. All the people will have their say. The people clearly like him. He visited Old Crow last summer, simply walked around town and met people. He told them he would come back later to hold a meeting about the pipeline. He returned last month to visit these people in their ratting camps in the Crow Flats, a series of small lakes north of Old Crow where people go to trap. The chief remembers and testifies, "I want to say this spring when you made the visit to the people in the Crow Flats, you seen how they make their living. Because of that I know you will listen to the people because you have seen how they make their living already." The people are not used to government officials taking so much time and showing so much interest; they have never been granted such an ear and now they are ready to speak.

Still more people come forward, sit down at the small table beside Jim Sittichinli, put their hands on a bible held by inquiry secretary Pat Hutchinson, and swear to tell the truth. They speak slowly and pause for translation. Next, surprisingly, comes Professor William Irving from the University of Toronto, an anthropologist who has been doing a dig in the area. He tells us these people have been here for ten thousand years. His words, although in a different language, echo the history as unfolded by the old couple of Old Crow. Professor Irving says seriously and sadly, "With heavy construction there will be a destruction of archaeological sites." But all day long these people have said, just as seriously, strangely politely, but firmly and powerfully, that the construction of the pipelines will destroy their village and maybe their lives. "Where will we get our food if the animals are gone? No Safeway here."

It is now two a.m. and the hearing is about to adjourn. A baseball game is announced. Last night there was a dance. "We will start again at one p.m. tomorrow. Those who haven't spoken will get a chance tomorrow," says the Judge. There is applause as we walk to the baseball game at the other end of town, not knowing whether to be more amazed at the midnight sun or at the sheer number of mosquitoes.

As the hearing starts again the next day, an old man of seventy-two asks about pipeline leaks. "What if there is a fire?" Representatives from the gas companies reply that there will not be a leak, but if there is, it appears that one and a half hours of gas will leak. There may be a fire, but they can control the fire. The old man looks on skeptically. Peter Nukon, young and strong at age twenty-five, is more demanding and articulate: "We do not want them to tell us the pipeline won't break. We have lived here long enough to see many things go wrong with white man's projects. We are told that when the pipeline breaks, a fire may start; now who is going to fight it?" There are more questions: about seismic lines, work camps and sewage disposal. And there is mention, by almost every witness, of the Native land claims and how they want them settled before there can be a decision on the pipeline.

Bertha Allen has a sister in Kenora, Ontario and she tells about fish being contaminated by mercury and eaten by the Indians there. "This is what the greediness of white people will do; they will do anything to develop the country." She now lives in Inuvik and is a little more bitter than the people of Old Crow. Another woman tells the story of her niece being carried off to Edmonton by a white man. "Mr. Berger, some white people are real good, and some are like dogs."

As the hearing goes on, commission staff members and press people occasionally drift out of the room to the adjacent one where some women of the village are serving hot coffee, sandwiches and boiled white fish. One witness says good-naturedly that there's already been some inflation—the price of bologna sandwiches has gone up 100 percent.

But the Judge sits there impassively. "I am Judge Berger. I am here to listen," he said at the beginning of the hearing. And listen he does, with dogged patience. He looks at each witness and doesn't interrupt. He is in his shirtsleeves now, his corduroy jacket on the back of the chair. An unused ashtray is there to gavel the meeting to start. "I find that I am learning a great deal from all that you have told me." When the attention begins to wane he will take a break, but until then he is alert for each witness. There is respect on both sides.

Charlie Abel, a highly respected man who was chief of this village for seventeen years, says, "Whenever the government wants to do anything, any kind of work, any kind of project in our land, they go ahead and do it. Even if we say *no*, it don't matter a bit to them." He talks about oil companies cutting seismic lines. "I saw the way they worked. They had their blades down and tore up the road wherever they went, and in the springtime wherever they went it is more like a creek, and in that way they spoiled a lot of good land where we used to trap. They never once told any of the Native people of the project they were going to work on." Other people speak of half-empty oil drums left to pollute creeks and about accidental creation of ice bridges blocking the fish in the creeks.

Some more witnesses come forward. All of them clearly love Old Crow: "You won't find very many places like this left in the world."

"We happened to be one of the lucky ones."

"I know what happened to the Indian people down south and I wouldn't want this to happen here."

Father Mouchet, who teaches the cross-country ski-ing team in Old Crow, speaks of the toughness, the way of adapting that meant survival against really tough odds, and the harmony and self-reliance it has produced. The people of Old Crow have a lot of pride and they are very industrious. He speaks of guarantees of protection if Old Crow is to jump into the modern society. (Two of those skiers, twins Shirley and Sharon Firth, were the first female Indigenous athletes to represent Canada in the Winter Olympics and won seventy-nine medals in the national championships).

We finally hear from the young people, the youngest being Harvey Kassie, aged eleven. The Judge listens to him with the same patience as with the older people. He is always polite, never condescending. Briefs are read in from the young people, and they speak of returning after school to a quiet peaceful town in an unspoiled land. They also echo some of the fears of the older people.

Again in the early hours of the morning, the hearing comes to an end. Chief Kaye thanks Judge Berger for spending three days with the people of Old Crow and he thanks our staff and the other people who came to attend the meeting. He announces yet another dance after the meeting. He says that every person who spoke at the meeting had something they wanted to tell the Judge and they all hope that it will help them in the future. "After you leave us and when you bring your message in the House of Commons, we look forward to hearing from you, and if you send a good message back to my people, everyone in Old Crow would be happy." The Judge is then given a present: some mukluks and mitts for himself, his wife and children.

Judge Berger thanks the interpreters and the people for the friendship they extended to him, his staff, the members of the CBC and press, and the participants in the inquiry. "These people from the CBC and the press come along with me to enable you to tell the people of the North and the people of Canada what you think." He explains that he's going on tomorrow to visit the whalers from Aklavik out on the Mackenzie Delta, and then he's going back to Yellowknife and later to Fort Liard in the southern Mackenzie to hold another community hearing. "I have to hear what all the people in the Mackenzie

Valley and the Mackenzie Delta and the northern Yukon think of the pipeline. Then I have to send a report and recommendations into the government, and when I am considering what I will recommend to the government, I will be thinking about what all of you have said to me over these three days about the land and about your way of life." His comments are interpreted and then there is applause. We have heard from eighty-one people in this village of 250. And we will visit another thirty settlements to hear people in five other languages. This surely must be one of the strangest hearings in Canadian history.

All told, Berger held hearings in log cabins, village halls, beside rivers, and in hunting and fishing camps throughout the western Arctic. There are 8,438 pages of transcripts in seventy-seven volumes and 662 exhibits from these "community hearings."

Southern Hearings

While Michael Jackson handled the northern community hearings, I was given the task of organizing hearings in major cities in southern Canada. We had originally thought we would go only to western Canadian cities that the pipeline would run near or through. However, I began to get requests for hearings from people in Nova Scotia and even Prince Edward Island. I took them to the Judge, who said in effect, "They are Canadians, and it's their North, too. We will go."

How could we inform people in the south about the project and its issues? This was before the Internet and twenty-four-hour news channels. Southerners were getting some TV footage, mainly of Indigenous people speaking to the Judge at community hearings. And they could read Martin O'Malley's reports in the *Globe*. I thought we could do more. The answer we came up with was to produce a short film about the inquiry, showing us at work in the North and introducing some of the big issues, that we would show before each southern hearing. I got a friend, Iain Ewing, to help make the film.

Ian and I had won a debating contest together at Victoria College, and we had even made a film when we were students. The film, *Picaro*, was the story of a young guy who took to the road for some coming-of-age adventures. I was the executive producer, so was responsible for the budget. Of course like a lot of Canadian films, we lost money, and when the bills kept coming to our suburban home in Etobicoke, my mother put her foot down. "Get someone else to do this," she insisted. When I left for British Columbia after law school, I gave the file to a fellow law student named Michael Levine. I thought he might be good at business because his father had a clothing manufacturing company. Michael became the top entertainment lawyer in the country, duplicating my experience with a young Clayton Ruby, who went on from working with me to become a top defence lawyer.

The crew for the film on the Berger Inquiry consisted of Ian and me. We made it on the cheap. One day we went out in the hot Arctic sun, tripod and camera in hand, to film a grader digging in the Inuvik dump. This would show the issues arising from building a pipeline in permafrost. On our way back to the Inuvik Inn, we saw some young people waterskiing in the Mackenzie River. When we were in our hotel room, swatting off flies and dust, we looked at each other and laughed. "Geez, they were Eskimo kids. We missed a good shot." We did, however, film all the main participants and scenes of the formal hearings at the Explorer Hotel ballroom in Yellowknife, as well as one community hearing in Old Crow. We were careful to be fair to all sides. I got Pierre Genet, the lawyer for Arctic Gas, to agree to the use of the film at southern hearings by including Vern Horte, the boss of Arctic Gas, telling his side of the story and by allowing them to sign off on the film before we showed it. Genet was a remarkable guy, rotund and amiable but no dummy. He was a good match for Ian Scott.

For me, the best scene was a shot of the Judge himself, standing out in the tundra in Yellowknife with some trucks moving in the far background. Wearing a Cowichan sweater and looking into the camera, Berger gave an off-the-cuff description of the inquiry and then summarized his view of its importance to Canada saying we are a northern people even though most of us haven't been to the North. His remarks were echoed in his final report. When we showed the film in southern Canada, it connected.

Berger saw our southern hearings as a means to educate southerners about the issues of the North and to raise awareness of the inquiry and the proposed pipelines. They got underway in the Hyatt Regency Hotel in Vancouver, where over five hundred people attended. I controlled the witness list and tried to get a balance of views, but I made a mistake in Vancouver by including the radical American Indian Movement (AIM), whose spokesperson went on about politics in the United States. Berger took a break, and on his way for coffee he whispered to Ian Scott and me, "You're trying my legendary patience." The rest of the witnesses stuck to the issues.

We covered ten cities in the southern tour including Vancouver, Calgary, Regina, Toronto and Charlottetown. All the hearings were well attended and we received over four hundred briefs. Martin O'Malley wrote that the inquiry heard from "priests, unionists, housewives, students, professors, company executives, politicians, doctors, Quakers, nuns, missionaries and organizations." Our last southern hearing went late into the night in Halifax. The next day I walked with the Judge through the park grounds of the Citadel in downtown Halifax. I was talking non-stop as usual, happy that we had got through the hearings without any big problems. The Judge just walked and listened, occasionally taking some small notepapers from the pocket of his old brown corduroy sport jacket, the same one he wore in Old Crow, and scribbling something.

An hour later, our team met before dispersing back to Toronto, Ottawa or Vancouver. "We have work to do," said the Judge. He pulled out a few of those yellow papers and proceeded to outline what we would be doing in the next few months. He said that the report should be written in such a way that it would be "accessible" to any Canadian who wished to read it. There should be as many photos as possible, and every person who spoke should get a copy. Finally, the French-language editor should be in the adjoining office with "pen in hand" as we wrote so the report wouldn't be delayed while it was translated. We all just looked at each other.

The Berger Report

When the hearings concluded on November 19, 1976, we had nine hundred pages of submissions, over forty thousand pages of transcript (ably and quickly put together by the Banister family, Ken and his dad, with employees like my long-time friend, Michael Robinson) and more than 1,500 exhibits. The inquiry cost $5.3 million, which is a remarkably modest amount given the magnitude of the task. On April 15, 1977, we released the first volume of Judge Berger's report, *Northern Frontier, Northern Homeland*, in both French and English (the French-language translator and his people were delighted to be "present at the creation"). The English edition was a mere two hundred pages, beautifully written and filled with stunning pictures of the North. Volume 2 followed on November 30, 1977 with more technical recommendations for if and when gas was to flow down the Mackenzie Valley.

Berger recommended that a pipeline be built down the Macken- zie Valley corridor, but only after a delay of ten years, which would allow time for the settlement of land claims along the route. Most of these are now settled, though it took much longer than ten years. The Judge recommended that there be no energy corridor in the northern Yukon. Instead he urged a national park be created in the area to pro- tect the calving grounds of the Porcupine caribou herd. The wilderness park Ivvavik was established in the northern Yukon in 1984 and another, Vuntut, in 1995. They are both part of the Inuvialuit (Inuit) and Vun- tut Gwich'in (First Nation) land claims settlement, meaning they're constitutionally entrenched: their character and boundaries cannot be altered except by Aboriginal consent or constitutional amendment.

Canada has done its part to save the migrating caribou, though of course, the calving grounds extend into the United States. On the Alaska side they are part of the Arctic National Wildlife Reserve, where the fight to stop oil and gas exploration has gone on for fifty years. In

December 2017, the Republican congress got President Trump to sign a tax bill that smuggled in the right to drill, putting the great caribou herd at risk.

In the early 2000s the Aboriginal Pipeline Group (APG), representing the Indigenous peoples of the Northwest Territories, signed a memorandum of understanding with a consortium of resource companies (Imperial Oil, Shell, ExxonMobil, ConocoPhillips) that gave the APG a stake in a new proposal for a pipeline that would run from the Mackenzie Delta northwest of Inuvik to Alberta. The proposal was approved by the National Energy Board in 2010, and when and if it is built, Indigenous people will be full partners.

In its time, *Northern Frontier, Northern Homeland* was a bestseller, unusual for a government report. I believe it is still the bestselling report ever published by the Government of Canada. *Le Devoir* described the French-language version as "la poesie veritable." The report continued to be available at public and university libraries or online, as well as the lecture given by Mr. Justice Goudge (my old friend Steve) at the University of Ottawa law school on September 29, 2015: "The Berger Inquiry in Retrospect: Its Legacy."

So What Did the Berger Inquiry Mean?

I have already commented on the important contribution the Berger Inquiry made in terms of intervener funding, ensuring that all groups with a stake in the project received financing that allowed them to participate equally. There were many other legacies of the proceedings, too. I can't list all of them, but I will describe some that I feel are most important. The second volume of Berger's report was divided into three parts, addressing People (social and economic concerns), Environment and Land, and the Project (including engineering and geotechnical considerations). In that last section, Berger included a lot of evidence from testimony on the issue of "building in discontinuous permafrost," including material on "frost heaves," which is now buried in the archives. This less-known part of the inquiry is relevant for future construction in the Arctic, especially as the effects of climate change become more apparent.

Commission counsel Ian Scott later wrote that for almost the first time in Canada, where the economy has historically been based on the exploitation of natural resources (including cod, fur, lumber, coal, minerals, oil and gas), companies had to justify economic development against the competing claims of a traditional way of life and the environment. Companies had to explain how they could construct a pipeline and its attendant infrastructure without damaging the culture and livelihood of the First Peoples and the fragile ecosystem of the Arctic.

It was Berger's idea to hold the bulk of the hearings in the North, away from Ottawa, a major departure from the way public inquiries were usually run. Ruth Carriere ran our office in Yellowknife and Shirley Callard ran our small office in Ottawa. The Judge's former legal secretary Pat Hutchinson quietly and effectively ran our budget. Of course I got the credit, but Pat was the steady hand. Any good lawyers will tell you their secretaries, now called assistants, are the key to a successful practice. Because the hearings were held far from the country's

Hunting muskrats in Crow Flats.

media and population centres, the extensive media coverage was crucial. No previous inquiry had been broadcast the way this one was, and only the Truth and Reconciliation Commission has had such coverage since then. Diana Crosbie opened the inquiry up to Canadians generally through her diligent work with the press. She later carved out a successful career in public policy media relations, and handled media relations for four other government inquiries.

Berger also wanted to ensure that what the Indigenous elders and others said at the community hearings was treated as seriously as the testimony of the oil company executives. Steve Goudge summed up my own feelings when he wrote, "As a southern Canadian lawyer, it was profoundly moving and a new way to gather wisdom. The community hearings gripped the North, and they profoundly captured the imagination of Canadians." Following the Judge's patient example, people actually listened to each other. The process led to the development of a whole generation of Indigenous leaders.

Nellie Cournoyea worked with the Committee for Original People's Entitlement, which represented the Inuit. I remember her as a striking, articulate young resident of Inuvik. Later she became a member of the legislative assembly of the NWT. Some years after the end of the inquiry, I visited her beautiful log house in Tuktoyaktuk on the shores of the Beaufort Sea. I was very sleepy and crashed for a nap on her couch. I woke up momentarily as she was putting a blanket over me and saw a number of people at her dining table in mid-afternoon. Nellie told me to go back to sleep—they were only holding a cabinet meeting! Nellie was premier of the Northwest Territories from 1991 to 1995, and later chaired the Aboriginal Pipeline Group and the Inuvialuit Regional Corporation.

Frank T'Seleie was a young Dene Chief who publicly challenged Bob Blair of Foothills Pipelines. He said he would put his body in front of the construction. Later, after land claims were settled, he became a proponent of the pipeline, which then included Indigenous people as partners. A boyish Stephen Kakfwi helped organize the Dene's presentations to Berger. He became president of the Dene Nation, premier of the NWT (2000–2003) and a supporter of the pipeline. A survivor of residential schools, he married Marie Wilson, a journalist in her own right and one of the commissioners of the Truth and Reconciliation Commission that held hearings across Canada to examine the devastating effects of residential schools. Watching the TRC chair, Judge Murray Sinclair, I could see echoes of Judge Berger. Dave Porter, who used to carry the equipment for the CBC crew, was a Yukon MLA in the 1980s and went on to be executive director of the Yukon Human Rights Commission and a negotiator for the Kaska Dene Council.

Jim Antoine, then the quiet but charismatic twenty-six-year-old chief of the Fort Simpson Dene, also later became premier of the NWT from 1998 to 2000. At our hearing in Calgary, Jim and I found ourselves at dinner with John Ralston Saul, the young assistant to the chair of Petro-Canada, who exclaimed the Peking duck at this Calgary restaurant was as good as or better than that served in Peking. Antoine and I just looked at each other. Saul went on to become a great Canadian writer, never at a loss for words. George Erasmus cut his teeth at the inquiry, appearing for the Indian Brotherhood of the NWT (later renamed the Dene Nation). He became national chief of the Assembly of First Nations from 1985 to 1991, and was co-chair of the Royal Commission on Aboriginal Peoples.

The young Indigenous representatives were, like me and many of the other lawyers and inquiry staff, in their late twenties or early thirties. The inquiry was the catalyst for their emergence as leaders in the conversation not only about the North, but also about relations between Indigenous peoples and the rest of Canada. We southern lawyers may have been the first to see a new generation of Indigenous people, both male and female, and their growing awareness of how to use their political power and collective strength.

Many of the lawyers who worked on the inquiry went on to major positions in the Canadian justice system. The four Commission counsels—Ian Scott, Steve Goudge, Ian Roland and Alick Ryder—carved out a unique role for later counsels: rather than tell the commissioner in private what they thought he should do, they made their final submissions in the same way all other parties did, in public before the Judge. Scott went on to be attorney general of Ontario from 1985 to 1990. Steve Goudge became a judge in the Ontario Court of Appeal where he presided over an inquiry into pediatric forensic pathology dubbed "the Goudge Inquiry." When I saw Judge Goudge sitting at the hearings, listening patiently, I knew where he had learned that from! Ian Roland and Alick Ryder went on to become successful lawyers in Toronto. Roland says the Berger years were the best. "It was like coming out of law school and going into the NHL."

Berger followed in a great tradition of judges in Canada's North, including Judge John Sissons, the first justice of the Territorial Court of the Northwest Territories (equivalent to a Supreme Court), and Judge William Morrow, who succeeded Sissons. What they all had in common was a deep respect for northern cultures and the land. Whether at trial or heading a government inquiry, they conducted themselves in such a way as to build trust among those who appeared before them.

The inquiry was unique, even revolutionary in Canadian history. Berger actually went out and talked to the people who were going to be affected by a massive construction project. These people told our government that they did not want to give up their rights or have them extinguished, and also showed us that people who lived on the land could know more than so-called scientific experts. I never forgot that in my subsequent practice as a trial lawyer when I dealt with expert witnesses. As we struggle with the issues of environment and the economy, pipelines and hearings, Canadians would do well to remember the lessons learned. The inquiry had taught me so much about so many issues I would come back to again and again—pipelines, energy, Indigenous rights, the Canadian North, caribou, the environment. I had made great friends and come to love the North. And I had fun.

CHAPTER 4

"Fix it. You're My MP."

DeCario and Waddell Lawyers

Life after the Berger Inquiry was a lot less hectic. I formed a law partnership with my friend Gerry DeCario in Richmond, a suburb of Vancouver that was a long way from Old Crow. Gerry was from northern
Ontario—South Porcupine, in fact. We met in the bar admission course
during my first year in Vancouver and used to hang out after classes
at a little restaurant in Gastown run by an Italian guy named Tony.
We would sit at the back of the restaurant and drink wine with Tony
after closing, listening to the winter rain falling outside. When we were
hungry, which was often, Tony would command his young assistant
Umberto to cook something for us. Tony later faded away from the
restaurant scene, but his assistant, Umberto Menghi, became a famous
chef with restaurants in Vancouver and Whistler.

Gerry is everything I am not: thorough, frugal, calm. All the necessary characteristics for a good solicitor. I was the barrister in DeCario
and Waddell, always in court and sparring with judges and Crown
attorneys. I tried to maintain a sense of humour, which I thought was
appreciated by most judges. Sometimes I did go over the top, as when
I represented a client charged with theft of a bucket of oolichans (oily
little fish). While speaking to sentence, I suggested it might be an act of
"ooliganism"! I got a laugh from the judge, and a low fine for my client.

I tried to keep my hand in at public law, receiving a small grant
from the Donner Foundation and working with my friend Andrew
Roman, who in 1976 incorporated the Public Interest Advocacy Centre
(PIAC). PIAC operated as a public interest law firm providing advocacy,

assistance and training for citizens' groups nationwide. Such services are normally available to corporate clients when they deal with government agencies. PIAC was designed to fill a gap legal aid wouldn't cover. For example PIAC, representing the National Anti-Poverty Organization, took on Bell Telephone, successfully arguing before the CRTC that Bell should roll back pay-telephone rates, saving consumers, many of them low income, some $14 million per year. By the mid-1970s there was a network of storefront law offices like VCLAS in a number of provinces, as well as Andrew Roman's national centre. This was our idea of law working for all the people.

In 1977 the BC Legal Services Commission was looking into the adequacy of legal aid. I was hired by the chair to be the commission counsel and to organize community hearings. Just before one of those hearings, the staff of legal aid went on strike and threatened to picket that night's hearing at the Hotel Vancouver. I told the commissioners at a private meeting that I would find it difficult to cross such a picket line. One of the commissioners, Duncan Shaw, a pretty conservative guy, was horrified. I was in a bind, so I phoned the great radical lawyer Harry Rankin to ask how I should handle my upcoming resignation and/or firing. Harry asked me the time of the hearing, then told me to arrive early and "to prepare adequately." It turned out the pickets never appeared, but I was *well* prepared for that hearing. Shaw later became a judge and showed some real courage on the bench, ignoring death threats after he ruled a portion of Canada's law against the possession of child pornography was too broad and unconstitutional—an unpopular but legally correct ruling.

Although I enjoyed this work, I missed the North and the great issues of environmental protection and Indigenous rights. A day after my fishing trip with Harry Chingee near Mackenzie, Jim Fulton, Jack Woodward and I flew over Williston Lake, created by the W.A.C. Bennett hydro dam, which had flooded 1,700 square kilometres and engulfed First Nations villages. Our destination was Fort Ware, on the northern shore of the lake, which was still a pristine village. Halfway up we stopped to refuel at Ingenika, a spit of land where there was an encampment of displaced Indigenous people and a group of American

Christian missionaries. I walked around the camp with Bob Maracle, son of a prominent Indigenous family in British Columbia, who was travelling with us. We found out that the people were squatting in Ingenika, living in tents with bad water and little food. Bob looked at me and said, "Now you've seen genocide in Canada, Ian."

I never forgot this, or my day with Harry Chingee back in Mackenzie when he told me the plight of his reserve. I was well aware that Aboriginal communities across the country lacked acceptable housing and access to safe drinking water. And Aboriginal people faced higher levels of food insecurity, unemployment, poverty, infant mortality, substance abuse, addiction and suicide than other groups in Canada, and they made up a disproportionately high percentage of the prison population. When I returned to Vancouver, I decided to run for the federal NDP nomination in Vancouver Kingsway. I told Gerry DeCario, "Don't worry. I probably won't win."

The Candidate

Phyllis Young, my main opponent for the nomination, was a former cabinet minister in Dave Barrett's provincial government. Phyllis and I had in fact put together the province's first-ever ministry of consumer affairs in my Robson Street apartment living room. She now had an election team that included former MLA Bob Williams, a young community planning student named Glen Clark and two local pub owners, Roger Tretanero and Ron Wickstom. Both Roger and Ron had grown up in Woss Camp, a logging community on Vancouver Island, and they were whip smart.

I got Jim and Elaine Duvall, two teachers who lived in the De Cosmos Housing Co-op, to run my campaign. To be honest, I really didn't know what I was doing, but I got lucky. First, I realized I had to neutralize Grace MacInnis, the former NDP MP for the riding. Grace was the daughter of J.S. Woodsworth, founder of the NDP precursor the Co-operative Commonwealth Federation (CCF) and a "saint" of Canadian politics. In 1968 she had been the only woman in the Canadian

House of Commons. She and her late husband Angus, himself a former MP for East Vancouver, spoke out against the wartime removal of Japanese Canadians from the Coast to internment camps in the BC Interior. Later she told me it was like standing against a tidal wave of public opinion. Now retired, she was suffering from arthritis but was still very sharp—and sophisticated (I knew her father, a Methodist minister and a longshoreman, had scraped together enough money to send her to the Sorbonne as a student).

I invited Grace for lunch and offered her the choice of a local Kingsway diner or a cool new downtown restaurant owned by a friend of mine. She chose the place downtown. The lunch was a good move. She agreed to remain neutral in the nomination fight, and later she was a great resource in my campaign. I also saw that some of the older members of the constituency association were a little uncomfortable with the group around Phyllis Young, so I drew on them for advice and encouragement—people like Gloria Levi, the indomitable wife of the former minister Norm Levi; long-time NDP members Ena and Jim Parsons; and New Westminster powerhouse Yvonne Cocke.

A week before the nomination meeting, Ron Wickstom called me to say his candidate was bowing out due to health issues. Bob Williams called me a day later to warn me that I had been insensitive to "the boys," Ron and Roger, and they might not even vote for me. But I won the nomination handily over Arnut Tuffs, a very gentle guy and a loyal New Democrat. Driving home from the nomination meeting with Margaret Birrell and Murray Rankin, I almost ran a red light; Murray had to take the wheel.

A few days later, Ron Wickstrom needed a ride to his pub, the Molly Hogan at 41st and Knight in Vancouver. As he got out of the car, I asked him to be my campaign manager. Ron had managed to get Dave Barrett re-elected to the provincial legislature after he lost the government and his seat in 1975; he also (with the help of Gerry Scott) ran Mike Harcourt's campaign for mayor of Vancouver and later, Mike's campaign to be premier of British Columbia, as well as Glen Clark's campaigns as MLA and as premier. Not a bad record. Ron was incredulous. "You just beat us," he said. I told him I knew little of street politics and I really needed his help. Getting Ron to be my campaign manager was one of the best decisions in my life. Ron and I became great friends. He always liked to kid me about my first speech at an NDP meeting when I opened my remarks with the phrase, "Putting policy and principles aside for a moment…"

The Vancouver Kingsway election race was a blur for me. The NDP owned the old Rio Hall on Kingsway, which we used as our campaign office. My job was to knock on doors and knock on doors and knock on doors. In those years, campaigns were sixty days long. At first volunteers answered our phones with, "Hello, Ian Waddell Campaign." Later, again luckily for me, Premier Bill Bennett called a provincial election, which started after our campaign began but ended nearly two weeks before the federal election. Suddenly the greeting at the campaign office was "Waddell, Barrett [Dave, the former premier] and Macdonald [Alex, the former attorney general] Campaign." Some people asked, "Who the hell is this guy Waddell?"

My main opponent in the election was Simma Holt, the Liberal incumbent. She had been a journalist at the *Vancouver Sun* since 1944, a time when few women were hired by newspapers. Simma did not cover "women's issues," but took on tough beats like crime and topics like prostitution. According to journalist Alan Fotheringham, she had the safest Liberal seat in western Canada. That assessment, and my fairly low profile, gave me little hope of winning the seat, but I figured I could put up a good fight and raise some of the issues I felt strongly about, like legal reform and Aboriginal rights. In hindsight, I realize voters were beginning to turn their backs on the Trudeau government, which was looking tired after just over a decade in power. Our leader Ed Broadbent got a lot of attention running a campaign in which he said the NDP was "for Main Street not Bay Street"—that is, for ordinary people, not big business interests. Our leaflets stressed "pocketbook" issues like jobs and living costs.

People like Cathy Lavery, Mike Gillan, John Nielsen (from IWA Loc 217), Andy Joe and almost five hundred others worked tirelessly for me. Now my job was to go around and show my face at polling stations. My friend Jim Wilson was assigned the task of going with me and

Stephen Lewis helps my campaign.

calming me down. We took my Fiat, but the starter was not working properly. At some polling stations we would park on a hill and get going with a rolling start. If there was no hill, we got a couple of locals to push us. At one poll, as we were preparing to push, I saw a group of Scottish seniors coming out of the station with Liberal poll cards. They waved and I said, "Well, I guess you voted for Simma; she's a good person." They waved back, and an elderly man shouted, "Are you kiddin', son? We voted for wee Waddle." Very Glasgow. The other thing I remember of that hazy day was Jim telling me never to speak to my constituents while wearing sunglasses. My constituents!

After the polls closed, I went back to the Rio Hall. Big sheets of paper were hanging on the wall. Poll results would be written on these sheets as they came in. Jim Wilson and I went to stand by them with Jack Nichol, the head of the Fisherman's Union. A volunteer came over with the results of the first poll. She marked a big 1 for the Marxist-Leninist candidate, 0 for an independent candidate, 18 for the Conservative, and 69 for Simma. Mine was the last name. The volunteer marked a big 1 and then another, and then paused. I thought, *I have eleven votes.* Then she raised her black felt pen and stroked down another big 1. I had 111 votes and was leading by a good margin. I became quiet;

Jim freaked and Jack Nichol shook my hand, telling me I was going to win big.

I did win, by 4,400 votes, and we had quite a party that night. Poor Gerry DeCario. I had to go back to Richmond and say our law partnership was over. To his credit he remained my close friend, and continued to practise successfully with Richard Scardina for the next thirty-five years.

Barbecued Duck

We were surprised by the size of our majority. Some of my campaign workers who analyzed voting patterns told me this was partly the result of the Chinese vote. Just as I came on the scene, Vancouver's Chinatown was regaining its reputation as a dynamic place. This was after decades of institutional racism that ignored the Chinese contribution to building Canada. In the 1880s, Chinese labourers accepted low pay and atrocious, dangerous working and living conditions to help build the Canadian Pacific Railway which united our country. After completion of the railroad, Chinese immigration was discouraged by a head tax and then an outright ban; those immigrants who were here already could not vote and were banned from many professions; and Chinese people born in Canada, some of whom served honourably in the First and Second World Wars, could not become citizens.

Things began to change after the immigration ban was lifted in 1947. More Chinese people came, especially younger people and women and they were able to take up professions, like law, that had been forbidden before. In fact, the law firm of Joe, Chong and Yee was at the heart of the renaissance of Chinatown. Andy Joe was the first Chinese lawyer in British Columbia; David Chong, more conservative, was a well-organized business lawyer; Bill Yee, later an alderman and judge, was an immigrant from Hong Kong. Alongside them were the somewhat older members of the Chinese Merchants Association and the new executive of the Chinese Benevolent Association (CBA). The CBA was the unofficial government of Canada for Chinese Canadians; until recently its

My Chinese-Canadian team.

executive had favoured Chiang Kai-shek's administration in Taiwan, but by 1979 the new group was looking to China and Hong Kong.

Enter barbecued duck. The shop owners in Chinatown wanted to prepare and sell barbecued meats in the traditional manner. That meant hanging the meat at the front of their store. *No*, said Health Canada. Storing the meat outside a refrigerator was a health hazard. The merchants appealed for the help of their MP, Simma Holt. She refused to meet with them and sided with Health Canada. My view was that merchants had followed this practice in China for thousands of years, and they didn't have a health problem. The shop owners gave me a Chinese name, *Chin chin wy do* (as it sounds in Cantonese), which I was told means, "Please elect the righteous way or true path." Great name. People I met at this time, including brothers Hain and Joe Wai, Rosanne So, and Andy's brother Ron Joe, became friends and supporters for life.

But here we were on election night, victorious at least in part because of Chinese support, and where were my Chinese friends? Not at our headquarters. Someone said they might be in a building owned by Andy Joe on the outskirts of Chinatown. I got into a cab with Wickstrom, one of my young campaign organizers Glen Clark and a tall teenaged

Scots lass, our piper, in a kilt. On arrival I instructed her to play "Scotland the Brave" as we walked up a long stairway and entered a room full of phones and beaming faces. My Chinese supporters applauded me and we applauded them.

Wake Up—Your Life Has Changed

The next morning my head was a little sore from our late-night victory party, but I was the first downstairs at the home on East 18th Avenue in East Vancouver that I rented with the Terry brothers, John and Brian. As I dropped a couple slices of bread into the toaster and put on the coffee pot, the old black phone on the kitchen wall rang. It was a man complaining that Air Canada, then owned by the Government of Canada, would not allow his father, suffering from terminal cancer, to get on one of its planes in Halifax. I listened patiently, if a bit sleepily. Finally, after he went on a bit too long, I interrupted him asking what he expected me to do about this. "Fix it," he said. "You're my MP!"

A week later, June 4, 1979, I was in Ottawa, officially sworn in to the 31st Parliament of Canada. You go into a small room with the clerk of the House, swear an oath and get your picture taken. My new Ottawa secretary Sarah Cloutier and her son joined me, as well as my constituency assistant Sharon Olsen and her kids, Dana and Darcy. Sarah had been Andy Roman's secretary at PIAC, and she efficiently set up my first Ottawa office. The next day the new members from British Columbia gathered in the Centre Block office of our House leader, the Honourable Stanley Knowles. Stanley was an icon in the NDP, recognized by all parties in the House of Commons as an expert in parliamentary procedure.

Stanley first entered parliament in 1942, taking over J.S. Woodsworth's seat. Rake-thin and slow-speaking, he stood by his old desk as we new members waited for him to hand out our office keys. One member—I think it was Margaret Mitchell, who was like a mother hen to the rest of us—smiled and asked about his filing cabinet where he was rumoured to have neatly filed every letter he received and every

Jim Fulton and I tease our leader Ed Broadbent.

case he dealt with. Stanley gave us an example, pulling out a letter from the 1940s. Of course, the files were a lesson to all of us: do your constituency work.

I noticed the famous tin of arrowroot biscuits and the tea set on his desk. Stanley took his tea and biscuits every afternoon. On the first-ever parliamentary trip to China in the 1960s, the MPs including Tommy Douglas found the Chinese food difficult, and made their trip bearable by raiding the Knowles biscuit box. When Stanley had handed out the office keys, we, like schoolchildren, dutifully thanked him. Any questions? Margaret Mitchell was still smiling; the rest of us were bewildered. "Any questions?" Stanley asked again.

"Where's the fridge?" replied Jim Fulton, our lovable "wild man" from the constituency of Skeena in northern BC.

"The fridge?"

"For the beer, Stanley, for the beer," barked Jim. Knowles, an ordained United Church minister, was a well-known teetotaller. Then Fulton went over and gave him a big embrace—though he later confessed that Stanley was so thin and brittle, he worried that some bones would break. There were a lot of new, young NDPers on the Hill. Bill Blaikie, Svend Robinson and Fonse Faour were twenty-seven, Fulton and Peter Ittinuar twenty-nine, Bob Rae was thirty, Terry Sargeant was thirty-three, and I was an old thirty-six. We were all products of the "movements"—environment, peace, gay, civil rights, Aboriginal and women (fifty-six-year-old Pauline Jewett and fifty-three-year-old Margaret Mitchell were also elected).

A Friend of China

Politicians should deliver on promises made to their electors. I'm not talking about the old idea of giving the "pork," or jobs, grants, et cetera to friends. No, I'm talking about the barbecued kind of pork, or duck, that may have helped me win against an incumbent. The merchants of Vancouver's Chinatown and I, now their member of parliament, met with officials from Health Canada. Nervous officials! I said, "Let them put the meat at the front of the store." Health Canada said they were worried about the temperature and the dangers of bacterial growth. Fred Mah, a firebrand activist in the Chinese community, whose day job was as a scientist for Environment Canada, saved the day. He said, "How about we put in some overhead heaters?" The guys at Health Canada jumped at the "compromise," and today you can see your duck before it is cut up.

Soon after I arrived in Ottawa, I was invited to dinner at the Chinese Embassy, which was in a former convent, an old grey building.

The invited guests were veteran politicians, the Ottawa elite. I was the youngest and newest, but the Chinese ambassador seemed to give me special attention. When I asked him why, he smiled, mentioned the barbecued meats and called me "a friend of China." Years later Glen Clark, by then premier of British Columbia, hosted a state luncheon for Zhu Rongji, former mayor of Shanghai and then the premier of China. During a lull in the conversation, I told my story of the barbecued meats. The premier's face lit up and he wanted to know all the details.

On June 16, 1980, the House of Commons passed my motion to recognize the contribution made to the Canadian mosaic and culture by the people of Chinese background. This was a debatable motion, but it passed unanimously. Stanley Knowles told me that only two or three of these motions pass in each parliament. I was able to speak of the history of the Chinese in Canada and expressed my hope that this history would be taught in our schools. My colleague Margaret Mitchell, MP for Vancouver East, fought the battle for redress on the Chinese head tax. In 2006, Canada finally offered an official apology and reparations for its anti-Chinese policies.

Into the Arena

The election was in May, but new prime minister Joe Clark waited until October to convene parliament. On the day before the session began I had Thanksgiving dinner with my mum Isabel, my new assistant Jack "Woody" Woodward and his parents, and Fulton's new assistant Gerry Scott. We sat in my small apartment using crates for furniture. The next day I made my way to the Parliament Buildings as the snow came down around me. Entering the House of Commons reminded me of my first time as a peewee hockey player. This time I went into a covered arena, but instead of ice and boards there were green leather-topped desks, each one seating two MPs in five stepped rows facing five other rows of desks. High above this political arena were the visitors' galleries where the fans sit, and above the galleries wonderful stained-glass windows that let in some real light.

My seat was the last one in the house. Indeed, I began my first question with, "Thank you, Mr. Speaker, for recognizing me without binoculars." I learned early in life that a little humour gets you a long way. As a politician I tried to follow the example of Tommy Douglas, who often used humour, sometimes against himself, to his benefit. The advantage for me was it softened my opponents; the disadvantage was that humour, combined with my small stature, meant people often didn't take me as seriously as I wanted them to. Of course, they might have been right not to! In any case, I had a new job in a new city; these were exciting times. My assistant Jack Woodward and I were quite a pair: big Jack and little Ian. We both worked around the clock.

A few days after being sworn in, I went to the old Press Club for lunch. Charles Lynch, Alan Fotheringham, Marjorie Nichols and a few more of the top press gallery journalists were dining together. Fotheringham remembered me from the Berger Inquiry—I think he had a soft spot for me as I babysat his kid one day in Yellowknife so he could get a seat in a helicopter with Judge Berger to attend a hearing— and he invited me to join them. Just as I did, I was paged on the public address system. When I got to the telephone it was Jack, calling about some mundane matter. I gave him hell and told him not to embarrass me again. As I returned to the table I heard Fotheringham tell his fellow journalists, "See, Waddell is already a pro. He gets himself paged at the Press Club. Now everyone knows he's here and important!"

I knew I wasn't really a pro, so I asked my friend Iain Ewing for some advice on media relations. Iain was an old debating partner who had helped me make the short film introducing the Berger Inquiry. One night I took him down to the darkened media room in the basement of the Centre Block. The big camera racks at the back were empty and there was a lone microphone at the front near a podium. We turned on the lights and I went to the podium. I explained to Iain that when I spoke there, I had to face the cameras but also talk to the print media reporters who held small tape recorders near me while asking questions. How was I to cover both? "You must look at the cameras," said Iain.

"But I have to look at the actual reporters, who may sometimes be annoying bastards, but are, after all, human beings." Ewing, who also used some cuss words, replied, "Look at the f— reporters briefly, then look and cut your clip to the cameras, and then briefly end by looking again at the reporters and say, 'Does that answer your question?'" Little did we know that the microphone was live and our conversation went right to the news outfits that filled a five-storey building across Welling-ton Street! In the days that followed I got a lot of ribbing both in and out of print, but the reporters gave me some credit for at least trying.

It took me a while to take Iain's lesson to heart about looking at the cameras. One early morning Jack and I drove my old Volkswagen Rab-bit to the Ottawa studios of CTV where I was to be interviewed from a Toronto studio. I sat on a stool and using an earpiece, faced a lone cameraman some distance from me. I did what I thought was a success-ful interview, but when I asked Jack what he thought of it, he said, "You were terrible. You didn't look into the camera." A few minutes later, unprompted, Jack said, "You were really bad. You didn't look into the camera." And again and again… We ran out of gas near a downtown gas station and were able to push the car to the pump. As we were doing so, Woodward again said the interview was terrible because I didn't look into the camera. "Woody," I said, "if you don't stop, I'm going to fire you." He just muttered. To this day, every time I have to do a TV or film interview I think of big Jack and I look directly into the camera.

FOI

When the NDP MPs arrived in Ottawa, our leader Ed Broadbent assigned us critic areas. I wanted to be the energy critic. After all, I had been special counsel to Judge Berger and knew a lot about pipelines. It was not to be. Cyril Symes, our member from Sault Ste. Marie, was named energy critic. I was the critic for communications and culture, which was considered low man on the totem pole. Funny that culture was always considered so unimportant. Lucky for me, one of the first government bills concerned freedom of information (FOI), which fell within my critic area. But I was torn. As a former storefront lawyer I had always supported and admired the work of Ged Baldwin, a frontier lawyer from Peace River, Alberta and long-time backbench Conservative MP who had worked for more than twenty years to make government information accessible to the people of Canada.

Finally a government, his government, was about to bring in a bill on FOI that might become a law. In my maiden speech to the House I welcomed the bill. I paid tribute to Baldwin, "a man twice my age who over many lean years in opposition was a lone voice in championing this cause." Then I had a parliamentary page carry a Christmas present over to the government House leader, an amused Walter Baker. The present was in two parts: first a rose, because we welcomed the bill after years of Liberal indifference; second a toy dump truck, "because if he will look closely at the exemptions, he will see that one can drive a truck through some of them." That got a shout from the House.

Looking back, this was a rare but important moment. Ged Baldwin's long crusade showed that a backbencher with perseverance could champion an issue and eventually bring it to a stage where it might become law. This particular bill died on the order paper with the defeat of the Clark government, but it paved the way for future legislation passed in 1982. My speech wasn't all wit. I went on to say we in the New Democratic Party believe in government, but a government that is "lean, accountable, workable and above all open." I still believe that a well-informed citizenry is the lifeblood of a democracy.

This speech came after my first intervention in the House, which was at question period. All new MPs see themselves as potential Perry Masons, the brilliant questioner. However, most go on too long asking rhetorical questions. (Tom Mulcair when NDP leader was a notable exception.) Ironically, my first question was directed to the minister of the environment, the Honourable John Fraser, from the riding next to mine, Vancouver South. He was of course my old friend who as a board member of VCLAS championed my class-action case against BC Hydro. I asked him about tankers off the BC coast. (Nothing changes!) I noticed reporters in the press gallery above the speaker's chair seemed to be dozing off.

My supplemental question was directed to the prime minister, asking that the government consult with the Americans on this important matter. To my surprise, in answering my question, Prime Minister Clark announced to the House that President Jimmy Carter would visit Canada. To his credit, Joe was always a House of Commons person. The press gallery immediately woke up and every pen was scribbling a note. I thought, *Wow, this is a big story and I raised it.* The next day it was the lead story in every newspaper in Canada. Each story mentioned the PM and the president. Somehow they forgot Ian! Welcome to the world of the backbencher.

Enter the Wheelchairs

We backbenchers were more successful on another issue. One morning a group of people with disabilities arrived at the Parliament Buildings to meet with MPs. Some members of the group were in wheelchairs, and there was no way they could get in through the front door. We met them at the freight elevator in the basement near the garbage. It got worse: Svend Robinson and I had to carry their wheelchairs into the dining room. We tried to get them into the visitors' galleries, but that was impossible.

One rare opportunity for parliamentary backbenchers was a procedure under Standing Order (SO) 43. In the fifteen minutes before the start of question period, the speaker would recognize individual MPs, who had up to a minute to introduce a motion requesting government action in some area. You would briefly describe the issue and then say, "I move, seconded by the member from X, that the House pass such-and-such." The speaker would then ask if there was unanimous consent. SO 43 said you needed unanimous consent for the motion to pass.

Bill Kempling, a really big, serious guy, was the government whip. His job was to keep government members in line. He was a war veteran who had seen combat and a man I came to respect a lot. His job in the fifteen minutes before QP, however, was to say "No" after each SO 43 motion. Near the end of the SO 43s, cabinet ministers would come into the House to take part in QP. On November 26, 1979, the speaker recognized the member for Vancouver Kingsway: me. I talked about our visitors being unable to enter the building by the front door, or to access the dining room or even the public gallery. Then I moved, seconded by the member for Vancouver East (Margaret Mitchell), "That this House notes the difficulties handicapped people face inside the Parliament Buildings and urges the appropriate authorities to investigate these facilities with a view to suggestions for correction." Knowles had helped me draft this motion.

Just as I started to speak, Prime Minister Joe Clark entered the chamber and caught my remarks. As I finished he nodded his head. When the speaker asked for unanimous consent, Kempling—"Doctor No" as we called him—hesitated with his standard "No." He didn't want to go against his leader. The clerk then passed my motion, which I had written out and filed, up to the speaker, who also hesitated. Hearing no "No" from Kempling, he read my motion and asked again for unanimous consent. Joe nodded in the affirmative and the speaker said, "Passed." Then we went on to question period as if nothing had happened!

Some of my other antics in that short parliament were not so productive and my friend, the irrepressible Jim Fulton, shared some of the blame. Prime Minister Clark had named Robert de Cotret to his cabinet as trade minister. However, de Cotret was a senator and senators are not allowed in the House. This meant he was not subject to questioning by MPs. Since trade was important for British Columbia, Fulton and I decided to go down the hall to the ornate wooden doors of the Senate while question period was going on in the House. As we tried to crash into the senate, we—meaning me, as Fulton held back—got into a scuffle with one of the senate guards. Things became heated and the guards called out for reinforcements. After a minute we heard the House sergeant-at-arms Gus Cloutier coming down the hall. He was a veteran with an artificial leg, and as he approached the senate he put his hands on his sword as if to pull it out. This had the effect of completely reducing the tension and prompting laughter from Jim, the senate guards and me.

Jim said we would withdraw, but he whispered to me that we could sneak up to the senate gallery and swing down from there to the floor where we could put our question to de Cotret. Wisely, I told Fulton this was enough. When I got back to my seat in the House, I rose on a point of privilege and complained about not being able to ask the trade minister a question. Then, stupidly, I went on to tell about our scuffle at the door of the senate. Stanley Knowles was scandalized, but most MPs hooted and some BC media actually congratulated us! I'm not sure the story would have the same ending today. If we pulled a stunt like that now, the call for reinforcements would bring a tactical squad and we would probably be shot.

Ain't Over Till It's Over

The election of 1979 had put me into parliament and Joe Clark's Conservatives into government. The era of Pierre Elliott Trudeau was over… or was it? In the election, the Conservatives and the NDP swept English Canada but Quebec remained loyal to Trudeau, so the new Conservative government was six seats short of a majority. Quebec also elected six Creditistes, what we would call Social Credit. This didn't seem to bother the Conservatives; they thought they would be in power for a long time. Joe Clark was only thirty-nine years old and had done what seemed to be the impossible: kept his notably fractious party together long enough to win an election after five losses in a row.

But young Joe had some demons waiting for him. He didn't seem to realize that the 1979 election was really a protest vote. As the powerful Liberal minister Marc Lalonde told me later, "By 1979 we were a tired government, and the electorate were tired of us." In his book on this period, *Discipline of Power*, journalist Jeffrey Simpson pointed out that because of their long period in opposition, the Tories had dug themselves into some unworkable policy positions. Now that they were in government they wanted to implement some of those policies, but they didn't take the time to build a new mandate for change among the public. This was especially true when it came to making change in energy policy. They were also overconfident, taking the support of the Creditistes for granted.

Clark's finance minister John Crosbie finally delivered a budget on Tuesday, December 11. Standing in a pair of mukluks, Crosbie presented with zest in his "Newfie" accent, cleverly hiding the fact that he was a gold medallist law grad with a degree from the London School of Economics. The Conservative backbenchers loved it. However on close examination, we could see the budget was not a Christmas present. It was all about reducing the federal deficit, but not by reducing expenditures. Instead, taxes were being raised by about 10 percent overall. This was at a time when interest rates had risen four times in the previous year, and the Organization of Petroleum Exporting Countries (OPEC) was forcing another oil crisis. To top it off, the Conservatives had been elected on a platform of reducing taxes and reducing interest rates. "Short-term pain for long-term gain," Crosbie explained.

MPs from each party meet every Wednesday morning for party caucus. The Liberals, after a boisterous Christmas party and a spirited debate in caucus, decided to oppose the budget even though Pierre Trudeau had announced he was going to retire. He had even visited his former finance minister Donald Macdonald, who was now practising law in Toronto, to tell Macdonald he wanted him as his successor as Liberal leader. My old friend Steve Goudge was to be Macdonald's executive assistant. Along with some Liberal MPs, Steve found it hard to believe the Liberals were actually planning to force an election.

And what were we in the NDP to do? We met as a caucus in 112N, a basement room of the Centre Block, to decide. The caucus agreed we could not support a budget that included the eighteen-cent-per-gallon excise tax on gasoline, and higher energy prices generally, all without adequate tax relief for low-income people. The majority of caucus agreed to a broad-based motion:

> This House unreservedly condemns the Government
> for its outright betrayal of its election promises to lower
> interest rates, to cut taxes and to stimulate the growth
> of the Canadian economy, without a mandate from the
> Canadian people for such a reversal.

Our finance critic Bob Rae would introduce this motion. Under parliamentary procedure we were allowed to make a sub-amendment to the Liberal amendment to the Crosbie budget. The vote on our motion would come first. John Rodriquez, the flamboyant and irrepressible NDP member from Sudbury, wanted to make our motion sound more radical in order to "jam the Liberals," but that didn't pass.

Most of the new NDP MPs, myself included, were led to believe that there would be no election. Surely the leaderless Liberals would choke, or the Creditistes would make a deal with Clark, or the government would somehow find a way to postpone the vote. Even so, as we hammered out our motion in caucus, I wanted to put up my hand and ask, "If this passes, do we really want an election?" But I was a rookie and held back; I believe other rookies did the same. That would be the last time I held back in caucus. The next day, Thursday, December 13, the government scheduled the first vote on the budget even though some Conservative MPs were out of town. Word was the six Creditistes would abstain. It looked like the Liberals were trying to get a couple of members back from their hospital beds.

Clark could have postponed the budget vote by changing the orders of the day after question period so the House would debate another government bill, or he could have made a deal with the Creditistes. He chose to do neither. I believe he didn't want to look weak, and given that there had been a recent election, he thought the Canadian people would give him a majority in a new one. But he was not thinking strategically. He had no agreement on energy with Alberta premier Peter Lougheed; his policy on Petro-Canada was muddled, as Broadbent pointed out in the House; and his proposed eighteen-cent-per-gallon tax on transportation fuels, on top of sharply higher gasoline prices, was hugely unpopular.

The speaker called the vote on our motion first, and the clerk called the name of each NDP MP as we rose to vote in favour: "Mr. Broadbent," "Mr. Knowles" and so on. When he called "Mr. Waddell," I rose, and that was the last of the twenty-seven NDPers. Then the clerk called out "Mr. Trudeau," and 112 Liberals stood one after the other. I wrote the result, and the date of the vote, on a piece of House stationery.

Every time I look at it, I remember clerk Bev Koester announcing the vote—139 for the "Ayes" and 133 for the "Noes." The House was silent for a few seconds. Then Prime Minister Clark rose in his place and solemnly announced he would visit the governor general the next day. The government was defeated and we were going to have an election on February 18, 1980. All hell broke loose as the House adjourned, and scraps of paper flew everywhere.

When I got to the lobby I phoned Ron Wickstrom. "Are you crazy?" he said. "You had the Liberals' heads under water, and now you let them live. They are your real enemy." I didn't know what to say. A couple of my colleagues joined me. Their excitement of a few hours ago, like mine, had turned to worry—we were facing a winter election. As we headed back to our offices in the Confederation Building, east of the main Parliament Buildings, I tripped over some construction and cursed. Jim Fulton looked at me and said, "Relax Wad, that's for the handicapped, the only thing this parliament actually did!"

What if we had not defeated Joe Clark on that cold December night? His Conservative government might have matured in time and found a balance between the red Tories and the blue ones. He was and is a fundamentally decent man. He respected parliament, treated the civil service decently and approved services for the handicapped. Later he became a very good foreign minister in the Mulroney government. His "community of communities" vision of Canada offered an alternative to Trudeau's more centralized federalism; perhaps Clark would have found ways to bring the provinces into better balance with the central government. All I know is that we can't rewrite history.

CHAPTER 5

The Big Leagues

The New Critic

"Well, welcome to the 1980s," Pierre Trudeau announced to a group of cheering Liberals in the ballroom of the stately Chateau Laurier hotel. He had decided not to retire after all and won a majority government in the February 18 election. Why did he change his mind? No doubt the master Liberal strategists Jim Coutts and Allan MacEachen were pretty persuasive. Maybe he read his own political obits and didn't like them. When journalists asked, he said it was his "duty." I'm not sure my campaign team was entirely happy about having to take part in a cold rainy campaign, but Wickstrom and company delivered. I increased my majority and returned to Ottawa as the member from Vancouver Kingsway for a new parliament. Some of my colleagues were not so lucky. While we gained seats in the West, we lost seats in the Maritimes and northern Ontario.

Chance is a strange beast. Our energy critic Cyril Symes had been publicly critical of former Sault Ste. Marie mayor Ron Irwin because Irwin, while an appointed member of the CRTC, had welcomed Trudeau to the Soo. Previously, Irwin had turned down Trudeau's urgings that he run as a Liberal candidate, but smarting from the criticism by Symes, he changed his mind and ran in the 1980 election, defeating Symes. To Cyril's credit, he stayed in Ottawa for a while and worked as an NDP researcher on energy issues. But it meant the NDP needed a new energy critic. This time Broadbent gave me the job—a bit reluctantly, I thought. I was confident I knew enough because of all I'd learned about gas pipelines from the Berger Inquiry. Little did I know what I was in for.

Ron Wickstrom drives "Red Shark" in campaign.

Soon after my appointment I was invited to be part of a panel at the annual conference of the Canadian Association of Petroleum Landmen at the Empress Hotel in Victoria. Landmen are the people who negotiate agreements for mineral rights and exploration, or research land or mineral titles. The panel at the conference included landmen, energy company executives and politicians—me. My new assistant David Levi, son of my early mentors Norm and Gloria Levi, wrote me a speech that among other things, called for the government to nationalize the oil and gas industry. A skunk would have received a better reception.

To make matters worse, I bombed when I tried to defend myself on the panel after our speeches. Especially fierce in attacking me was Bill Richards, a senior executive with Dome Petroleum. Dome, of course, was held up as a paradigm of private enterprise, even though in truth it was a corporate welfare bum, using its insider status to get government grants and other handouts from Ottawa. "Smiling" Jack Gallagher, Dome's CEO, had convinced the Liberal government in 1977 to introduce the Frontier Expense Allowance, which allowed energy companies and their investors to deduct two-thirds of the expenses over $5 million on a well. In August 1979 the *Calgary Herald* had calculated that of the $150 million spent on oil exploration in the Beaufort Sea in

1978, Canadian taxpayers had contributed anywhere from $130 million to $140 million in the form of foregone tax revenues.

Laurier LaPierre, the moderator of the panel in Victoria, was a friend of mine. He had been an unsuccessful NDP candidate in the 1968 federal election. Before that he was co-host, with Patrick Watson, of the hit CBC-TV show *This Hour Has Seven Days* from 1964 to 1966. LaPierre and Watson took turns interviewing the newsmakers of the week, but they were often in trouble with CBC management for being too opinionated and sensational. After Laurier cried on air while interviewing the mother of Stephen Truscott (Truscott had been convicted of murdering a young schoolmate though he was acquitted of the charge nearly fifty years later) the program was cancelled and Laurier returned to academia. Laurier could be flippant, overly dramatic and supercilious, but he was a strong federalist who loved Canada, and he was also one hell of a cook.

After the panel discussion and my goring by Bill Richards, Laurier invited me to his hotel room for a drink. Patrick Watson happened to be visiting Laurier, and both of them lit into me, telling me that if I was going to play in the big leagues, I had to know my facts even better than other people. I should have known this myself. I used to give the same advice to the young storefront lawyers, telling them we had to be better lawyers than the big downtown types. I decided I would do my homework and learn all I could about energy companies and energy policy. Maybe someday I would get another shot at Richards.

Canadian Energy Policy: A Short History and an Energy Crisis

The first things I learned about energy were one, that from Confederation in 1867 until oil was discovered in 1947, the energy question was really a land question; and two, the issue of resource control has divided Canadians since the opening of the West. The four original partners of Confederation—Ontario, Quebec, Nova Scotia and New Brunswick— retained full control of their own resources. So too did British Columbia, which joined Canada in 1871, and Prince Edward Island (1873).

However, when the prairie provinces entered confederation (Manitoba in 1870, and Alberta and Saskatchewan in 1905), the federal government retained legal control of their land, water and mineral resources.

The prairie provinces' fight for control over their resources was unsuccessful for a long period because they were isolated. Ottawa stubbornly retained control because it wanted to flood the West with immigrants; instead of giving the three provinces legal control over land, it gave them financial subsidies to help with road construction, education and other provincial responsibilities. Of course, the subsidies were "never enough." Other provinces didn't support the prairie provinces' demands for control arguing that they, as part of Canada, had "paid" to purchase those prairie lands when the Hudson's Bay Company sold Rupert's Land to Canada, and the revenue from prairie lands, water and minerals was payback. It was not until the 1930s that this question was settled when Prime Minister Mackenzie King and the premiers of Alberta, Saskatchewan and Manitoba signed agreements handing control of resources to the provinces.

This little bit of Canadian history is instructive if you want to understand why western Canadians are so possessive of their natural resources, exercise control over them so jealously and are so suspicious of the federal government. As an aside, there is an old joke I first heard told by the professor in my first-year political science class: an English citizen, a French *citoyen*, an American and a Canadian are each asked to write an essay on the role of the elephant. The English citizen wrote about the role of the elephant in the British Empire, the French *citoyen* about the sex life of an elephant, the American how to make a bigger and better elephant—and the Canadian? She wrote about the role of the elephant in federal-provincial relations.

When you apply this history of fraught federal-provincial and inter-provincial relationships to the huge question of energy, especially oil and gas, you can see the problem. Canada is unusual in having producers and consumers of oil and gas within the same country. For the most part, consumers are in vote-rich Ontario, Quebec and southern British Columbia. Production is done mostly in Alberta, Saskatchewan, northeastern British Columbia and offshore Newfoundland, where there are fewer people. You don't need to be an expert to figure out the politics of this. The actors in the drama change, and you can make the issues more complicated, but it always comes back to producing provinces versus consuming provinces, and the federal government trying to implement policy that it thinks is fair for all Canadians.

My seat in the House of Commons.

To add another layer, many of Canada's energy companies were (and still are) subsidiaries of foreign multinationals, and much of the oil used in eastern Canada was cheap foreign oil imported from Venezuela. Throughout the 1950s, Alberta oil producers were trying to get a bigger piece of the eastern Canadian market where there were more people, more cars, more industry and more money. They lobbied Ottawa for an import tariff on oil, which would make the foreign oil more expensive and the price of Alberta oil more attractive. But easterners didn't want to pay more for oil. Prime Minister Diefenbaker's compromise in 1960 was to divide the country into two markets: east of the Ottawa River, consumers in Quebec and the Atlantic provinces would have cheap imported oil; Ontario and the western provinces would use more expensive Alberta oil. Westerners had been using Alberta oil all along, so they had been paying more all along, too, but it meant people and businesses in Ontario were suddenly paying more—and paying more than their counterparts in Quebec.

Ten years later, Canadian exports to the United States started expanding. US oil production peaked in 1972, so thereafter the US began importing millions of barrels of oil each day to meet demand. This was great for the Alberta producers, but other Canadians began to get nervous that so much oil was leaving the country, especially in 1973 when the price of oil shot up. The oil cartel OPEC (Organization of Petroleum Exporting Countries—a group of countries in the Middle East, Africa and South America) was pushing up the world price for oil by cutting production and announcing they would not sell oil to the United States, Canada and other nations that supported Israel in the Yom Kippur War. I remember taking a holiday to Los Angeles at the time. I rented a car, and as I pulled off the Santa Monica freeway to fill up my tank, there was a huge line of cars waiting. Welcome to the "gas jam"! The price of oil nearly quadrupled, from about US$3 per barrel at the start of 1973 to US$11.65 at the end of the year.

The price instantly went up at Canadian pumps, though it didn't rise as high as the US prices. Donald Macdonald, the federal energy minister at the time, froze the domestic oil price and put an export tax on western crude. This made Alberta oil more expensive to export, the idea being that it would keep more oil in Canada. The move infuriated the western producers, who had hoped to benefit from the rising prices. To make matters worse in the eyes of Albertans, Macdonald made these changes without consulting the Alberta government in advance. Most Canadians at this time may not have understood that they were paying oil prices well below the going world rate.

The rise in the price of oil involved a number of actors. Peter Lougheed, the new, smart premier of Alberta, wanted to increase the royalties paid to his provincial government by the companies taking oil out of the ground. Ottawa wanted its share of the money. Consumers resisted any increase in price at the pump. The big oil companies wanted to export like hell and pay as little tax as possible. Think of four points to a square—Trudeau (and Joe Clark briefly) in Ottawa; Peter Lougheed leading the producing provinces; largely foreign "Big Oil" companies; and you: the consumer and voter. Sometimes the four points fought each other, and at other times they were on the same side of an issue.

Much has been written about the great Tommy Douglas, the father of medicare in Saskatchewan and later in all of Canada, but people tend to forget that when he resigned as leader of the federal NDP, he remained in parliament as NDP energy critic under David Lewis and then Ed Broadbent from 1972 to 1979. Unlike most MPs, Douglas understood the provincial viewpoint. He had been premier of Saskatchewan for seventeen years. When Donald Macdonald introduced legislation giving Ottawa power to fix the domestic price of Canadian oil, Douglas said he would support the move, but he also suggested it would be better for the feds to seek a deal with the western oil-producing provinces before invoking this power. Of course, the Liberals did just the opposite.

By mid-1974, OPEC had ended its embargo of sales to Western countries and resumed regular production, but oil prices continued to rise. People realized how important oil was to their lifestyle and to the economy, and could see how easy it was for supplies to be disrupted. They began stockpiling oil and gas, but also started looking for ways to conserve energy. The 1973 oil crisis, and a similar crisis in 1979–80 that followed the Iranian Revolution and the Iran–Iraq War, sparked the push for fuel-efficient cars and trucks, energy-efficient appliances, better insulation and energy-efficient building techniques for houses, the search for renewable energy sources and many other ideas we take for granted today.

In the midst of the 1973 oil crisis, when Pierre Trudeau was leading a minority Liberal government, Tommy Douglas introduced a bill to create a government-run oil company. Because the Liberals needed NDP support to retain power, and because the idea meshed with their own economic nationalism, they backed the bill. Both NDP and Liberals feared that because so much Alberta oil was controlled by American corporations, it would be shipped to American markets, potentially causing oil shortages in Canada. As well, Canadians would not benefit from rising oil prices because a lot of the money was going to foreign oil companies.

The Liberal government established Petro-Canada as a Crown corporation in 1975. It started operations in 1976 with $1.5 billion in capital and a head office in Calgary. The federal government moved quickly, transferring its 45 percent share in Panarctic Oils Ltd. and its 12 percent share of Syncrude to Petro-Canada, which also took over Atlantic Richfield, Pacific Petroleums, Petrofina and BP Canada. This put Petro-Canada and the government in the field (Pacific Petroleums), on the frontier (Panarctic Oils and Atlantic Richfield), at the tar sands (Syncrude) and at the refineries and gas pumps (BP Canada, Petrofina). With a powerful player in the thick of the oil patch, the feds could better understand the industry, fashion policies to protect Canadian jobs, get a fair share of the exploding revenues and, as much as possible, keep the industry Canadian. The intention was not to nationalize oil and gas but simply to give the federal government a window into the industry. Even so, Petro-Canada met with huge resistance from private oil. When the company built a new headquarters with red granite, detractors dubbed it "Red Square." The CEO of Petro-Canada was a dynamo named Bill Hopper, an oilman to his cowboy boots. Yet when I was NDP energy critic in the 1980s, Hopper told me he could still feel the chill when he left his "Red Square" office, even on a summer night.

When Joe Clark's Conservatives formed government in 1979, they promised Canada would achieve energy self-sufficiency by 1990. I bet Clark thought that with six Conservative provincial governments, federal–provincial relations would be easy. But Clark couldn't get a deal with Peter Lougheed. Even within his federal caucus, western and Ontario MPs clashed over energy. Prairie provinces wanted Canadian oil prices to move to world levels. Eastern Canada resisted higher prices. Like the NDP, the Conservatives had a history of struggling to balance the role of the federal government versus that of the provinces. When Joe Clark talked about Canada as a "community of communities," Pierre Trudeau, a stronger nationalist, called him the "head waiter of the provinces," implying that Clark would be taking orders from the provincial premiers.

There were ideological differences as well as regional stresses. "Red" Tories saw a role for the state in solving social problems; they were opposed by the hard-line "free enterprisers" who wanted to curb the powers of the state. Poor Joe. He struggled with Premier Lougheed of Alberta and was also undermined in various speeches by Premier Bill Davis of Ontario. Both were Conservatives who should have been supporting him! And logically, the eighteen-cent-per-gallon tax on transportation fuels in John Crosbie's budget was correct policy in that it began moving Canadian consumers away from cheap oil, but there was no clear vision for the role of Petro-Canada and no attempt to bridge the gap between producing and consuming sections of the country. That was left to the newly resurrected Pierre Trudeau government of the early 1980s.

Let the Eastern Bastards Freeze in the Dark!

I became the NDP's energy critic just in time to take part in the biggest battle between Ottawa and Alberta over the National Energy Program. There are a lot of lessons to be learned here. On the morning of finance minister Allan MacEachen's first budget for the new Liberal majority government in the fall of 1980, I got a call from Ed Broadbent's research director Marc Eliesen. Somehow Eliesen had heard that a group of high-level bureaucrats from the energy and finance departments had secretly been working on some new energy policy. I was to join Bob Rae, the NDP's finance critic, in the budget lockup to see what I could find out. On the day of a national or provincial budget, journalists, stakeholders and opposition politicians are literally locked in a room where they are able to read the budget documents. These documents are only made public when the minister of finance rises in the House of Commons and gives the budget speech.

In 1980, the centrepiece of the budget was essentially the National Energy Program (NEP), with its stated goals to promote oil self-sufficiency and security for Canada, and to ensure Canadians shared in the benefits of the industry, with revenue sharing and fair pricing across the country. The NEP created a "blended price" for oil, combining cheaper imported oil and more expensive domestic oil. It offered grants or tax incentives to encourage exploration for oil and gas by Canadian companies on Canadian lands—that is, lands on which mineral rights were controlled by the federal government (for example, the Arctic). It gave Petro-Canada an automatic 25 percent share in every new oil development. And it levied new taxes on gas and oil at the wellhead, the refinery and the pump.

In short, the NEP tried to increase Canadianization of the oil industry and achieve self-sufficiency through conservation measures. It tried to develop the frontiers and the tar sands, and diverted money away from Alberta to the federal treasury. It was a progressive policy in that it finally taxed "Big Oil," those American-owned companies that were doing business in Canada and benefiting from Alberta's resources. But it was all being implemented by a government that had gained its majority by winning more seats in eastern and central Canada while electing no members west of Manitoba. So of course, all hell broke loose in western Canada, especially in Alberta, Saskatchewan and northern British Columbia where the oil industry was particularly active.

At the press conference in the National Press Theatre after the budget speech, energy minister Marc Lalonde briefed the media. As he was leaving his chair at the table in front of all the journalists, David

Levi poked me and told me to get up there and give the NDP position (i.e. "The Liberals didn't go far enough"). This was a brash move, but I did it. When I got back to my office, Levi had me working the phones to newspapers in western Canada. The next day I was all over the press talking about the budget. Suddenly I was in the big leagues.

My job was made difficult by the fact that on the one hand, a central NDP tenet was support for government intervention in the economy: we had supported—indeed, moved the original bill for—the creation of Petro-Canada, and we wanted to tax Big Oil. On the other hand, a lot of our seats were in western Canada where our predecessor the CCF had been born, and where people wanted the feds to leave their natural resources alone. "Give me a one-handed lawyer..." Taking Tommy Douglas's advice, I tried very hard to consult with our provincial New Democratic parties on energy policy. Given the obvious producer-consumer differences in the country, this was a challenge.

But I was especially helped by my close friendship with Alberta NDP leader Grant Notley and his energy advisors Blair Redlin and Davis Swan. I recall David Levi and me meeting with Grant's team and a group of Premier Alan Blakeney's staff for a weekend in Edmonton, trying to crunch the numbers on a national energy policy of our own. We consulted Ontario MPP Jim Foulds, who was most helpful, and we came up with an alternative energy policy to Canadianize the oil industry, grow Petro-Canada, institute a fair tax regime, and split the wealth fairly between Ottawa and the producing province. (We never dreamed that Grant's daughter Rachel would one day become the first NDP premier of Alberta. I hope we were nice to her then!)

Of course, it was easy for the Conservative opposition in the House. They simply railed against the whole of the NEP. But we had to be subtler. First, I pointed out that Douglas was right. The Liberals should have at least consulted the western provincial governments and tried to get an agreement before taking unilateral action. Then I threw a reference to Lester Pearson's notion of co-operative federalism at the Liberal government. I was very happy when Bob Rae quietly whispered, "Well done." When the Tories accused Marc Lalonde of being a socialist, I defended him, refuting the accusation that he was a socialist and calling him a Stalinist instead. This provoked a great Duncan Macpherson cartoon in the *Toronto Star*, giving poor Lalonde a big Stalin moustache and a hard hat. (Many years later Lalonde and I had a huge laugh over this.)

The NEP was made up of a whole slew of energy bills that were brought to the House of Commons for debate. They kept my staff of Levi, Erin Berger, Ted Glass and Danielle Page very busy. At one point the Liberals tried to pass them in one omnibus bill, and the Conservatives filibustered, even letting the bells of the House ring for a week without coming in for the vote. They forced Lalonde to split up the bills. This is how parliament is supposed to work, except one by one, the procedural mechanisms available to the opposition have been eliminated, and today we would not be able to prevent this kind of undemocratic tactic.

Meanwhile in Alberta, Premier Lougheed reacted by announcing a constitutional challenge, a freeze in approval of tar sands megaprojects and a cutback in oil production. In hindsight, Lougheed may have realized he should have made an energy deal with Joe Clark's short-lived government. Lougheed distrusted federal bureaucrats, as most western politicians do, and he thought he was smarter than Clark, so didn't deign to negotiate with him. Big mistake! After the return of the Liberals he had to deal with Trudeau, Lalonde and company, whose political base was in eastern Canada. These were tough guys who like Lazarus, had just come back from the dead and were smart as hell to boot. To be fair, though, Lougheed was no slouch either.

Bumper stickers sprouted on cars: *Let the Eastern Bastards Freeze in the Dark*. The West rightly felt there was a double standard at work. Ottawa would never have dared to set prices, control exports or impose taxes on hydroelectric power, the majority of which was produced in Ontario and Quebec. Did the prairie provinces have the right to control their non-renewable resources or not? Did the federal government have the right to impose a tax at the wellhead? Economists John Helliwell and Anthony Scott wrote that each level of government "had substantially enough power to thwart the other." This is what happened. In August 1981, Lougheed and Trudeau finally signed an NEP agreement setting a series of oil and gas price increases and revenue sharing. A deal with Saskatchewan followed a year later. Douglas had been right: the feds needed to negotiate with the provinces to reach a deal; unfortunately, the Liberals had got it backwards.

There is still ferocious rhetoric whenever the National Energy Program is mentioned in the West. Exploration activity dramatically declined in Alberta, Saskatchewan and northern British Columbia after its announcement in October 1980. There were 390 drilling rigs operating in Alberta in January 1981, but by April 1982 the number had dropped to sixty. But was this the result of the NEP? Or was it caused by a capital strike as American companies pulled back into the United States because they saw some measures in the NEP that favoured Canadian companies over them, and they were not used to paying more in royalties and taxes. Lalonde told me later he was under a lot of American pressure from the Reagan administration in particular.

But I believe the real reason exploration slowed, and the NEP did not have the positive effect the Liberals expected, was because the whole policy was based on the price of oil rising. But it fell. Once again the "experts" were wrong, and all oil-producing countries in the world experienced a dramatic reduction in exploration and production. Sound familiar? The lesson is that with oil and gas, nothing is predictable except the fact that one day we'll run out of the stuff and will have to switch to renewables.

Could We Have Done Better?

I wonder now, looking back, if we could have done better as a country. Perhaps it was flawed in its implementation, but the NEP was a visionary policy. Its authors were all very smart guys, perhaps too smart. The idea of Canadianizing our oil and getting proper economic rents from Big Oil made a lot of sense. Lougheed's Conservatives were generally considered to be good governors of the industry (especially in comparison to their successors), but was their absolute determination to protect their oil a blind spot? After all, it is only by chance that vast reserves of oil were in one part of Canada and not spread equally throughout the country. Good policy would be to share. We could have done it differently.

We needed to find new sources of oil. This meant figuring out how to extract oil from the Alberta tar sands and finding new supplies in the frontiers, whether that was the Arctic or offshore (remember, this is 1980). We needed to restrict the amount we exported to the United States. We needed to increase the price to promote conservation, keeping in mind that this hurts low-income people disproportionally. We needed to change the tax system that had allowed some oil companies to pay little tax. We needed to recognize the feds were increasing the deficit to finance lower Canadian prices. And we needed to do all this when the existing system favoured large, integrated, multinational oil companies at the expense of smaller Canadian ones.

We also needed to figure out how to fairly distribute the money that came from increasing oil prices and taxes on oil companies. How much would go to Ottawa? How much to Alberta or Saskatchewan? How much to the oil companies (because they need to make some money or they won't bother operating here)? How can we help the lower-income consumers, because the higher prices and taxes are all coming from their pockets? Finally, we had to begin switching from oil to natural gas and, later, to renewable energy.

Many people hold Norway up as an example of what Canada could have done (though bear in mind that Norway doesn't have to worry about balancing federal and provincial rights). In 1972 Norway set up a state oil company, Statoil, that participated in the oil developments in the North Sea. This was what the government-owned Petro-Canada was supposed to do in Canada. The Norwegian government also set up a sovereign oil fund, the Petroleum Fund of Norway (now the Government Pension Fund Global) as a place to store the profits from its oil riches and save for future generations.

The fund is largely financed by high oil taxes. Oil companies are taxed up to a whopping 78 percent on their profits from Norwegian oil. Big Oil told Norway it would leave if this tough taxing regime was implemented, but in the end these same energy companies backed down, stayed in the North Sea and paid the taxes. (In contrast, when Canada was pressured by the US government and the oil companies threatened a capital strike, we folded.) The Norwegian government spends only 4 percent of the fund's assets each year, which means it is now worth over US$900 billion. In addition, Norway has no debt and offers its citizens free education.

Lougheed did set up an Albertan "rainy day" fund, the Alberta Heritage Savings Trust Fund, putting in some of the money collected from taxation of the oil companies. However, no more resource revenue was added to the fund after the late 1980s, and later Conservative governments in Alberta used this fund like an ATM. So even though Alberta produced much more oil than the Norwegians, the fund has barely more money now than it did in the 1980s. To paraphrase Andrew Lloyd Webber, "Don't cry for me, Canada"!

Revenge

They say revenge is a dish best served cold. So it was in a small committee room in the basement of the Parliament Buildings, that W.E. "Bill" Richards appeared before the House Energy Committee at 9:25 a.m. on a May morning in 1982. The committee was investigating Bill C-104, *An Act Respecting Petroleum Incentives and Canadian Ownership*. According to Peter C. Newman's book *The Acquisitors*, Richards, then Dome president and second-in-command to chairman Jack Gallagher, received a 1980 salary of $602,377 and held Dome stock worth $33 million. But Jack Gallagher and Bill Richards had recklessly overreached by buying Hudson Bay Oil and Gas Company from Conoco, first with a loan of $1.68 billion from four of the big Canadian Banks, and later by another loan of $1.8 billion from the Citibank group. Within a year Dome was on the verge of a default and had to be bailed out.

At committee, when it was my turn to ask questions, I paused, looked around at the packed room that included many journalists, and said that as a "poor social democrat," I welcomed Mr. Richards. At the end of the long table Richards was smiling faintly. I said I would begin

Fighting big oil.

with a joke. The room was silent, no doubt wondering if I was a bit crazy. The smile came off Richards's face.

"A Dome Petroleum employee walks into corporate headquarters and says, 'There is good news and bad news,'" I began. "'The good news is Imperial Oil will sell all its Canadian gas and oil holdings in the Mackenzie Delta and the Beaufort Sea for $300 million. [Short pause.] The bad news? They want $25,000 cash down!'" Many people in the room started to laugh; others were quiet, as they no doubt grasped the import of the joke. Here's how one of those present that day, journalist Jamie Lamb, put it in his May 5, 1982 column in the *Vancouver Sun*:

> The premise of the joke—a shortage of ready cash despite billions of assets—runs like a bass counterpoint under his remarks to the energy committee. With the oil sands projects down and out, the House of Commons about to go into an all-night emergency energy debate, and the dream of Canadian energy self-sufficiency by 1990 fading like an autumn leaf, Mr. Richards's company has become the hope and salvation of the government's National Energy Plan.

During my questioning, the extent of Dome's debts became apparent. When the Liberals had introduced the NEP two years earlier, Dome Petroleum reinvented itself as Dome Canada so as to take advantage of the generous Petroleum Incentives Program (PIP) grants, government handouts offered Canadian-owned companies. Under questioning, Richards said Dome expected $150 million in PIP grants for 1981, another $250 million in 1982 and at least $250 million for 1983. Asked if that wasn't a lot of money, Richards shrugged and said, "The more you give, the more you get." He also agreed that Dome was the largest beneficiary of PIP grants. Finally, I noted that Dome might be doing the bulk of its successful drilling in Ottawa and not the Beaufort Sea. Richards just scowled at me.

Natural Gas

Oil and gas go together in Canada's energy picture as they both involve pipelines. In 1978 the Parliament of Canada had passed the *Northern Pipeline Act* approving the building of a pipeline to carry gas from Alaska through Canada to the southern United States. As the Trudeau era was drawing to a close, the Liberal government approved by executive order—that is by regulation rather than legislation—the "prebuild" of the southern portion of this pipeline to take Alberta gas to the US.

The problem was that the *Northern Pipeline Act* specifically said the pipeline was for Alaska gas. Now the government was authorizing a shorter pipeline from Alberta, which would suck up all that cheap Alberta gas for quick export, without changing the *Act*. The executive order made a mockery of any rational Canadian energy strategy, which should have been to get eastern Canadians to switch from expensive imported oil to Canadian natural gas—the ultimate aim being energy self-sufficiency for Canada. Surely exporting Alberta gas was not what parliament intended when it passed the *Northern Pipeline Act*. I believed the government was short-circuiting the *Act*, and I said so quite loudly.

Energy minister Lalonde replied that the larger northern pipeline would be built later. Indeed, he was seeking "ironclad guarantees" that the whole line would eventually be built. He got a general resolution to build from the US Congress, but not one red cent committed to construction. The resolution didn't bind private companies, the guys who would actually build the line. I said the bigger line to carry Alaska gas would probably never be built. (I was right.)

It was time for a man to bite a big dog. I decided to hold up the House of Commons for a few days before the summer recess. I got good at "procedure." The Liberals sure took notice. Then I made a deal to force a debate (because I had to get the public aware of the complicated issue). My motion said that construction of the controversial prebuild portion of the pipeline should not commence until complete financial guarantees for the whole pipeline had been obtained and an agreement was reached with the US government to replace Canadian gas exported in the prebuild with US gas from Alaska when the complete line was finished.

Then I sued the Canadian government. I got Jack Woodward to draft the legal papers, the writ. We sued the whole cabinet, naming each one of the ministers but beginning with the governor general. It sure looked strange: "Waddell vs. Schreyer et al." I'm sure Ed Schreyer, a former NDP premier of Manitoba, was smiling. We sought a court ruling on whether the federal cabinet had power to alter the *Northern Pipeline Act* in such a major way. We said the project had been changed from a pipeline carrying Alaska gas to, at least in its initial stages, a pipeline exporting surplus Alberta gas.

I thought I had a good legal case. If the government wanted to legalize a "prebuild," they should have brought in legislation to amend the *Northern Pipeline Act* (which would have been debated in parliament) and not just do the same thing by government regulation. As *Globe* columnist Michael Valpy recognized at the time, the flaw in the prebuild was that there was no ironclad guarantee that the American section of the pipelines would ever be built, and thus no guarantee that there would be Alaska gas to replace the Canadian gas sold south of the border.

The lawyers for Foothills Pipelines responded by moving to have the court throw out my action on the grounds I didn't have "standing" to bring it to court. My lawyers, Paul and David Rosenberg and Jack Woodward, with the help in court of John Laxton, argued that as an MP, an energy critic, and a plain old Canadian citizen and potential consumer of that gas I did have the legal standing to at least bring the lawsuit. Justice George Murray of the Supreme Court of British Columbia agreed. The Foothills Pipelines lawyers then appealed all the way to the Supreme Court of Canada, which held for us. I proudly told the media, "We are on first base!"

Later, in the publicity around the lawsuit, I said we were on third base, then back to second. Eventually, in the trial itself, we lost. The judge was Justice Ken Lysyk, whose background was pretty left wing, but he gave a judgment in favour of the government. I think he may have been what my old law professor John Willis called a "government man," which meant he was prepared to give the government broad discretion within the *Act*. But I had at least put the issue in the news. Years later Robert Holmes QC, who was a young lawyer junioring with the government at the time, wrote this to me: "While not the most successful venture in your career... I admired your courage in bringing the case to court and the optimistic attitude toward everything... It was obvious that you were all enjoying your role as young activists out to reform the law and the world."

Unfortunately by the end of the 1980s the great defenders of the rights of parliament—John Diefenbaker, Ged Baldwin, Stanley Knowles and Gordon Fairweather—were gone. My fight on the prebuild was about energy policy, but in my mind it was also about parliament. There was a lot of editorial comment about this at the time. My favourite was a column in the *Vancouver Sun* by Allan Fotheringham, who mentioned that northern journalist Abe Okpik, "a droll Eskimo who sports a crewcut, a vast belly the size of Lake Athabasca, and a gimpy leg," had christened me "SikSik," meaning the Arctic squirrel. Foth concluded his article about my pipeline fight with "The squirrel is alive and digging."

CHAPTER 6

The Constitutional Promise

In the 1980 referendum on Quebec's sovereignty, Pierre Trudeau led the federalist side against Parti Québécois premier Réne Lévesque and the separatists. Canada was lucky to have him there. When he was prime minister, Joe Clark had decided to leave the fight to the province's opposition leader Claude Ryan. It's impossible to predict what might have happened without federal involvement, but Trudeau and other federal Liberals campaigned actively against separation, and on May 20, 1980, just three months after Trudeau's Liberals regained power, the "No" side against sovereignty won 59.56 percent of the vote.

In a speech he gave in Montreal during the campaign, Trudeau stated that the referendum indicated the need for change and pledged that if the result were "No," he would work with the premiers to "renew" Canada's constitution. Trudeau was mindful that in the 1980 election his Liberals won only two of seventy-five seats in the four western provinces. They didn't have a seat west of Lloyd Axworthy's in Winnipeg. Even though he had a majority government, Trudeau knew he would have more influence in the constitutional discussions if some members of his cabinet came from the West. To this end, he was in talks with Ed Broadbent about taking some of our western NDP MPs into the government as cabinet ministers, though we MPs were not aware of this.

On the night of the press gallery dinner in May, I was invited to the *Toronto Star* pre-party. From there I went to the dinner and then the after-party at the Press Club in the wee hours of the morning. I have only been drunk a few times in my life, and this was one of them. I faintly recall standing in the Press Club, across Wellington Street from the Parliament Buildings, with the prime minister's chief of staff Jim Coutts in our group. I learned later he was a serious teetotaller. He was talking to me about my background with Berger and the environment. I looked at him, turned around, and ran to the toilet to barf. That's as close as I got to a federal cabinet post.

The New Constitution

A constitution is the fundamental law of any country, the rules by which it governs itself. In 1980, Canada's constitution was essentially the *British North America Act* of 1867, which was an act of the parliament of the United Kingdom. Any significant changes to that constitution had to be made by the British parliament. In the wake of the Quebec referendum, Trudeau's plan was to "patriate" the constitution—to bring it home so we could make changes ourselves rather than running over to London to ask politicians there to do it for us. However, when Trudeau sat down with the provincial premiers to discuss how to bring the constitution to Canada, they couldn't reach an agreement. They couldn't, for example, agree to an amending formula, which set out how the first ministers would change the thing once it was a Canadian law.

After numerous meetings with the provincial premiers, and numerous tentative agreements that failed when provinces backed out or refused to support him, Trudeau rather courageously offered his own constitutional package, which included a Charter of Rights and Freedoms and the promise of a national referendum on the amending formula. He introduced his proposal in the House of Commons on October 6, 1980. Of course this stirred up a furious debate among politicians and also among the citizens of Canada. Trudeau soon found that only two provinces, Ontario and New Brunswick, supported his plan. The others, the "gang of eight," were vehemently against it. Quebec wanted a veto on any constitutional amendments; Saskatchewan and Manitoba were against a court-interpreted Charter; Alberta, Newfoundland and Saskatchewan wanted protection of provincial resource control embedded in the constitution; and so on.

Ed Broadbent came out rather quickly in support of Trudeau's package, to the consternation of many MPs in his caucus. Jim Manly, Jim Fulton and I wanted Aboriginal rights included in the Charter, while Pauline Jewett and Margaret Mitchell wanted women's rights included. Svend Robinson wanted the Charter strengthened generally. Lorne Nystrom and Simon De Jong wanted Saskatchewan's concerns addressed.

When Ed came to British Columbia to speak at a fundraiser in late 1980, I invited him to join me at Nibbles restaurant, near Vancouver City Hall, after the event. I was a regular at Nibbles and knew the staff. The restaurant was owned by Laurier LaPierre, a staunch Quebec federalist and invaluable sounding board for Svend Robinson and me during the constitutional debates. So I figured this was a good place to take Ed. But the two of us got into a loud debate. I told Ed that a lot of us in the caucus could not support Trudeau's constitutional package. Ed's handlers got really nervous about our noisy argument, especially when a group of off-duty CBC reporters showed up (it turned out they were more interested in eating and drinking than listening to Broadbent and me).

With Ed Broadbent, one of the most remarkable Canadian politicians.

Ironically, as we argued, I was also asking the Nibbles staff to find a cigar for Ed. You could smoke in restaurants then, and Ed liked Cuban cigars. Chris Price, a great waiter and another friend of Laurier, ended up going down the street to find a cigar. When he returned, I lit Ed's stogie while we continued ferociously arguing. Ed was not happy when I told him his MPs from western Canada were not going to go along with the deal. He was, overall, a democrat, and as a former professor he was prepared to argue issues without taking it personally. That night amidst the cigar smoke, the scared assistants, the loud discussion and nearby journalists, neither of us changed the other's mind.

NDP leaders in western Canada were also outraged by Broadbent's support of Trudeau's package. They were each in a difficult position. Grant Notley had been under pressure from federal NDPers in his province to publicly support the National Energy Program, which was hugely unpopular in Alberta but was seen as a progressive policy by rank-and-file members. Premier Allan Blakeney of Saskatchewan, a highly intelligent and principled man, represented those in the NDP who didn't like the idea of unelected judges making law, which would happen when judges interpreted a Charter of Rights. Blakeney also wanted the principle of provincial control over non-renewable resources to be nailed down in the constitution.

Ed flew into Calgary secretly to meet with the western leaders, including Notley, Blakeney, Saskatchewan attorney general Roy Romanow, Howard Pawley of Manitoba and Dave Barrett of British Columbia. The meeting, held at the Delta Hotel by the Calgary airport so the press wouldn't see Broadbent, was tense. The westerners felt Broadbent had not consulted them adequately before jumping to support the constitutional package. Peter Puxley and Davis Swan were present as Ed's advisors. When Puxley attempted to take notes, Barrett grabbed his pen. Poor Ed was under a lot of pressure, and I'm not sure if the Calgary meeting provided any relief.

Getting the British Ambassador Kicked Out

The House of Commons debate over the constitutional package continued into the new year. In February 1981 I was at another party (not wanting to sound like a party animal here, even though I am one). This was a skating party at Ed and Lily Schreyer's house in Ottawa. Of course, their house was stately Rideau Hall because Schreyer, a former NDP premier of Manitoba, was the governor general of Canada. At one point I found myself in a group discussing the Trudeau constitutional package. A chap with a British accent asked me why the NDP, with a majority of its MPs from western Canada, was supporting Trudeau when it seemed against the interests of the West. I couldn't reveal how divided we were, so I gave a weak defence, concluding lamely with, "It will be passed by Britain anyway."

"Don't be too sure of that," replied the well-dressed Englishman.

"Why do you say that?" I asked.

"Because I'm the British High Commissioner." I was speaking to the UK ambassador to Canada! Jim Manly was standing beside me, and we were both a bit shocked. Next morning at caucus I offhandedly mentioned the incident to Ed Broadbent. I was stunned when later that day in question period, Ed put a question to Mark MacGuigan, secretary of state for external affairs, mentioning UK ambassador Sir John Ford and me by name. One of my first thoughts was, *Nobody is going to invite me to another cocktail party!*

Sir John called a press conference, and Trudeau complained to British prime minister Margaret Thatcher behind the scenes. Editorials in most Canadian papers protested Britain's involvement in Canadian affairs. The one in the *Toronto Star* said, "End British Meddling"; the *Montreal Gazette* accused Britain of "over-stepping bounds." Trudeau had more of a sense of humour, making a quip about the current *Star Wars* instalment, *The Empire Strikes Back*. Sir John was recalled to London, or so I thought.

I had my second drink with Sir John Ford thirty-three years later at the home of his sister, former Vancouver city councillor Marguerite Ford. I was a little apprehensive. Did he think I'd got him kicked out of Canada? He laughed and told me he had already been planning to retire, and the government was well aware of that. Sir John had gone on to a career in the private non-profit sector. We had a nice chat, and he gave me a unique insider's look at a history I had been part of. Sir John had just been doing his job. The political atmosphere at the time was tense, and he may have been using me to get a message to Trudeau. The Kershaw Report in the UK had recommended that the British House of Commons not pass Trudeau's package. Trudeau didn't have the votes in the mother of parliaments, and Sir John thought he should know that.

The Birth of Section 35

Tired. I remember being very tired. The lethargy seeped into my eye sockets. My legs were sore. I was dragging myself from the floor of the House of Commons out to the granite lobby and up six floors to Ed Broadbent's office, 653C, then over to my parliamentary office in the Confederation Building, west of the Centre Block. There the phone wouldn't stop with calls coming from my constituency office almost five thousand kilometres away in Vancouver.

At the same time I felt that my mind had never been so alert. I was exhilarated even as I fought off the body fatigue of two tumultuous years with two long election campaigns, the travel back and forth to Ottawa, and my new parliamentary critic role during a looming energy crisis. I was exhilarated because the movement for constitutional renewal had given me a cause. I was fighting for the rights of Canada's First Nations. Most of the calls from my constituency office dealt with immigration problems, many of them involving Chinese Canadians and South Asian Canadians who made up a majority of my constituents. None dealt with Aboriginal Canadian matters. But that didn't matter. As Tom Berger had said to me in Yellowknife years earlier, "You've got the religion."

My involvement, indeed passion, for Indigenous issues came about unexpectedly. As a young Scottish immigrant to Canada, I first saw Indigenous peoples when I was a teenager, and then only fleetingly as my dad drove us through a small reserve near Lake Couchiching north of Toronto. It was not until I was a young criminal lawyer in Vancouver at Main and Hastings that I began to appreciate the tragedies and injustices that enshrouded Canada's Indigenous peoples. As counsel to Tom Berger during the Mackenzie Valley pipeline inquiry, I began to see an answer to their plight: Indigenous peoples could regain real political and economic power within the modern Canadian framework through the recognition of Aboriginal and treaty rights.

The scope of those rights became clear to me during Judge Berger's countless meetings from Old Crow to Fort Smith as the people spoke of their love of the land, and their use of that land for hunting and fishing from "time immemorial." I heard that they had governed themselves for generations before the arrival of the white man; that they had never surrendered the title to their land. But they had lost access to the land and the resources that went with it. As Henry Chingee had told me a few years earlier, they wanted "a piece of the action." Fellow lawyers Jim Aldridge and Don Rosenbloom were keeping me up to date on their work with the Nisga'a in northern BC, whose Calder case heard before the Supreme Court in 1973 established that First Nations did have title to the land when colonizers arrived, but didn't determine whether that title still existed. I came to realize this moment of constitutional renewal might be the opportunity they needed.

In the latter part of 1980 the constitutional debate was taking place in joint hearings before the Senate and House of Commons. My friend Jack Woodward had appeared there as counsel for the loquacious and determined Chief George Watts of the Nuu-chah-nulth Tribal Council, who was arguing for a clause protecting Aboriginal rights. In the midst of this, I attended a ball hosted by Governor General Schreyer at Rideau Hall. As I returned to my table with a glass of red wine in each hand, I came face to face with Prime Minister Trudeau. "Oh," he said, "here's the fighter for the Indians!"

Perhaps it was the fact I couldn't use my hands; perhaps it was my legal discussion just the weekend before with Rosenbloom and Berger; or perhaps it was fate. In any case, I blurted out an impassioned plea: "You know, Prime Minister, you don't have to take the side of the reactionaries in the justice department. You could go with the progressive reasoning of judges like Spence, Hall and Laskin in the Calder case."

"Well the NDP, your leader, has given the package his support."

I was now holding the two glasses like swords, waving them slightly. The wine was almost spilling. "Don't be sure it will pass our caucus," I stammered. (It's not well known, but unlike other political parties the NDP caucus operates on the principle of a majority vote, so the MPs may decide not to follow the leader's decisions.) At this point one of my colleagues grabbed me and moved me away, remarking that my face was as red as the wine.

Now Trudeau was the man who in 1969, before the Calder decision, had called Aboriginal rights "historical might-have-beens." To his credit, Trudeau did change his mind. This may have been because he needed the NDP's backing for his constitutional package—he had only two provinces on board, and no support from western Canada. But whatever the reason, he sent his loyal lieutenant, Justice Minister Jean Chrétien, to negotiate our support. That is why I found myself in Broadbent's office a few days later. As chance would have it, Don Rosenbloom was in Ottawa and I asked him to join me, Ed and Marc Eliesen. Jack Woodward happened to be back in Ottawa, and I put him to work as well. Eliesen concentrated on drafting the amendment (now Section 92A of the Constitution Act, 1867) which clarified that the provinces controlled their resources. This would bring Blakeney and Notley on board. I concentrated on the Aboriginal rights amendment.

Chrétien was at first reluctant. "I have to report to the boss, you know," he said. But he hung in there. We discussed the issue and its potential ramifications. I also knew that he was under intense pressure from Aboriginal groups who were literally camped in offices, buildings and even tents around downtown Ottawa. A vote was called in the House, so we took a break from the negotiations. Then I scurried back to my office in the Confederation Building to find Woodward at the typewriter drafting a clause himself. He was the only one of us who knew how to type. I took his draft back to Rosenbloom. Don and I thought the wording was too general, so Don went next door to Ed's secretary's office and called his office in Vancouver.

NEW WORDING FOR AMENDMENT ON NATIVE PEOPLES'

WOODY

The aboriginal and treaty rights of the aboriginal peoples of Canada as they have been or may be defined by the courts are hereby recognized and affirmed. Any power which the government of Canada or a province may have to enforce, create, amend or extinguish these aboriginal and treaty rights can only be modified by amendment.

Sug Am.
The aboriginal or treaty rights of the aboriginal peoples of Canada (as they have been or may be defined by the courts) are hereby recognized and affirmed and (can be modified only by amendment).

Confirmation of aboriginal and treaty rights	XX. (1) The aboriginal and treaty rights of the aboriginal peoples of Canada, as finally determined from time to time by the courts, are hereby recognized and affirmed. (to continue)
Amendment of aboriginal and treaty rights	YY. The rights recognized and affirmed by Section XX may be modified (a) in the case of rights of the aboriginal peoples of Canada within any province, in accordance with the appropriate procedure for amending the Constitution of Canada; and (b) in the case of rights of aboriginal peoples in areas of Canada outside the provinces, by the Parliament of Canada.

My draft of Section 35, now in our Constitution.

He talked to Tom Berger and came back saying Berger had advised us to keep the wording general in order to give the courts space to develop the law. We took Jack's draft and tweaked it—made it simpler, really, and that eventually became Section 35. Here is the tweaked version: "The aboriginal and treaty rights of the aboriginal peoples of Canada [as they have been or may be defined by the Courts] are hereby recognized and affirmed [and can only be modified by amendment]."

We gave this to Chrétien, who took it to the joint parliamentary committee co-chaired by MP Serge Joyal and Senator Harry Hays. The bracketed parts were removed as redundant. Harry Daniels, president of the Métis National Council and the Native Council of Canada, had been attending the committee hearings representing the NCC. He grabbed Chrétien by the lapels as he was going into the committee and told him not to forget the Métis. Svend Robinson, a member of the committee who was standing nearby, scribbled down a definition—"'Aboriginal peoples of Canada' includes the Indian, Inuit and Métis peoples of Canada." I have always thought that if there is a heaven, a prominent place should be reserved there for Harry. I suspect Svend doesn't believe in heaven, but if he does end up there, he should also get a prominent place!

The Native Peoples Have Not Come This Far to Turn Back Now

The House of Commons passed the draft constitutional agreement in February 1981. However, several provinces challenged Trudeau's plan to unilaterally patriate the constitution. When the Supreme Court ruled in September 1981 that such an act might be legal but violated existing constitutional conventions, the prime minister was forced to go back to the premiers one more time. On November 5, 1981, the feds finally reached a deal with the provinces—all except Quebec. In the process, the clauses that had entrenched Aboriginal and treaty rights, and women's equality rights, in the new Constitution were somehow removed. What was affirmed in February was rejected in November. Tom Berger responded to this in a speech he gave at Guelph and later in an op-ed piece he wrote for the *Globe and Mail*:

No words can deny what happened. The first Canadians—a million people and more—have had their answer from Canada's statesmen. They cannot look to any of our governments to defend the idea that they are entitled to a distinct and contemporary place in Canadian life. Under the new constitution the first Canadians shall be the last. This is not the end of the story. The native peoples have not come this far to turn back now.

Judges are not supposed to speak on political matters, as they must be seen to be impartial. But should a judge remain silent when, by speaking out, he may prevent a great injustice to a minority? Tom Berger put his judicial career on the line.

George Addy, a conservative judge on the Federal Court, complained to the Canadian Judicial Council about Berger's actions. And on Jack Webster's TV show in Vancouver, Trudeau was asked whether a judge should speak out on a political issue. The prime minister gave the standard answer, "No." When pushed, he added rather petulantly that he hoped the other judges would do something about it. This drew headlines and put Berger in an almost impossible position. On December 15, 1981, I wrote to Trudeau in Berger's defence:

> I am writing to you to ask you to recall our short conversation on the evening of the historic vote on Canada's new Constitution. You may recall that, at that time, I asked you about your recent criticism of Justice Berger.
>
> I got the impression that you were unaware that at the Annual Meeting of the Canadian Bar Association on September 2, 1981, Mr. Justice Berger defended your original constitutional package during the course of a panel discussion. His remarks were widely circulated in the lawyers' journals and appeared in the press in western Canada. He was virtually the only voice in western Canada to so strongly support unilateral action.
>
> You may be right that, as a judge, Justice Berger should

not have made comments on native matters during the constitutional debate but you must remember the absolute special place Justice Berger has in the hearts of our native people. Your government had the foresight—as it turns out—to appoint him to the Mackenzie Valley Pipeline Inquiry which now has given Canada a worldwide reputation as a country that honestly tried to struggle with the implications of development on the frontier.

Who knows what the future holds for the eventual settlement of matters concerning our native people, but I remain convinced that your initiative in putting the native guarantees in the Constitution (no matter how much criticized now) will be seen as a statesmanlike act. Judge Berger takes that view and said so. He also defended your Charter of Rights. Considering his position of trust among native people, Canada may need him in the future to work with our native people.

Your remarks could potentially undercut his position and I would hope that, at some time, somewhere, in your future public remarks you might take the opportunity to temper your criticism with some positive comments. Otherwise, I feel an injustice may be done.

Trudeau responded:

You are right: I was unaware of Justice Berger's statement to the Canadian Bar on September 2, 1981. It was a superb statement, and I am thankful that you brought it to my attention.

But it was made late in the game, and in a forum scarcely designed to get wide coverage. Whereas Berger's attack on that accord was made in the *Globe and Mail*, and at that time when even your Party was not certain of supporting the accord so painfully reached.

The paradox remains. Berger supports us in an esoteric

forum, perhaps as might befit a member of the Judiciary. But Berger attacks us in a hostile "national" political newspaper, as hardly befits a judge.

But have no fear. I have no lasting grudges, nor have I the disposition to pursue them. And Berger will suffer no injustice on my account!

I made public the response, and the Judicial Council eventually cited Berger for an "indiscretion," contrary to the Council's committee report, which had advocated his removal from the bench. Chief justice of the Supreme Court Bora Laskin wouldn't let the matter drop and spoke out against Berger. In the end Berger resigned from the bench. He spoke out and he paid the price. That's what civil disobedience is all about. It probably cost him a future appointment to the Supreme Court of Canada, which was a great loss for Canada. But his unique voice made a difference in the constitutional debate.

Bora Laskin was my law professor, Tom Berger my mentor and Pierre Elliott Trudeau my opponent whose intellect I secretly admired. One was the Jewish son of a Thunder Bay jeweller, another the Protestant son of a Saskatchewan RCMP officer, and the third the Catholic son of a Quebec businessman and Scottish mother. I had the privilege of knowing all three of them up close. They couldn't have been more different, but they shared almost exactly the same federalist view of Canada.

If the Judicial Council had tried to impeach Berger, or if the government had failed to put Section 35 back into the constitution, I believe Broadbent and our NDP caucus would have withdrawn our support for Trudeau's package, which would have tied the House of Commons up in knots! As it was, Aboriginal leaders and allies like Vancouver lawyer Louise Mandel flocked to Ottawa by train, the "Constitutional Express." They forced Trudeau and the premiers to restore Aboriginal and treaty rights in what is now Section 35. The word "existing" was added to placate some premiers, but that had little effect. In fact, courts have subsequently said that the word reinforces the phrase "recognized and affirmed." The rights truly exist! So this actually helped Indigenous people. Here is how the clause we wrote now reads:

RIGHTS OF THE ABORIGINAL PEOPLES OF CANADA

Recognition of existing aboriginal and treaty rights

35. (1) The existing aboriginal and treaty rights of the aboriginal peoples of Canada are hereby recognized and affirmed.

Definition of "aboriginal peoples of Canada"

(2) In this Act, "aboriginal peoples of Canada" includes the Indian, Inuit and Métis peoples of Canada

As I look back on the negotiations, I think of the moral courage of Ed Broadbent, who had to step back from his original approval of the package and tell that to a no-doubt-angry Trudeau. I think of Tom Berger, who put his judicial robes on the line. And there was Pierre Trudeau himself, who had the intellectual courage to listen and change his mind. There were George Watts, Jack Woodward, Don Rosenbloom, Jim Aldridge and Jean Chrétien, who all worked tirelessly. Above all, there was the steadfastness of the Aboriginal people, not only their leaders in offices throughout Canada, but also the voices and the drums that I had heard in all those villages and fish camps. They beat away our fatigue and kept us going that fateful January night in Ed's office on Parliament Hill.

CHAPTER 7

Our Constitution Comes Home

The Bino's Accord

During that intense period in early 1981 when the joint parliamentary committee was hearing submissions about the constitution and the Charter of Rights and Freedoms, Tory MP Perrin Beatty moved that the draft Charter include a clause guaranteeing the right to the "enjoyment of property." Robert Kaplan, a genial Liberal cabinet minister, said he was prepared to acquiesce. The idea of including property rights as a fundamental right seems seductively simple and politically popular. But in 1981 the provinces, particularly Saskatchewan, were strongly opposed. Property is mainly a provincial jurisdiction, and the premiers feared including property rights in the constitution would give the courts an opening to interfere in that jurisdiction, particularly as it applied to natural resources.

Svend Robinson, my fellow MP from neighbouring Burnaby, and Saskatchewan MP Lorne Nystrom were the NDP representatives on the joint committee. They were determined not to let a vote on the motion be called the day it was introduced, which was Friday. If they could stall until the end of the day, they would have the weekend to drum up enough provincial opposition to get the Liberals to back down. Svend and Lorne began filibustering, talking about anything and everything to delay proceedings. However, they were up against the Tory's big guns, people like Jake Epp, John Crosbie, David Crombie and Harvie Andre, who were trying every procedural motion in the book to end the filibuster.

With about ten minutes left in the Friday afternoon session, Svend was on his feet, ragging the puck. Tory MPs were calling on the chair

Serge Joyal to put the question. Svend was running out of things to say. He paused. The Conservative MPs just looked at him, mouths open but quiet. Then Svend began speaking again. About what? The family farm! The Tories started to shout. Joyal finally banged his gavel and adjourned the committee to Monday. The Tories went crazy. But it was over. Next to suggesting the wording for the Métis clause, I think this was Svend's finest moment in the constitutional debates: talking about the "family farm" and the looks on the faces of those Tory MPs!

We thought we'd driven a stake through the heart of property rights, but in April 1983 they rose from the grave. By this time, many provinces had had a change of heart and now supported the idea of including property rights in the Charter of Rights and Freedoms. Given this provincial support, motions that would amend the Charter to include property rights, or at least send them to committee to be studied, were introduced in the House.

Svend and I were concerned that our NDP caucus was about to fold to the pressure to put property rights in the new constitution. We were strongly against this because of the history of property rights in the United States, where the courts used this concept to protect large corporations from government regulation. We argued that an individual's right to property was already protected in English common law. After all, "an Englishman's home is his castle," as the popular saying goes. If the government wants to expropriate or even encroach on your property, it has to have some public purpose for the expropriation, follow a fair procedure and compensate you at market value.

However, if governments were not allowed to "interfere with the enjoyment" of corporate property, they might not be able to honour First Nations land claims, legislate minimum wages, preserve parkland, regulate health and safety measures in the workplace, or set rent controls. Take a recent example in Vancouver, where city council stopped the destruction of 317 pre-1940 character houses; the city bylaw survived a legal challenge, even though it lowered the properties' values and impinged on the rights of the owners. That might not have happened if the owners could cite a property rights clause in Canada's constitution.

On the weekend before the motions were to be voted on, Robinson and I met for lunch at the Bino's restaurant across from my constituency office on Kingsway in East Vancouver. Bino's was a small chain and the food was, well, just average. We agreed that we would work together to make sure our NDP caucus had the backbone to resist the pressure. We would tag-team—that is, one of us would always be in the House until the "danger" passed. Our "Bino's Accord" worked. One or the other of us was in the chamber at all times, ready to say no. And to its credit, the NDP caucus did not fold. As a postscript, BC NDP leader Dave Barrett, who was in the middle of a provincial election, was furious with us. He wanted property rights entrenched in the Charter. Most of our caucus was pretty mad, too, including Broadbent who had agreed to give the unanimous consent needed for a Conservative motion to incorporate property rights. But the anger passed.

Trouble in the UK

When Canadian officials first presented Trudeau's constitutional package to British Prime Minister Margaret Thatcher in 1981, she slyly asked, "What is this Charter of Rights?" Of course she had been well briefed before the meeting. Indeed, she had already sent her defence minister to Canada. He was supposedly discussing defence issues but was in fact learning about Trudeau's proposals. At this time, Trudeau only had the support of two provinces, and many members of the "gang of eight" were asking the courts to rule on the federal government's right to unilaterally patriate the constitution. The feds were pushing ahead regardless, and a worried Trudeau set up an elite team of four people, including journalist Jonathan Manthrope and civil servant Dan Gagnier, to be his eyes and ears in London. They reported to Michael Kirby, deputy clerk of the Privy Council, in Ottawa.

Trudeau also sent two of his ministers, Mark MacGuigan and Jean Chrétien, to brief the queen, Canada's constitutional monarch. MacGuigan was one of my old profs at U of T law school, so I asked him about that lunch with Her Majesty. He told me the queen spent most of the time feeding her corgi dogs under the table and giving her son Andrew a bit of a scolding. The prime minister at first wanted to take a hard line with Britain, effectively: "Hold your nose and pass this." At the time though, Thatcher was on shaky ground with the British public and her own backbench. She probably couldn't have whipped the Tories to pass the package even if she wanted to, and since she was no big Trudeau fan, she probably didn't feel like sticking her neck out to do him a favour.

Those British MPs were being lobbied like mad by various groups opposed to the package. Delegations of First Nations chiefs had gone to London, and the province of Quebec had a strong contingent there. The Parti Québécois government held great cocktail parties, much appreciated by British MPs. And the feds were fighting back. I know because I happened to be in London at that time and was invited for lunch by a man from the Canadian High Commission. It was like a scene from a John le Carré novel. I met the fellow at the church of St. Martin-in-the-Fields near Trafalgar Square and was taken to a lavish brunch at a restaurant patio on Hampstead Heath, no doubt paid for out of Kirby's budget. Canadian embassies don't usually lay on that kind of thing for backbench NDP MPs.

What seemed to turn the tide was the Supreme Court's ruling on unilateral patriation. As mentioned earlier, the court held that that such an act might be legal but violated existing constitutional conventions. Trudeau was in Seoul, South Korea when the verdict came down, and even on TV I could see he was troubled. He would have to go back and negotiate with those damn provinces. After more negotiations and Trudeau's deal with nine provinces, the package was put before the British parliament. Luckily for Canada (unluckily for many soldiers) this was during the prelude to the Falklands War. That had the effect of shifting the focus of British legislators elsewhere. They held their noses and gave Canada back its constitution.

Of all the UK political insiders who tried to predict the votes of the Conservative backbenchers, including party leaders, whips, journalists, veteran MPs, et cetera, Sir John Ford told me the most accurate was the queen. She really does pay attention to Commonwealth matters. And I'm sure she was happy not to find herself in the impossible position of being advised by her British ministers to reject the Canadian package while being advised by her Canadian ministers to accept it.

The Queen and the Kilt

Door-to-door canvassing to meet constituents can be one of the most frustrating parts of a politician's job, but it can also lead to memorable encounters. It's frustrating because it gives people a chance to actually talk to a real candidate, and most are pretty passive. Sometimes you get people who will ask you questions, tell you amazing details of their lives, or give you their unvarnished opinions. Other times you see a different kind of residence. As I approached a basement apartment in East Vancouver, I saw through the window a woman working at a sewing machine. A number of Scottish kilts were scattered about the small

Sharon Olsen and I, later on in life, at Rolling Stones concert in Cuba.

room. Turned out my constituent was Irene Donegan, and she made those beautiful kilts for the Vancouver Ladies Pipe Band and the SFU Pipe Band.

We had a little talk at the time, and I made a special note of this address. Later, when my Aunt Sadie in Scotland sent me some beautiful material to be made into a kilt, I took it to Irene. When I went to pick up the finished product, Irene asked me for a ridiculously small amount in payment. I offered a lot more. "No," she said, "but you can do me a favour." She told me she had made a similar kilt twenty-five years earlier for a Senator Reid. He had worn it in front of Queen Elizabeth, and she had approached him and said she liked his kilt. Irene asked me to wear the kilt if I were ever to meet the queen.

In 1982, Queen Elizabeth came to Ottawa to publicly sign the documents that brought our constitution back from Britain. Madame Sauvé, the speaker of the House of Commons, invited all members, with guest, to an afternoon reception. My constituency assistant Sharon Olsen was in Ottawa, and I invited her to go with me to the reception in the big Railway Committee Room in the Centre Block. As I was getting dressed, I remembered my promise to Irene. So I put on my kilt with a Harris Tweed sports jacket, a white shirt and a tartan tie. After all, it was an afternoon reception so not ultra-formal. Turned out I was the only kilted member there.

The Queen, with Speaker Sauvé at her side and Prince Philip slightly behind, walked in a roped-off section down the centre of the room. She stopped briefly to speak to the prime minister and even more briefly to speak to the leader of the opposition. The media were kept out of the room, but they could look through the open double doors. As the queen came by us, she stopped, looked at me and said, "I like your kilt." A weak laugh escaped from me and she frowned slightly. I said, "I'm sorry, Your Majesty. You said the same thing twenty-five years ago."

The duke quipped, "Has it really been twenty-five years?"

"Can I explain?" I stammered.

"Please," the queen said with a smile.

I then briefly told her the story of how I got my kilt and the promise I had made.

The queen listened and said, "You tell her, Mrs. Donegan, that I like this kilt, too." With that the queen was off, and Sharon and I soon left the Railway Committee Room. Just as I turned into the corridor, I heard a voice say, "Excuse us, Mr. Waddell. Just a couple of questions?"

"Scrum" is the modern word for a group of journalists with their notepads, microphones and cameras in the face of a politician who often looks like a deer in headlights. I was pretty calm, as I had nothing to spin this day and had already had a good glass of single malt scotch. I had done a few scrums in my time, but nothing prepared me for this! There must have been a hundred journalists, many foreign.

I heard a woman's voice with a soft British accent. "Mr. Waddell [pronounced the British way as in "waddle"], Mr. Waddell, the queen spent one minute with the leader of the Opposition, two with the prime minister and three minutes with you. What did you talk about?" Before I could reply a Canadian reporter piped up. "Did you talk about Prince Andrew being sent to the Falklands?" I heard a blur of questions from other reporters. Then I heard clearly a veteran Canadian reporter yell at me: "We know you are a bit of a maverick, Mr. Waddell [this time properly pronounced]. Did you mention Mrs. Thatcher and the Falklands?" When I said we talked about my kilt, most of them just shook their heads. Luckily, Sharon is tough and she pulled me away, suggesting it was time the wee Scot had another drink, which he did. Oh, and Mrs. Donegan was pleased.

Focus on Asia

After the most intense period of my life, first as energy critic during the National Energy Program, and then as a participant in the patriation of our constitution, I thought I should spend some time looking after my riding. Being me, I also wanted to travel! It turned out I could do both and still accomplish a few things I wanted to get done in the House of Commons. John Bruk, a Vancouver businessman who had made his name in the mining industry, was one of the first people to really talk about Canada's future being a Pacific one. He wanted to create a foundation to promote mutual awareness of the cultures, histories, religions, philosophies and languages of Asia-Pacific countries, including Canada. The foundation he envisioned would also promote economic, business, and academic ties and connections within the Asia-Pacific region.

That foundation, like nearly all others, could have been incorporated by filing under the *Canada Corporations Act* if not for a conversation Bruk had with his neighbour Tom Berger. To show the world, as well as all Canadians, the importance of this region now and in the future, Berger suggested the incorporation be done more formally by an act of parliament. I approached minister for external relations Jean-Luc Pepin and Conservative trade critic Pat Carney, and we all supported Bruk. So it came to pass on Friday, June 1, 1984, that Jean-Luc Pepin introduced a bill to incorporate the Asia-Pacific Foundation of Canada.

In an editorial the following Monday, the *Vancouver Sun* said, "The speedy all-party approval in parliament for the Asia-Pacific Foundation of Canada is welcome recognition of the need to build a new bridge across the Pacific. In parliament, the Liberals, Conservatives and New Democrats for once cooperated magnificently to give the foundation official, physical status." According to the *Sun*, Pat Carney and I "worked hard and spoke persuasively for the bill," and the paper paid special tribute to Mr. Bruk, an "energetic and persistent" private citizen—and an immigrant from Europe to boot.

I had taken an interest in John Bruk's proposal because Asia-Pacific issues were becoming more and more important in British Columbia, particularly in Vancouver. Much of the workload in my Vancouver Kingsway riding on Vancouver's East Side was made up of immigration issues, many involving Southeast Asia and South America (think Hong Kong, Chile and the Punjab). Sharon Olsen carried most of that load, though I would do "legal open houses" at the Rio Hall on alternate Saturdays. It was like being a storefront lawyer again. Those long Saturdays after a full week in Ottawa and a gruelling flight home were tough, but it sure helped to be young. We got a reputation as fighters for our constituents. I always reminded Sharon that the government officials worked for us, not vice versa. Sharon alternately charmed the immigration officials or scolded them. She had some huge successes, including saving one constituent's relative from death. Like me, Sharon came out of the activist movements of the 1960s, so helping our constituents was not just another job for her; it was a cause.

We were both strong personalities, and inevitably we clashed. One time she publicly poured a pint of beer over me at an NDP convention because I was "becoming too Ottawa." At another point I phoned her from the lobby of the House of Commons and we argued, she suggesting I fire her and I suggesting she quit. Not an hour later, NDP house leader Ian Deans approached me and offered me the NDP position on an all-party delegation to the People's Republic of China. I phoned Sharon and asked her to come with me. She was a single mum with two kids, Dana and Darcy, and she had to arrange for someone to look after them while she was away, as well as someone to run the busy constituency office. When I saw her exhausted on the trans-Pacific plane ride, I realized how hard constituency assistants work.

Near the end of our trip, Sharon was given the opportunity to make a toast at an official dinner in Shanghai. She was warned to keep it short and non-political. "To the women of China," she shouted. The Chinese wives and daughters there jumped up and joined her. I had the feeling that the Chinese officials hadn't seen anything like this before. To this day, Sharon "has my back."

Our delegation had gone to South Korea first and then Hong Kong, which was a British dependent territory at the time. But already negotiations were underway between Mrs. Thatcher and the People's Republic of China, as the colonial lease would end in 1997. In Beijing our delegation was hosted at a meeting with vice foreign minister Zhou Nan, representing the Chinese government. In those days, China took Canada seriously. Chinese officials talked about Dr. Norman Bethune, our grain and Pierre Trudeau's early recognition of their regime.

A few days earlier when I was in Hong Kong, I was reading the *South China Morning Post* when I noticed that Zhou Nan was one of the senior Chinese officials negotiating the handover of Hong Kong to China. At our Beijing meeting he said he was open to questions. A Conservative MP asked him if the Rotary Club could come to China.

No problem. A Liberal MP asked about China's relations with South Korea. Zhou gave a diplomatic answer but spoke of good relations with both Koreas.

I was next. I prefaced my question by saying some of my constituents, not rich people, had families and property in Hong Kong. What was going to happen to Hong Kong? I recall looking at the faces of two Canadian diplomats in the room with us. They looked bored. Zhou Nan answered by stating firmly that full Chinese sovereignty over Hong Kong was non-negotiable, and British newspapers got it wrong when they wrote about Britain retaining some degree of administrative control. Our diplomats still looked bored and were getting ready to leave, as was our chair, who was about to end the meeting.

Zhou Nan paused for a few seconds and then continued. He said we could tell our British friends not to worry. China would agree to a series of special administrative measures. The legal system would remain unchanged, except colonial appeals to courts in England would end (as had happened in Canada). The Hong Kong dollar would retain its role as an international currency. Hong Kong could carry on its economic relations with the outside world; China would take over the diplomatic relations. China would not send officials to Hong Kong to govern it; the local Hong Kong people would do that. Finally, breaking into a big smile, he concluded, "If they want their nightclubs and racetrack, they are free to do so." There was nervous laughter in the room from everyone but the Canadian diplomats. They were scribbling notes like mad!

Zhou Nan ended his remarks by saying he had recently met with Cyrus Vance and Henry Kissinger in Washington, and they said China was being "especially magnanimous." The two sides should be able to achieve a solution, he stated. And they did pretty much as he predicted, reaching an agreement in principle and having a peaceful handover on July 1, 1997 (130 years after Canada ceased to be a British colony). On my return to Canada I crossed the floor of the House and spoke to Prime Minister Trudeau asking whether Canada would get involved in the negotiations. He said it would not be wise, but he did ask for my notes.

Eighteen MPs from BC after 1988 election.

In retrospect, it was thrilling to have even a little glimpse into this historic event. During the federal election the next year, I milked it for all it was worth. Candidates from all parties attended a big meeting in Vancouver's Chinatown where they were asked, "What have you done to help Chinese Canadians?" All said they loved Chinese Canadians; one said she was born in China; another praised Chinese food (no kidding); and Margaret Mitchell pointed out her part in the fight to save Chinatown from destruction by freeway. Up to that point, Margaret got the most applause. I was last to speak and I told the story of the settlement of the future of Hong Kong. Of course, I told it in such a way that I was a major player! There was silence, then huge applause. Sharon Olsen just looked at me.

One more Asia-Pacific connection developed while canvassing for my first election in Vancouver Kingsway. I was invited into a house where Kieko Lasky, a Japanese Canadian woman, lived with her Canadian husband. Kieko told me that in 1945 she was a fifteen-year-old nursing student living in her parents' basement in Hiroshima. At eight a.m. on August 6, 1945, the US air force dropped an atomic bomb on the city of Hiroshima, effectively ending the Second World War but killing

140,000 people. Later the USAF dropped a second atomic bomb on Nagasaki, killing another 75,000 people. That morning, Kieko said she saw a flash at the window of her basement room. When she looked out, she saw images of people frozen on the walls of buildings. We became friends, and a few years later I helped welcome a group of Japanese scientists into Canada to study the health of the "hibakusha," the survivors of those terrible bombs.

A Prairie Stage

My travelling wasn't always overseas. I tried to support the NDP in other provinces as much as possible. In particular, I supported Cathy McCleary who ran many times in Calgary and became a great friend to Sharon Olsen and me. I also developed a strong friendship with Grant Notley, who was much admired in Alberta, even by people who didn't vote for him. In the 1980s, as Cathy will attest, Alberta was not fertile ground for the NDP.

During one provincial election I dropped in for a huge rally in Edmonton where Grant spoke. When he found out later that I had been in the audience and he had not acknowledged me, he was very apologetic. It didn't bother me; I liked the Alberta NDP's role as giant killers and was happy to watch. But Grant wanted to reward me somehow. He asked me to accompany him to Ponoka, a farm town in central Alberta, and invited me to share the stage at the nomination meeting with him, the local candidate and Tommy Douglas. To share a prairie stage with the great Tommy, the father of medicare and a fellow Scot! Are you kidding? I showed up and was piped into the basement of a church hall with the platform party.

I sat on the stage at one end of the hall and looked out at a crowd of about two hundred smiling faces. The emcee introduced our candidate, who was apparently a hog farmer. Then Grant. Then Tommy. Finally me. I did get some polite applause. I was asked to speak first, and I was just beaming as I brought greetings from Ed Broadbent and the NDP caucus in Ottawa. At that point I looked toward my fellow

With the greats: Grace MacInnis, Tommy Douglas and Stanley Knowles.

stage politicians. Seeing Tommy must have done it. I proudly said I was very pleased to be here in Ponoka, *Saskatchewan*. Looking out at the audience, I saw smiles vanish and eyelids tighten. For the rest of the meeting I was ignored. After the speeches, over coffee, no one talked to me. I guess they thought I was some latte-drinking dude from Kitsilano.

Yoga, Then and Now

When I was a young lawyer, my filmmaking friend Iain Ewing had taken me, his young wife Gita and my friend Michael Robinson to a yoga retreat in the Bahamas. We drove in an old truck from Toronto to Florida, then flew over to the Nassau ashram where Gita was to dance. This was in the 1970s, and most westerners knew little about yoga.

I hated my first visit to the retreat in Nassau. I got sick, and then I couldn't cope with the standard regimen: wake up at six a.m., meditate and chant until eight a.m., yoga (always the same simple asanas) until ten a.m., vegetarian breakfast, then free time, which was mostly swimming and sunning on one of the most beautiful beaches in the world. We would do yoga again from four p.m. until six p.m., have a vegetarian dinner, which we all helped cook, and then more meditation and chanting, with a lecture by the swami until 10 p.m. and lights out. We all wore tattered shirts and shorts. No one had yet invented fashionable yoga outfits.

The next year I went back to the ashram in Nassau and actually came to love it, returning many times. I would bring my tent and do yoga twice a day, sleep, meditate, eat good food, drink only water and take at least the first step to what yoga is actually about—that is, seeking a state of tranquility from the world. I came to understand that the yoga positions or asanas are just a means to proper breathing, leading to the goal of spiritual enlightenment. My problem was that I would go to Nassau just after Christmas, meet the same crowd year after year (a lot of very smart and fun Jewish people from New York), have a great holiday and return to Ottawa and parliament totally refreshed. Within a month I was back to hamburgers, chips, Coca Cola and House of Commons coffee.

In his lectures at the ashram, Swami Vishnu often spoke about the dangers of nuclear war. This was greeted by the tired yawns of people who'd been up since six doing yoga and swimming, but he was right on. History tells us there was a real danger of nuclear war between the two great superpowers of the time. Swami Vishnu didn't just talk about peace. He learned to fly, had psychedelic artist Peter Max paint his twin-engine airplane, and then flew "peace missions" over Israel, Northern Ireland (with Peter Sellers) and the Berlin Wall. He should have been arrested, but the local security forces thought a flying swami was a bit crazy.

In fact, he was crazy, but he was also courageous and right. Swami Vishnu's biggest contribution to Canadian and world society was that he was thirty years ahead of his time. Through a "yoga teachers' training course" given at Val Morin in Quebec, Nassau and his other ashrams educated some forty thousand yoga teachers. He should have been given an Order of Canada.

One beautiful June day, Swami Vishnu came to Ottawa. His assistant called me in the morning and invited me to come to the Centennial Flame in front of the Parliament Buildings where the swami and some followers were going to stand on their heads for peace. I had actually become quite good at standing on my head in the yoga pose and often did it after a couple of drinks at private parties. As I was leaving my office to go to the flame, my staff of three lined up at my office door, sort of like the BC Lions defensive line. "We know you, Ian," they said. "If you stand on your head at the flame, we all will resign immediately."

I didn't know why they were so worried. When I got to the flame that morning, two big, young guys were doing full headstands with the magnificent Parliament Buildings as a backdrop. Swami Vishnu was there, and he asked me to do a headstand. After all, he had taught me how to do it. To humour my staff, I demurred, citing a sore back. "But Swami, is there anything else I could do for you?"

"Well," said my Swami, "you could introduce me to Prime Minister Pierre Elliott Trudeau."

"Okay," I said. "Call my assistant and he will take you to the members' lobby just after the end of question period at three p.m." I had to say something! It so happened that it was a slow day in QP. Most of the questions were about fisheries, and only one long-winded question about the possible regulation of fishing boundaries between Canadian and international waters went to the prime minister. Trudeau's response was a quick "The problem is, Mr. Speaker, fish swim." He was clearly bored. I scribbled a note asking Trudeau to meet my swami in the lobby outside the house after question period, and had a page deliver it. I got a quick note back.

So you do yoga. Can you stand on your head here in the House?
How do I recognize the guy? PET

I sent another note: "Yes to headstand but not here. You can't miss him—white hair, brown face and an orange sari." Trudeau unfolded my note, put on his reading glasses, smiled and gave me a thumbs-up. I realized that he and I were likely the only MPs in the House who had even heard of yoga, never mind were practitioners!

After QP I had to hurry back to my office as I was returning to Vancouver that night on the six p.m. flight. I got a call at the airport from the swami's assistant. They were very happy. They got their photo op with Trudeau, and the picture would go in their next members' letter. (The swami had a good grasp of North American marketing.) Thanks to the time difference between Ontario and BC, I arrived in Vancouver with plenty of time to meet with Sharon Olsen, receive a briefing on some constituency issues and adjourn to our neighbourhood pub, the Molly Hogan at 41st and Knight Street.

As I sipped what I thought was a well-earned pint, a few of my constituents joined our table. They too had just got off work. One, a drywaller in apartment construction, asked me how my sore back was doing. I told him I didn't know what he was talking about. He replied that he had just seen me on the TV news telling the "weird Indian guy at the flame" that I had a sore back. I understood then what my politically wise staff had been getting at. This was the 1980s after all. Yoga was thought of as a bit "out there," especially among working-class people, which was the huge majority in my riding. My supporters would have thought me crazy to be standing on my head in such company. Even worse would be to have my picture taken with the swami and Trudeau, who in those days was not liked in western Canada.

Today on "Yoga Wednesdays" you can see hundreds of people doing asanas on the lawn in front of the Parliament Buildings, some with some pretty expensive yoga outfits. The old house on Point Grey Road where I celebrated being called to the bar in 1969 is now owned by Chip Wilson, founder of Lululemon Athletica, rebuilt for about $30 million. In retrospect, if I had stood on my head I would have been thirty years ahead of my time. And had I realized that our old yoga pants could have been updated, I would be a billionaire. Okay, at least I was re-elected in Vancouver Kingsway by a huge majority. But sometimes you are courageous and ahead of the game; other times you are not.

A Walk in the Snow

In early 1984, Pierre Trudeau took a "walk in the snow" and resigned. John Turner took over as prime minister and called a quick election. The problem was that he looked a bit rusty after being out of politics for a while. The new Conservative leader, Brian Mulroney, was a fresh face and a very good campaigner. This was one of my easiest campaigns. When the tide is running in, everything's easy; it's when the tide inevitably runs the other way that you are in trouble, as I was to find out later. But in 1984 the Liberal vote under Prime Minister Turner was collapsing. In Vancouver Kingsway, where the Liberals were our main opponents, this was good news.

My campaign manager was a tough, self-assured, young guy. I remember him barking out orders to my staff and telling them he would fire them if they got out of line. His name was Glen Clark, and he went on to become an MLA, finance minister, premier and later president of the Jim Pattison Group, the largest privately held company in Canada. We had a solid organization in Kingsway, as I had kept in close touch with my Chinese Canadian allies. With people like Kashmir Dhaliwal, Henry Hundel, Hardev Bal and others working for us, we could count on the support of the Indo-Canadian community as well. Sharon Olsen organized the canvass and filmmaker Debbie McGee did our election day.

The campaign was going so well that they had to find something different for the candidate to do. Glen sent me into the schools to talk to the kids in grade five. He figured the population in the riding was quickly shifting from Anglo/Scottish/Irish constituents to newer immigrants who didn't speak English. But their kids did speak English, and the kids would talk to their parents. So I went to talk in the public schools. What do you say about politics to a grade five student? After a few stumbles I decided to tell them a story—a story about a king who got his head cut off. That got their attention.

It went like this. A king by the name of Charles needed some money to run his kingdom, so he got some men (the women finally came later, but unfortunately it was a lot later) chosen by local townspeople to meet in a big building near the Thames River in London, England. They called their meeting hall a "parliament," or a place where they could speak. They wanted to tell the king about some of the people's problems in the kingdom before they voted to give King Charles the money he wanted. They called the money by the name of "taxes."

The problem was that the king was impatient. Some of the members of this parliament wanted to tell the king what to do, but King Charles took some of his soldiers down to the entrance of the parliament to hurry the people up. He was met at the door by the "speaker" of the parliament, one of the members who had been chosen to speak for the group. When this speaker said the king couldn't come into the parliament, the king got really mad. He said he was responsible only to God, and he could go anywhere in his kingdom. So he and his soldiers pushed the speaker aside and rushed into the big room where the parliament members were meeting.

Little did the king know that two very strong members, one called Oliver Cromwell and the other John Pym, had fled out the back door, then down a long staircase and into a boat which rowed them down the Thames River to safety. They then raised a big army of men. That army got into a huge battle with King Charles's army, and they beat the king. Then they took the captured king back to the House of Parliament, now called the House of the Commons—that is, the house of common people, not a house for the king or his rich friends called lords. They put the king on trial, found him guilty, took him to the Tower of London prison and cut off his head.

So what is the moral of the story? A lot of young hands shot up. Eventually we agreed that the commoners, the ordinary people, were more powerful than the king. "Is there one place where the present-day queen or king can't go in their kingdom of Canada or Britain?" I asked the students, and I ask it of you, Dear Reader… Of course the answer is the House of Commons. That is why the speech from the throne, which outlines the government's program for the coming parliamentary session, is given by the queen or her representative, the governor general, in the Canadian senate and not the House of Commons, the only place in Canada where she can't go. The grade fives loved the story and told their parents, and we won the election by over ten thousand votes.

Postscript

The period from 1980 to 1984 was the most intense of my life. Looking back, a lot of events stand out, but the moment I remember most clearly and fondly was taking part in the revision of the constitution, truly a once-in-a-lifetime experience. It was exhilarating, sometimes exhausting, often even mystifying. I believe my fellow MPs and I were often asking ourselves, *Are we really up for this?* The consequences of getting it wrong would be dire. With thoughts like that weighing heavily on my mind, I left the House of Commons after a late-night sitting on a snowy January night.

We had been debating the final draft of the constitution, and I decided I needed some fresh air. I would walk home to my tiny apartment in Sandy Hill, not far from Parliament Hill. The members' door was closed by then, so I had to walk down to the central foyer to exit like a tourist from the main door. It happened that coming from the opposite direction, from the senate side, was a small older man with a neatly trimmed moustache. I recognized Eugene Forsey, an independent senator who was Canada's foremost constitutional expert, in his last year in the senate. I introduced myself to him and suggested we walk together down Wellington Street to face the storm.

"I know your name, Mr. Waddell," the formidable senator said. As we walked, I asked him about a couple of constitutional issues that Svend and I were struggling with. He thought a moment and answered, "Sir Robert, he struggled with that problem."

"Sir Robert?" I said. "Who?"

"Sir Robert Borden," he replied. He was referring to Canada's eighth prime minister, who held office from 1911 to 1920. Borden had been born before Confederation. In spite of the cold, in spite of the snow flurries around my head, in spite of the fact that I was shielding this older man from the extreme elements, I felt a warm glow—something about being a Canadian and part of Canada's history.

CHAPTER 8

The New Prime Minister

I returned to Ottawa and was sworn in again as the member for Vancouver Kingsway. That night I went to a party thrown by the governor general. My date this time was my mother Isabel who looked lovely in a green Indian silk dress. The RCMP band was starting up near the dance floor and my mum dragged me over to dance. By chance, newly elected prime minister Brian Mulroney was standing alone nearby. He greeted me with "Hello, Ian," as if I were his best friend, even though we had never met before. I introduced him to Isabel and he smiled, looked down at my small mum and complimented her on her dress.

"Your fathers were both electricians"—Mum and PM Brian Mulroney.

Her response, in her thick Scottish accent, was "You and my son have something in common."

Mulroney and I looked at each other. "What is that, Mrs. Waddell?" Mulroney asked with a bit of hesitation.

"Your fathers were both electricians. [pause] Don't either one of you forget that!" Mulroney's father worked in the small Quebec town of Baie-Comeau and my dad John "Jock" Waddell wired up the Hearne generating station in Toronto, today reborn as a big cultural centre.

The PM's photographer took our picture and sent me a copy. It showed Mulroney at six foot one and my mum at five foot zero. I was in between. We were all talking at the same time. I got the picture framed and gave it to Isabel.

"What am I going to do with this?" she asked me.

I replied, "Hang it up in your apartment. After all, he is the prime minister and I'm your son."

"What would my girlfriends say?" she exclaimed.

I kept the picture.

More Kilt

"Mr. Speaker, I rise on a point of order, and it concerns what I am wearing, my kilt." It was Friday morning, January 25, 1985, the celebration of the birthday of the Scottish national poet Robert "Robbie" Burns. The speaker that day was actually the deputy speaker, a young Conservative MP from Quebec named Jean Charest (later premier of Quebec), who was perplexed when I raised my point of order.

When Pierre Elliott Trudeau retired in 1984, Sheila Finestone succeeded him as the Liberal member for Mount Royal. Once she found her feet in parliament, Sheila became very effective and persistent in following several issues. Our paths crossed as we were both on the House communications committee, where she proved to be informed and articulate. Her problem was that she had succeeded Julius Caesar, so to speak, and was getting almost no publicity compared to him.

This is why I had asked Sheila to meet me just before the House opened on January 25. I was wearing my kilt, and I told her I would rise on a point of order to ask the speaker for permission of the House to wear the kilt in the ensuing debate, arguing for this right on the grounds that the French Canadians and Scots were the founders of the country and this was national dress. Sheila would then also rise on a "point d'ordre" and ask, "What is worn under the kilt?" I would reply, "Nothing is worn, Mr. Speaker; it's all in perfect working order."

Well, I got up on my point of order, Sheila rose on hers, and I made my response. But as Burns himself wrote, "The best-laid schemes o' mice an' men gang aft agley" (that is "often go awry"). Members started rising on their own "points of order," and it got a bit crazy with talk of bird's nests and other things under the kilt. Finally the speaker had had enough. He gave me permission to wear the kilt, then moved on to the regular business of the House. In the lobby Sheila asked me, "What was that all about?"

"Have patience," I replied. "You will get some publicity." To be honest, I only half-believed what I was saying. But the Saturday papers ran the following item in the entertainment section, right next to the sports section:

> In the Ozark Mountains JANE FONDA is visiting DOLLY PARTON and is making a movie about DOLLY'S life. In Ottawa Canada, meanwhile, SHEILA FINESTONE MP rose in the House of Commons to ask kilt-clad IAN WADDELL MP what was worn under his kilt. Nothing apparently, all was in perfect working order IAN told a smiling SHEILA.

On Monday morning, Sheila met me in the lobby again. She could barely contain her mirth. We had made every paper in Canada and some in the United States, and we were in the entertainment section, which people actually read. Sheila's phone hadn't stopped ringing all weekend, and she had made her mark on the political map. Such is the power of the kilt.

Clearing the Air

Lynn McDonald was elected to parliament as an NDP MP after Bob Rae
left to become NDP leader and later premier of Ontario. Lynn became
a voice for people who suffered from exposure to cigarette smoke and
had no recourse in law. A generation before her, in 1963, Judy LaMarsh
was the first minister of health to raise the issue in Canada. But little
changed. At that time you could smoke almost anywhere, including on
airplanes, in restaurants, bars, government buildings, and even in hospi-
tals. It really was a different world.

McDonald and her staff assistant Cynthia Callard were determined
to change that. So too were the Non-Smokers Rights Association,
based in Toronto, and Physicians for a Smoke-Free Canada. We "boys"
in caucus were a bit skeptical. But Lynn persisted. In 1986 she drafted a
private member's bill that restricted smoking in any workplaces under
federal control, including aircraft, trains, ships, banks and government
offices. She got the NDP caucus to approve the bill, even though some
of our members were heavy smokers.

Lynn was also lucky. All private member's bills, including hers, go
into a lottery. Even among those that are drawn, only a few make it
onto the parliamentary agenda. After Lynn's bill was drawn, she had to
go before a committee of MPs, dominated by Conservatives, and convince them to choose her bill for debate. Again she persisted, and somehow the Bill C-204 was chosen for debate and a vote, even though the
Conservative government was not supporting the bill and Mulroney
was being intensely lobbied by the tobacco industry.

The bill came up for second reading one night in the House. Deputy
speaker Steve Paproski from Edmonton, a former Canadian Football
League player and a Conservative in the mould of my friend John Fraser,
called the question. We "yeas" bellowed out, and then the "nays" shouted
in reply. The deputy speaker said, "The 'yeas' have it." At this point, under
the House rules, any five members could stand up and force a recorded
vote (which would likely have been "nay"), but a lot of the Conservative
members were "sleeping" in their lobby just outside the House and they
didn't rush in. Paproski quickly declared McDonald's bill carried.

That meant it would go to a legislative committee for study. Lynn and Cynthia made sure experts appeared at the committee stage to present their research on the health damage done by smoking. They also cleverly used the committee to build public support by getting groups like the Lung Association, the Canadian Cancer Society and others to make presentations. McDonald got a lot of press over the claim she threw a committee ashtray into the garbage can (people were allowed to smoke in parliamentary committee rooms in those days). The committee couldn't bury her bill, though it took its time to report out: private member's bills are allotted only one hour of committee time per month, so it took over five months for the bill to come back for third reading.

McDonald was helped by Conservative MPs Arthur Malone and Paul McCrossan, who fought for it in their caucus. McCrossan even convinced a fellow Conservative MP from a tobacco-growing constituency to vote for the bill because that MP was by profession a doctor. The bill came back to the House for a final vote on May 31, 1988. After the NDP caucus voted for it, a group of us stood in amazement when the clerk announced that thirty-two Conservatives, twenty-four NDP and twenty-one Liberals had voted for it—seventy-seven members in total defeating the fifty-eight who voted against. We were all a bit stunned. Unfortunately, within six months Lynn was defeated in an election, but a few of us remembered her efforts and we pushed for proclamation of Bill C-204, which became law in 1989.

As a result of the passage of both Lynn's bill and a government bill that banned tobacco advertising and strengthened health warnings on cigarette packages, Canada led the Western world in restricting smoking and cigarette advertising. The work of one MP, her assistant and volunteer community groups made a difference, and since then country after country has followed our lead.

Nothing's Free Except Trade

Despite winning a huge majority government in 1984, Mulroney was in trouble with the electorate three years later, mainly because of his imposition of the Goods and Services Tax (GST). His salvation was the Free Trade Agreement (FTA) with the United States, our biggest trade partner (further negotiations resulted in NAFTA, the North American Free Trade Agreement, which included Mexico). Nobody but policy wonks had paid much attention to the trade file until the Mulroney government said free trade would bring huge economic benefits and an increased self-assurance to our soon-to-be-more-competitive Canadian companies. I took that with a grain of salt, but I was concerned that the United States under President Ronald Reagan was targeting Canada's Achilles' heel: our dependence on American markets.

Mulroney had opposed free trade during the 1984 election, following the example of Canada's first Conservative prime minister John A. Macdonald, who brought in a "National Policy"—essentially high tariffs on foreign goods—to protect Canadian companies. But ever the political animal, Mulroney soon saw the advantages of having a clear market-oriented policy with broad appeal for his political base in western Canada and Quebec. Thus, in early 1985 Mulroney unilaterally killed the National Energy Program, or at least what was left of it, by signing the Western Accord with British Columbia, Alberta and Saskatchewan. That same year he emasculated the Foreign Investment Review Agency, renaming it Investment Canada and making it easier for American corporations to take over Canadian companies. And in March of 1985, at the so-called "Shamrock Summit" in Quebec City, Mulroney was singing "When Irish Eyes Are Smiling" with President Reagan, signing the Canada–US Declaration on Goods and Services, and talking about free trade between the two countries.

The FTA, signed on January 2, 1988, turned out to be his political salvation. A strong coalition of labour and environmental groups opposed the deal, arguing it would drive down labour and environmental standards, and would restrict government's ability to regulate such standards. As well, it would send Canada's high-paying manufacturing jobs to low-wage right-to-work states in the American South (and later under NAFTA to Mexico, where workers were paid poverty wages). The Liberals and NDP also opposed the deal, and the November 1988 election was fought on the issue of free trade rather than on the government's record. Unfortunately, the two opposition parties split the vote, and Mulroney's Conservatives were returned to power with another majority, albeit slightly reduced. Soon after the election the FTA legislation was passed by parliament, and it came into effect on January 1, 1989. NAFTA came into force on January 1, 1994.

The biggest problem with the FTA and NAFTA is that they entrench in international treaties virtually unrestricted freedoms for corporations while hampering governments' powers to actively shape economic and social development. Mulroney often cited the Royal Commission on the Economic Union and Development Prospects for Canada as the inspiration for the FTA and NAFTA. Ironically, this commission was led by a former Liberal finance minister, Donald Macdonald, who did indeed support free trade, calling it "a leap of faith." However, Mulroney forgot to add that the Macdonald Commission report recognized that free trade combined with privatization and deregulation would hurt some Canadians, particularly the working poor. The commission suggested that Canada needed new social and labour market policies to go along with free trade. Today we can see the flaws of these and other trade deals: our manufacturing jobs have gone to Mexico and to China, there is more economic inequality, and corporations' ability to sue governments who try to regulate them discourages the implementation of labour and environmental standards, just as opponents predicted.

Free trade didn't just affect manufacturing. In 1984, Mulroney's pick for minister of communications was Flora MacDonald. Flora was a "red Tory," a strong economic nationalist and very progressive. She knew that in 1971 a Liberal government had introduced a law that required Canadian radio stations to devote a percentage of airtime to Canadian musicians. The private broadcasters hated it, but it worked. Chances are you can name five Canadian musicians without difficulty, but I'm betting you'd have a much harder time naming five Canadian filmmakers. MacDonald wanted to help our film industry, so she prepared a bill that would reserve 15 percent of the screens in movie theatres for Canadian movies.

Just as MacDonald was on the verge of tabling her film bill in the House of Commons, President Reagan, backed by Hollywood lobbyist Jack Valenti, started pressuring Mulroney to pull the bill, threatening to stop the FTA negotiations if he didn't. Mulroney, who had shown courage in standing up to Reagan and UK prime minister Margaret Thatcher over sanctions against apartheid in South Africa, felt he had no choice. The bill was dead. Later the Conservatives claimed culture was never on the table in the free trade deal. Guess again.

Since I'd had a long-time interest in film, I tabled a copy of Flora's original bill as a private member's bill. It went nowhere, of course, and it is still extremely difficult to get a Canadian feature or documentary into a Canadian theatre. But turn on your radio and you will hear Nelly Furtado, Carly Rae Jepsen, Feist, Nickelback, Avril Lavigne, Michael Bublé, Ron Sexsmith, et cetera.

A Lake Called Meech

I have to admit, while I disagreed deeply with most of his policies, I personally liked Mulroney. He was a compassionate guy, often calling MPs of any party when they were ill or in trouble. He worked with Jim Fulton to create South Moresby National Park in Haida Gwaii. In 1988 he convened the first international conference on climate change. He appointed Stephen Lewis as Canada's ambassador to the United Nations. What I didn't like was Mulroney's free trade deal with the United States, his dismantling of the National Energy Program and above all, his speeches in the House about the Canadian constitution and how illegitimate it was. He was referring, of course, to the *Canada Act* and the *Constitution Act* of 1982, which had been signed by nine provinces. Mulroney's claim that it was illegitimate was based on the fact that a separatist Quebec government had not signed on. Mulroney wanted to have the Province of Quebec endorse the *Constitution Act*—a good idea if it were possible, but at what cost?

The cost was the Meech Lake Accord, which was negotiated by Mulroney and all ten provinces. "Negotiation" may not be an appropriate word. On April 30, 1987, Mulroney and the ten provincial premiers met privately, without support staff, in a picturesque government lodge on a small lake in Gatineau Park just outside downtown Ottawa. By the end of the day, after nine hours of discussion, presto, they had a major constitutional deal. At first there was widespread public euphoria. My own leader Ed Broadbent and the Liberal leader John Turner said they would support the agreement. And although there was some hesitation among the provincial leaders when they met to sign the official document on June 3, 1987, they all put their signatures on the agreement. After that, the federal and provincial leaders had three years to have the accord ratified by their respective legislatures.

In spite of the initial public and political support, I believed that Meech was wrong for Canada. When Senator Lowell Murray, spokesman for Mulroney's Conservatives, said they were not open to any amendments, the federal NDP caucus still agreed to support the deal, hoping to get changes in the future. I thought this was wishful thinking. When the NDP's Yukon MP Audrey McLaughlin was given "permission" to vote against the bill because it would prevent the Yukon from ever becoming a province, I thought it was absurd and illogical that it was a whipped vote for the rest of us.

When I indicated I might buck the NDP caucus and vote against Meech, our constitutional critic Pauline Jewett haughtily told me I didn't understand the accord and should go and do my homework. (This was the standard government line against critics.)

So I did go away to a cabin in the Gatineau Hills—ironically, not far from Meech Lake—owned by my good friends D'Arcy and Nancy Thorpe. I locked myself away with all the documents I could get my hands on, including Eugene Forsey's testimony before the House of Commons committee on the accord and a letter from Tom Berger.

Countless articles were appearing as Canadians began to understand the ramifications of this deal for the future of the country. As one commentator noted, had this agreement been in place twenty years earlier, there would be no national health care program and probably no unemployment insurance as we know it today. Other writers remarked on the speed with which the accord was reached. After all, the constitutional process in 1980 took nearly two years and involved extensive public debate, several federal–provincial conferences and even a reference to the Supreme Court of Canada. How did this new agreement happen so fast? According to *Vancouver Sun* journalist Marjorie Nichols, "There was nothing novel about the formula for this alleged success. The provinces demanded and the federal government acceded."

Marjorie Montgomery Bowker, a former judge of the Family Court of Alberta, wrote the clearest summary of the Meech Lake Accord in a "self-financed" booklet. "In order to control costs," she wrote, "only two hundred copies are being distributed. You are at liberty to make duplicate copies." Many, many people did—this was social media before the Internet! In plain language, Bowker told Canadians about our present constitution. She described how the Meech Lake Accord came about, explained what it said, set out the arguments for and against, described possible alternatives and summarized her position. Her conclusions were simply and clearly written but were devastating for the accord.

She wrote that the process that created the accord was undemocratic, and the agreement's content represented a radical shift of power from the federal government to the provincial governments. It gave the provinces greater control over immigration, federal spending on shared-cost programs, nominations to the senate and nominations of judges to the Supreme Court of Canada. It also gave all provinces a veto on future constitutional amendments, making senate reform almost impossible. Since the accord failed to give precedence to the Canadian Charter of Rights and Freedoms, the rights of women, minorities, First Nations and northern Canadians could be at risk in the future. Finally, in order to bring Quebec into the constitutional fold, the federal government and the other provinces had agreed to Quebec's demands that it take control of what had been federal responsibilities. And in order to get the nine premiers to agree to these concessions being granted to Quebec and to the recognition of Quebec as a "distinct society," the federal government gave similar powers to all the provinces.

I emerged from my cabin after studying all this material and returned to the House of Commons to speak on the evening of Thursday, October 22, 1987. I'm proud of this speech; I think it was my best. I said that in good conscience I could not vote for the Meech Lake Accord. It was flawed, and the process of agreement and approval of the accord had been rushed and undemocratic. I acknowledged that my leader and caucus would support it, and I respected them and their position. I quoted CCF founder J.S. Woodsworth and his daughter Grace MacInnis who wrote that her father recognized the right of the minority, even a minority of one, to express its own position. I pointed out that there were a lot of people, especially in British Columbia, who shared my opinion.

"It is important to get the signature of the Quebec government on the Canadian constitution. However, it is not sufficient a priority that nothing else matters. The real priority is a good and sound constitution for Canada." Then I went on to dissect the deal in detail and to show how when it came to the senate, the Supreme Court, the entrenched First Ministers Conferences, the treatment of the North, the shutting out of Aboriginal peoples, the right of provinces to opt out of national social programs, and the restrictions on federal spending programs that would make future social programs like childcare impossible, the Meech Lake Accord was a power grab by the provinces.

I said I was not against recognizing Quebec as a distinct society in order to protect the French language and culture there, but I asked, "Have the other provinces really said 'yes' to Quebec? Or have they just grabbed at power over federal institutions and [run] away with those powers?" I spoke of Laurier's vision of the federal government's role in protecting Quebec's distinct society as well as "the French fact" in Canada, a reference to Francophones living in other provinces. I quoted Henri Bourassa and Tommy Douglas, who said that "the whole basis of national unity is founded on the principle of equal treatment for all and special privileges for none."

There was not a lot of notice of my speech as that night's debate was lightly attended. I got a couple of questions. But a fellow NDP MP, Steve Langdon, who would be voting for the Accord with the rest of the caucus, rose to say he appreciated my speech. I could feel the unease of my fellow members, and I was glad of Langdon's support. Not too long after this, the BC NDP repudiated the federal party's line. Letters of support for my position poured into my office. Unlike the short tweets of today, these letters were often long, articulate and well thought out.

We were debating Meech and the FTA at the same time, and some people believed Canada couldn't afford both free trade and Meech. I was one of them, saying in the House and in an interview that "Mr. Mulroney has given one half of the country away to the provinces through Meech Lake, and he's given the other half to the Americans through free trade." Perhaps it was a bit over the top, but a number of academics wrote to say they agreed with me.

I lost my critic's position for a while but later, when the dust settled, Broadbent reinstated me. I have no doubt he had good reasons for his position on Meech. I believe he thought it was necessary to have Quebec sign the constitution in order to stop the separatist movement. But once again, as when we were debating the original constitutional package, he understood dissent. He may not have liked it, but he was a big enough person to understand.

Over the next three years, public opinion turned against the deal and it died. Was I right? I admit I have struggled with my decision to disagree with people like Bill Blaikie, a thinker whom I have always admired and later supported as an NDP leadership candidate. And of course Ed was no intellectual slouch, either. When in the 1990 referendum Quebec came within a percentage point of voting to leave Canada, and the failure of Meech was blamed for providing ammunition for the separatist cause, I again wondered if I was wrong. But after seeing some more history, and thinking about it long and hard, I believe I was right for three reasons:

- It was a myth that Quebec was shut out of the *Constitution Act* in 1982. After details of the Meech deal were released to the public, Pierre Trudeau attacked it and some commentators said he was out of touch with Quebec. I asked a retired, relaxed Trudeau about this over coffee at his Montreal law office. Up to then he had been smiling, but suddenly his eyes narrowed and he said, "I did win seventy-three out of seventy-four seats in Quebec in 1980!"
- It was also a myth, and wishful thinking, that the passage of Meech would have ended the separatist cause.
- Judge Bowker was absolutely right that Meech was bad in both procedure and substance.

The Cheshire Cat: The Fight to Save Vancouver Kingsway

In the midst of the free trade and Meech debates, a parliamentary page approached my desk in the House with a note to call my office immediately. I was not prepared for the unpleasant surprise I received from my assistant Brian Burke. The Electoral Boundary Commission had just released its report, and the commission had eliminated the electoral riding of Vancouver Kingsway! Its territory was to be divided among four other Vancouver ridings. It's one thing to lose an election, quite another to have your riding disappear. Every ten years, after the census is conducted, electoral districts and their boundaries are revised to reflect population shifts and growth. Stupidly, we had not paid attention to the work of the commission. Now we had to appeal to the commissioners to change their minds.

I began to organize our fight. My chief ally was the relatively young mayor of Vancouver, Gordon Campbell. On February 22, 1987 he brought council members together with Vancouver MLAS and MPs over a lunch at Brock House. It was the first time elected representatives from all levels of government sat down together and discussed Vancouver city issues, only one of which was redistribution. Bob Williams, NDP MLA for Vancouver East, called it "very productive and non-partisan." Glen Clark, the second NDP MLA from Vancouver East (a dual-member riding until 1991) was also there. He and Campbell would run against each other for BC premier less than a decade later, but right now they were both helping me.

We decided that our argument to the Electoral Boundary Commission would be that the City of Vancouver needed proper representation. By reducing the number of the city's seats from five to four, and making the remaining ridings long strips running east and west when demographic divisions naturally ran north and south, the commission was ignoring community interests. I appeared before Vancouver city council and got a resolution to that effect, proposed by Don Bellamy on the political right and seconded by Bruce Eriksen from the political left. Tom Berger and I met with Mayor Campbell, who agreed that the city would finance a lawsuit challenging the constitutionality of the

The Cheshire cat.

commission's decision. We argued, among other points, that the principle of representation by population was violated.

Unfortunately, Supreme Court Chief Justice Allan McEachern ruled against us, and Vancouver Kingsway was gone. The *Province* newspaper ran an editorial cartoon featuring a fading image of me in a tree, like the Cheshire cat in Lewis Carroll's *Alice's Adventures in Wonderland* whose body occasionally fades out from tail to head, leaving nothing but its distinctive grin! I was determined not to fade out. The Electoral Boundary Commission amended its report to create the riding of Burnaby–Kingsway, which meant in theory that Vancouver lost only half a riding.

The problem was that Burnaby was Svend Robinson's turf. I thought the solution would be for Pauline Jewett to run in Port Moody–Coquitlam, Svend to go to New Westminster–Burnaby and me to run in Burnaby–Kingsway. For some reason, though—perhaps my stand on Meech Lake—Pauline decided to run in New West–Burnaby. Svend jumped into Burnaby–Kingsway. So I sold my beautiful little house on Trout Lake and moved to the suburbs.

The people of Port Moody, Coquitlam and Port Coquitlam welcomed me, especially Gwen Ranger, Dawn Black, Linda Aspergierson, Ann Cardus and Michael Farnworth, a young city councillor whom I hired as one of my constituency assistants. I bought an apartment, and Mark Rose, Dawn and Gwen patiently taught me to love the suburbs. Given that I grew up in the suburbs of Toronto, I was a quick learner. When I got up early to watch my neighbours head off in their cars for the commute to the city as the sun came up, I remembered driving from Etobicoke to the University of Toronto back in the 1960s—and got a new appreciation of the issues faced by suburban families.

My experience in debating really paid off, and I was able to get on the local map pretty quickly. *Coquitlam Now* newspaper quoted me as saying the struggle for the future of Canada was between Mulroney's vision, which was pro big business, with submission to the United States and a market economy, and the NDP's emphasis on ordinary people, independent foreign policy and the use of government to spark economic growth. I highlighted the opposition to free trade. I wanted to make it clear I was the anti-government candidate. Looking back, it seems the issues have not changed much.

With Sharon Olsen leading my campaign team, which included Adrian Dix, Mike Farnworth and David Perry, I was elected. Once again my mother Isabel was a big asset. My staff and NDP members loved her energy and honesty. At my fiftieth birthday party, which was, of course, a fundraiser in the riding, my mum was asked to give her explanation for how I had managed to have such a successful political career. She told a story of leaving my pram outside our Glasgow home one day. When her husband came home, he found the baby covered with bird poo. He was not happy, but her defence was that in Scotland, having a bird poop on you is seen as an indication of good luck. "So don't give him too much credit for hard work," she said in her thick Scottish accent. "He has been damned lucky all his life!" She stole the show.

The Perils of Question Period

One day in June 1986, the NDP caucus executive committee finally gave me permission to ask a question at the end of question period. At the time I was the NDP critic for fisheries, so I was supposed to ask something about fish. During the course of that question period, though, the Liberal opposition had been asking Prime Minister Mulroney about his travel expenses, accusing him of "spending taxpayers' money on hotels, airplanes, videos, limousine rentals, caviar and champagne, as if he had won the 649 Lottery." He had spent $3,400 a night for a hotel room in Paris (which was even more money in those days than it is now). He refused to answer, instead getting a junior minister to reply.

Finally my turn came: "Mr. Speaker, my supplementary question is to the president—rather, to the prime minister. Is he denying that the room cost $3,400, and can he tell us what you get for $3,400? Do you get chocolates on the pillow, for example?" Mulroney waved his junior minister down, stood up and flippantly replied, "Mr. Speaker, for that amount of money you get the NDP member for Kenora–Rainy River down the hall." Not Mulroney at his best, but the House exploded and I knew I would be on the national news that night.

In retrospect, I should have stuck to my original question on fish, but I knew by then that the eyes of the journalists in the press gallery would glaze over. Do you know the story of the scorpion and the turtle? The scorpion asks the turtle to give him a ride on its back across a big river. "But what if you sting me?" asks the turtle. "Impossible," replies the scorpion. "If I sting you, we will both drown." So the turtle gives the scorpion a ride. Halfway across, the scorpion does sting the turtle, and they both drown. As they slip beneath the surface, the turtle asks, "Why did you do that?" With his last breath the scorpion replies, "It's my nature."

A few years later I was putting a question on copyright legislation to the prime minister and ended up being a little too clever. Somehow the question came out like, "We know that the prime minister can sing, we know that the prime minister can act in a manner of speaking and we know that the prime minister thinks, at least, that he can direct. The artists want to know whether he can produce." Mulroney rose, looked at the speaker and then at me, smiled and replied. "The question is, can I produce? That is a sexist question but I will answer it anyway. Four kids and two majorities." Pow!

A Bas Bandidos

What does an MP do in his vacation time? Since I didn't have a big family, and I had what I thought was a pretty secure riding, I used my air miles to go to Zimbabwe, where one of my uncles had once lived. In Harare, the capital, I stayed with Frank Rutter, the *Vancouver Sun* correspondent for Africa (they did have such things in those days). He was travelling to South Africa to do a story on apartheid, which was still in force, so I had his apartment to myself.

I got to know Canadian ambassador Roger Bull, a tall, distinguished-looking man whom even Hollywood would have cast as a senior Canadian diplomat. Underneath that conservative veneer was a man of great principles and even a few radical ideas. His wife Therese Bull, an Irish redhead with endless energy and compassion (Angela Ricker, her equally energetic daughter, later worked for me), convinced me to join her when she persuaded a Zimbabwean air force plane to take her to neighbouring Mozambique, where there was an ongoing civil war. The Mozambican rebels were supported by the apartheid regime in South Africa.

In terrible heat and humidity we visited a refugee camp, our plane hugging the trees to land at a remote airstrip so we wouldn't be shot at. In the camp we saw people who were starving to death. That scene has stuck in my mind forever. How far away, and how lucky, Canada looked from there. When we got back to the coast, a Mozambican army unit took us around to visit a few villages where the residents were safe and had food. At each village a group of women would sing and then yell, "Viva President Chissano [then the President of Mozambique], viva Comrade President Mugabe [of Zimbabwe], a bas bandidos [down with the rebels]." (I thought I heard "A bas bandidos," but in Portuguese the phrase would be "Em baixo com as bandidos.")

At the last village I was asked to respond to the women's toast. I said, "Viva President Chissano, viva Comrade President Mugabe," but what was I to do about a Canadian leader? I thought of the governor general or the queen, then I thought of the prime minister and I even considered Ed Broadbent. I finally settled on "Viva Canada! A bas bandidos." All to a big cheer, I might add.

Returning to Ottawa on a Friday morning, I went straight to my parliamentary office to do some work. It was a lazy Friday afternoon on Parliament Hill, and the phone rang. A *Globe and Mail* reporter asked what I knew about an issue that was being talked about while parliament was in recess. I told him quite honestly I couldn't help him as I had just returned from Africa. When he asked me if anything interesting had happened there, I made a pitch for good Canadian diplomacy, especially our support of anti-apartheid forces. I then made the mistake of telling him the "A bas bandidos" story. I should have remembered what Tom Berger taught me: nothing is off the record. The story that appeared in the Saturday *Globe and Mail* was not about Canadian diplomacy, but about my dilemma of deciding what to cheer.

When I entered the House on Monday morning, Ed Broadbent came up to me at the NDP caucus meeting, smiling, and said, "'Viva Ed Broadbent' would have been about right." As I left the House, I was tapped on the shoulder by, of all people, a laughing prime minister. "'Viva Mulroney might have brought down the house,'" he said. A few months later I flew on a Canadian armed forces plane. Governor General Jeanne Sauvé was on the same flight. She sent an officer to ask me to come up to her compartment, where she greeted me warmly. Her first comment? You guessed it: "Viva the Governor General, a bas bandidos." Canada is a small country.

CHAPTER 9

A Busy Time

On March 4, 1989, at an NDP meeting in Toronto, Ed Broadbent announced he was stepping down after ten years as federal leader. "It's time for renewal," he said. People were shocked and saddened by Ed's decision. He was truly loved in the party and deservedly so. On issue after issue, both in caucus and in the House, Ed always took the high road. He was and is a true social democrat in every sense of the term. NDP MPs felt Ed did us proud when he was our leader.

We in British Columbia loved the results of the 1988 federal election—we had won a record nineteen seats—but I suspect Ed was disappointed. Although the NDP had forty-three MPs, our best result ever, we had no seats east of Ontario. Not long before the election, the NDP had been first in the national opinion polls, with 44 percent of Canadians saying they would vote for us, but this hadn't translated into seats. During the campaign, Ed had to deal with the fact that Ontario was generally against free trade and Quebec was in favour of it. He was criticized by some NDP members for not taking a firmer stand against free trade as Liberal leader John Turner did, but as far as I could see, certainly from a western Canadian NDP view, there was no pressure for him to step down.

On the Monday following his announcement in Toronto, Ed unexpectedly returned to the House of Commons. There was an empty chair beside him, and the whip told me to put my bum in it so Ed didn't look like he was sitting alone when the TV cameras picked him up. Member after member on both sides of the House got up to praise Ed. As they were doing so, he whispered in my ear, "You know what a statesman is? A dead politician!" He looked relaxed.

My Run for the Leadership

The media said there was no obvious successor to Ed Broadbent, and they were right. Stephen Lewis declined. Bob Rae had gone to Ontario (and within the year would be premier). Many in the party establishment wanted a woman as leader, possibly Alexa McDonough of Nova Scotia, but she also declined at this time. I looked at Broadbent's strengths. He was flexible enough to keep the various factions in the party together, he was realistic on the economy and he had a good—and in private a biting—sense of humour. He once informed a group of serious NDP policy wonks that a lot of ordinary people actually like to have fun. I knew I had a sense of humour. As well, I was proud of my efforts as energy critic to maintain East–West party unity, and I always talked as much about creating economic growth as I did about spending on new programs. I decided to run for the leadership.

I was pretty oblivious to my weaknesses. I didn't have much money, had no real organization and no caucus support. Moreover, I had never dealt with my sexuality and simply decided to keep that aspect of my life private. Those were different days. Columnists referred to me as a "bachelor." Looking back, I realize I sublimated much of my energy into my work. But things did start to change on February 29, 1988, when a courageous Svend Robinson publicly announced to Canadians that he was "a member of parliament who happens to be gay." I never thought I could win the leadership, but I saw the race as an opportunity to speak seriously about the environment, energy and Aboriginal rights in a very public forum. Also I was good at "biting dogs": presenting the issues I believed were important in such a way that they drew media attention and a wider audience. I had tons of energy and loved a battle.

It looked like MPs Steve Langdon, Howard McCurdy and Simon De Jong would enter the race. When Dave Barrett indicated he wouldn't run, I decided to announce quickly to pre-empt any other BC candidates. Most of my fellow BC MPs were backing newcomer Audrey McLaughlin, who had only been an MP since 1987. People like Bob White and Svend Robinson, who would have been serious candidates, decided not to run themselves and were basically saying it was time for a woman leader. I liked Audrey personally, but given that she had been in the House for only two years, I thought it was too soon for her to take on the leadership. Looking back, I regret that judgment. As I got to know her better, I saw she was a tough, smart woman whose wit could match anyone's.

I declared my candidacy at a press conference in Ottawa. I tried to highlight my ideas, especially those on the environment and energy, and I criticized the Mulroney government for giving us the double whammy of free trade and the Meech Lake Accord, which would make it difficult for a strong federal government to enact the industrial strategy that Canada needed. I also stressed party renewal, including the direct election of the leader. Here I overshot, saying the NDP suffered from hardening of the arteries. This was a good clip for the press but too glib for a real leader. Broadbent's response to my comments was diplomatic, but I made it difficult for him. However, I did believe that our message in the 1988 election was not strong enough, and I said so. We talked of "fairness" when we should have talked about fighting the emerging inequality in our economy. I also tried to bring the labour wing of the party and the environmentalists together by reaching out to both in my campaign stops and speeches.

Mum, Armeda McDougall and Jeanette Leitch.

My campaign manager was my twenty-five-year-old executive assistant Adrian Dix, who basically took nothing and made it into a good campaign. I got endorsements from Tom Berger, Eugene Forsey and Grace MacInnis, and I felt I handled myself well in the cross-country debates. At one point I thought I might finish second to McLaughlin but then in October, a month before the convention, Dave Barrett entered the race. Dave was probably past his prime, but he and Stephen Lewis were the best public speakers in Canada. At his best, Dave was up there in the Obama league.

The convention on December 2, 1989 was a lot of fun for me. A kilted bagpiper piped me in and I gave my speech. I called on the NDP to return to its roots as a "movement" and then focused on my issues: Aboriginal rights and the environment. Global warming was just coming to public attention in 1989. I know it was a good speech, but I could deliver it better now. On the first ballot I got 213 votes, which was about 10 percent and respectable given that there were seven candidates. I wanted to continue on to the second ballot, but Adrian took me to a quiet area away from all the cameras and the delegates, and told me it was time to quit.

I didn't want to hear it and Adrian knew that, but he told me anyway because he knew it was the right decision. That's why, when Adrian was running for premier of British Columbia twenty-three years later, I told the press that this quiet guy had a tough inner core and would be a good premier. When I bowed out, I had to decide whom to support. I let my delegates go their own way, and I went to Barrett. I saw him as a strong interim leader who, quite frankly, could probably save my own seat.

Audrey McLaughlin won. She was inexperienced but she ran a solid campaign. After we returned to Ottawa, she made a genuine effort to welcome all the leadership candidates into her team. It was then that I began to see what a genuine and fresh person Audrey was. Unfortunately Barrett didn't join us, and some of her labour supporters were of little help as she struggled to rebuild the NDP, which had so much relied on Broadbent's glow. I didn't see it, but at the leadership convention my mum gave a press interview, defending me on some point, and was a big hit. On my return to the Commons I got personal notes from Prime

Minister Mulroney and Liberal leader John Turner. Both of them mentioned Isabel. Mulroney said, "Conventions are strange animals—you confronted the beast and emerged unscathed, honour intact." I guess he would know.

Gwaii Haanas

One issue I consistently raised through my leadership campaign and in election campaigns was the need for Canadians not to take our land, water and clean air—in short, our environment—for granted. When it came to preserving and protecting land and water, I knew a good place we could start was one of the most beautiful and mysterious places in Canada and indeed on Earth: the Queen Charlotte Islands off the northwest coast of British Columbia, which today is known as Haida Gwaii.

My first visit to these islands was in the late 1970s when the Berger Inquiry was winding up. I went there with Ted Knowles and Jon King who worked with me on the inquiry for a time. We visited the home of lawyer Carey Linde in Queen Charlotte City; met the young Haida carver Gary Edenshaw who later became the powerful chief Guujaaw; and then went to stay in Liz and Jim Fulton's cabin on the Tlell River. On that first visit I learned about the incredible land on South Moresby, the southern part of the archipelago, known to the Haida as Gwaii Haanas. This is the ancestral home of the Haida people. Here lie virgin rainforests, including some of Canada's largest and tallest red cedar, Sitka spruce and western hemlock. Think of the paintings of Emily Carr with aging totem poles in the rainforest.

Shortly after I was elected in 1979, Murray Rankin, one of the student lawyers I'd met when I returned to the University of Toronto in 1974, wrote an op-ed piece for the *Globe and Mail* in which he outlined the plans of Rayonier Canada to log in the rain-swept fiords and rugged mountains of South Moresby. In those days Canada didn't have specific legislation to protect wilderness areas, so when Murray mentioned the Berger Inquiry's proposal to protect the northern Yukon as a wilderness park, suggesting South Moresby should be treated the same way, it caught my eye. Even as Murray was writing his op-ed, Haida people and environmental activists were working together to create the South Moresby Wilderness Proposal to protect the area. The battle was on.

Jim Fulton, by 1979 the MP for the region, was also determined to preserve South Moresby. Jim and I decided to work together, he on the ground in his riding and me in the House. That was why on May 2, 1980, I introduced Bill C-454, *An Act Respecting a National Park on Moresby Island and Its Adjacent Islands*. My assistant Jack Woodward had parliamentary counsel draft it. The bill never came to a vote, but Jim and I—mainly Jim—kept the issue alive in the House well into the 1980s.

Members of the Haida Nation put themselves on the line for their land in 1984 when dressed in traditional red button blankets, they blockaded a logging road to protect the trees of Lyell Island from chainsaws. Seventy-two people, many of them elders, were arrested and twelve were charged with contempt of a court injunction. But the logging stopped and negotiations began between the Haida and the federal government, the feds and British Columbia. It helped that in 1981 the United Nations declared the southernmost part of the archipelago a UNESCO World Heritage Site. But the negotiations weren't easy as the Province of BC claimed it owned the land (although the Haida denied this), and there were logging and mining interests in the mix.

One night I was sitting in the House with "Big Jim" Fulton. A page came over and told us the prime minister was on the lobby phone for Jim. He told the page to go to the phone and tell his staff to stop joking with him. She returned and said the voice insisted it really was the PM. Fulton was dubious. About a year earlier he had smuggled a salmon into the House and put it on Mulroney's desk during question period to protest federal policy on commercial, First Nations and sport fishing (unfortunately, Mulroney wasn't in the House that day, but Fulton got a strong reaction from the Conservative MPs... and the speaker) so he was used to playing pranks and having pranks played on him. Fulton and I went to the opposition lobby, where Fulton picked up the phone and yelled into it, "Don't bullshit me." There was a pause and Fulton began speaking a little more quietly.

"I'm listening, Brian," he said to my horror. When he got off the phone, Jim told me that Mulroney wanted him to put forward a motion to transfer jurisdiction for South Moresby from the province to the federal government. Mulroney would guarantee government support. We asked Liberal MP Brian Tobin to speak to his leader, John Turner, to arrange Liberal support. So when Jim got up to speak to the motion, we knew we had the unanimous support of the House. Here is the motion that Jim Fulton introduced on May 14, 1987:

> That this House calls upon the Government of British Columbia to co-operate in setting aside the South Moresby area of the Queen Charlotte Islands as a National Park Reserve; and
>
> Further, that the federal government provide for compensation to those interests affected by a National Park Reserve; and
>
> Further, that the House confirms its intention to ensure the continued participation of the Haida people in matters affecting South Moresby.

Note how delicately this was done. It's a "Park Reserve," not a national park. As Miles Richardson, Jim's great Haida pal, later said, this status respects the Haida position that the land was and is actually owned by the Haida Nation. The feds, who are always the guys with the big money, were prepared to compensate the loggers and miners for the jobs and resources they lost. And the pressure was on the Province of British Columbia that, after an initial resistance, finally came through and transferred the islands and surrounding waters to federal jurisdiction.

After introducing the motion, Fulton put everything he had into a brilliantly emotional speech, his best. He spoke about how nearly ten thousand Haida lived in the South Moresby region until 1884, and how within six years that population declined to five hundred as a result of the ravages of smallpox and measles. He reminded us that these were people who travelled as far as California and Mexico in their huge trading canoes. Jim mentioned that the UN had already designated Anthony Island a World Heritage Site:

> I know many members of this House have been to Anthony Island and seen the rare and deeply moving beauty as you come into the pebbled bay and see the totem poles and longhouses standing in the area. I am sure members are aware that in that immediate vicinity there are ten species of whales, killer whales and others. It contains the largest rookery of Steller's sea lions on the west coast of North America. It has a large seal population and 250,000 breeding pairs of seabirds. There are rare peregrine falcons, large populations of bald eagles and the world's largest black bear populations. The area has all kinds of endemic species of plants not found anywhere else in this part North America because that area, for a variety of reasons, was not covered by ice during the last ice age. It is a truly important area to the Haida people, to all Canadians, and to all people of the world to have preserved in as pristine a state as possible.

Jim quoted Bill Reid, a Haida and one of Canada's best artists (his *Spirit of Haida Gwaii* sculptures welcome visitors to the Canadian embassy in Washington and to Vancouver's airport), who said, "The forests of South Moresby should be treasured like the great cathedrals of Europe." Jim also quoted Miles Richardson, president of the Council of the Haida Nation, who said, "You have never fought us in a war and we have never surrendered. This is our land." And Jim cited the Constitution: *"Members should not forget what this House did in 1981 and 1982 by including Section 35 in the Constitution Act.* We recognized and affirmed Aboriginal rights and title... Today we are demonstrating our intention to recognize that and affirm the real Aboriginal rights of the Haida people in the area south of the Tangil Peninsula and those islands."

No one moved or made a sound, and the young parliamentary pages seemed to be leaning toward Jim's corner of the House, mesmerized by his words, as he concluded that this was *"one of these unique and rare oases on the planet Earth, where there is a multiplicity of life that is still interacting as it has been, not just for decades or centuries, but for thousands of years since the last ice age. It is a truly remarkable area."* Powerful rhetoric aside, Jim also stated that he had sought and received support from the International Woodworkers of America (IWA), the loggers' union. And so it was that one of the few opposition motions in Canadian history passed with unanimous support. It showed that politics and politicians are not all bad!

In 1993 the Government of Canada and the Council of the Haida Nation signed the Gwaii Haanas Agreement, which established Gwaii Haanas National Park Reserve and Haida Heritage Site, cooperatively managed by the Haida Nation and the federal government. Those magnificent trees still stand today, sustainably bringing in more tourist revenue and jobs than logging did, as they will continue to do for—as the Haida would say—"time immemorial."

Death with Dignity

I was of course always interested in legal issues. From 1990 to 1994 I was the NDP's justice critic, and I spoke in debates on justice for individuals who had been wrongly convicted, on law reform and even on judges' salaries. On February 17, 1993, I introduced a motion to decriminalize euthanasia:

> That, in the opinion of this House, the government should consider the advisability of introducing legislation on the subject of euthanasia and, in particular, of ensuring that those assisting terminally ill patients who wish to die not be subject to criminal activity.

Earlier BC Chief Justice Allan McEachern, a well-respected and by no means radical jurist, had called on the government to "consider the advisability of introducing legislation to permit assisted suicide," adding, quite rightly, "I can only hope that parliament in its wisdom will make it unnecessary for further cases of this kind to be decided by judges." This plea was part of his dissenting opinion in the case of Sue Rodriguez, a courageous woman who went public with her suffering as a result of ALS (amyotrophic lateral sclerosis). She challenged the law prohibiting assisted suicide, saying it violated the Charter of Rights and Freedoms, and even though the Chief Justice agreed, the BC Court of Appeal ruled against her. Rodriguez took her case to the Supreme Court of Canada.

Her challenge was before the courts when the House of Commons voted on my private member's motion, which was defeated by a vote of 145 to 25. The debate on the motion was intense on both sides but civilized, illustrating the best aspects of the House. Most of the MPs ducked the vote, but at least we talked about giving people the right to choose their moment of death. Sue Rodriguez lost her appeal to the Supreme Court of Canada in December 1993, and she subsequently took her own life in February 1994. In her fight for her rights, and in her death, she showed great dignity and courage. My colleague Svend Robinson supported her to the end and also introduced motions that would have made assisted suicide legal.

In my view, the Conservative government's reluctance to heed Chief Justice McEachern's plea and introduce legislation was a result of pressure from ideologues in the new Reform Party. However as predicted, even as Rodriguez lost in the courts, other cases came forward that argued for the right to "death with dignity." The issue was out in public, and both the Supreme Court and public opinion evolved over the next twenty years.

In a unanimous decision on February 6, 2015, the Supreme Court of Canada struck down the provision in the Criminal Code giving Canadian adults who are mentally competent and suffering intolerably and enduringly the right to a doctor's help in dying. The court gave the government twelve months to amend existing laws or introduce new ones, but the Conservative government of the time under Stephen Harper, did nothing. When Justin Trudeau's Liberals won the October 2015 election, the Supreme Court granted them a four-month extension to address the issue and on June 17, 2016, a bill legalizing and regulating assisted dying was passed in parliament. We sure have come a long way. But at the time, for Svend's and my troubles, a columnist in the *Ottawa Sun*'s parliamentary bureau called the NDP "Death's party of choice."

A Mother's Love

Another legal issue I had some involvement with involved a miscarriage of justice that took more than two decades to set right. On a snowy winter day in 1969, a sixteen-year-old kid named David Milgaard was travelling from Winnipeg to Alberta with a couple of friends. Along the way they stopped in Saskatoon to pick up another friend, Albert Cadrain. On the same day, police found the body of a twenty-year-old nursing student in a snowbank near Cadrain's home. The woman had been raped and murdered.

Under public pressure to find the culprit, Saskatoon police charged David Milgaard with the crime. Cadrain, who received a $2,000 reward for information, told police that he had seen blood on Milgaard's clothes the day of the murder. Milgaard was convicted and sentenced to life imprisonment in 1970. He lost his appeal of the conviction and his application for a new trial, but he never lost his mother Joyce. She believed he was innocent and became a tireless campaigner for his release from prison. In her lobbying to get justice for her son, Joyce Milgaard was everywhere. In May 1990 she tried to hand justice minister Kim Campbell a report from a Vancouver forensic pathologist. Campbell brushed her aside and later, on February 27, 1991, turned down Milgaard's request for a review of his case.

In August 1991, Milgaard's lawyers filed a second application to Campbell. Joyce still didn't give up. She managed to buttonhole Prime Minister Mulroney, who said he would speak to the minister of justice. Mulroney later told David Asper, who had taken on Milgaard's file as a law student and saw it through, that he did indeed pressure Campbell to stop stonewalling the case. Joyce Milgaard also approached a number of MPs, including Lloyd Axworthy, John Harvard, Russ MacLellan and me.

I took an interest in the case. As a student at the University of Toronto law school, I was privileged to hear a lecture by G. Arthur Martin. He was the top criminal lawyer of the day, and his book on the Canadian Criminal Code was *the* text. I learned two important things at the lecture. First, if you trace events leading up to an incident, they tend to fall into a rational order. And second, witnesses who at first seem credible can often turn out to be unreliable. Martin also said that when the police are under pressure to find a suspect quickly, they can leap to conclusions and charge innocent people. In Milgaard's case, when I looked at the events leading up to the incident, it didn't make sense. Here was a young person who had smoked a little dope and had some truancy problems as a youth, but he had no history of sexual assault. An ordinary kid like that doesn't suddenly go out and randomly kill someone.

Therefore during question period on September 17, 1991, I rose in the House of Commons to put a question to Minister Campbell: "The prime minister recently told Mr. Milgaard's mother that he would speak to the minister about the case, which, if I may say, was a very decent and humane reaction. Has the prime minister done that? Has the minister decided to act in what appears to be a situation where justice is not only not done, but there appears to be compelling evidence that Mr. Milgaard did not commit this crime?"

Campbell did acknowledge that Joyce had got Mulroney's ear, however briefly, and that Mulroney had spoken to her about it. She also noted her concern that a lawyer and officer of the court like me would "stand up in the House of Commons and appear to prejudge a case with which he is completely unfamiliar." In a way Campbell was correct. I was saying that Milgaard was innocent, even though he had been convicted by a jury, had lost appeals to the Court of Appeal and had the Canadian Supreme Court refuse to hear his case. I was indeed sticking my neck out. But talking to Joyce, with her passion and faith in her son's innocence, and also hearing the impressive facts and new information she and her lawyers had dug up, had its effect on me.

On October 24, 1991, I followed up the question with a statement in the House and one day later with a debatable motion urging a new trial for Milgaard. Finally on November 28, 1991, Campbell referred the Milgaard case to the Supreme Court of Canada. In April 1992 that court, on the basis of new evidence, quashed Milgaard's conviction and ordered a new trial. He had served twenty-two years. There was no new trial, so Milgaard was free, but his name had not been cleared. That took another three years, when new DNA evidence cleared Milgaard. The new evidence incriminated Larry Fisher, a man who had an extensive criminal record that included sexual assaults, and who had been renting the basement of Albert Cadrain's house when Gail Miller was killed.

Fisher was ultimately convicted of her rape and murder in November 1999, and in 2008 a Saskatchewan commission of inquiry concluded that the criminal justice system had failed David Milgaard, who was financially compensated for his ordeal. What's the lesson? Sometimes innocent people are convicted. And when miscarriages of justice occur, politicians can raise the issue in the House, questioning the government and prodding it to act. Lawyers like Hersh Wolch and David Asper can keep plugging away until they find the evidence that will help their client. But in this case, the real champion was Joyce Milgaard. You can't beat a determined mother and her love.

I'm a Macist not a Racist

Sometimes my passion for certain issues got me into trouble. Once it got me national headlines and a place in Canadian parliamentary history. On October 30, 1991, I flew back to Ottawa from my riding. When I turned on the television in my office to check what was happening in the House, I saw they were debating a private member's bill dealing with the taxation of seniors. This was an issue I was following closely and I wanted to take part in the debate, so I got on the green bus that takes opposition MPs from their offices in the Confederation Building to the main Parliament Building.

On my arrival in the House, I was shocked to see the acting whips had engineered a quick vote and were in the process of adjourning the House. In those days they had that power during private members' business. I was furious. The normal fifteen-minute period between calling the vote and actually voting had been cut down to four minutes. What's the point of being an MP if you are not allowed to vote? I called out a point of order, but to no avail. The acting speaker was leaving. Thinking he hadn't heard me, I rushed down the aisle to catch his ear before he left.

When the House adjourns, the sergeant-at-arms rises, takes the mace from its cradle and leaves the House. Unfortunately for me, the sergeant-at-arms was between me and the acting speaker. He was also carrying the mace. I tried to reach the acting speaker. In doing so, I grabbed the mace. It was actually a light touch, unlike the situation when British MP Michael Heseltine grabbed the mace in the midst of a heated debate and wielded it over his head! The sergeant-at-arms paused, turned slightly, looked at me and continued on.

Representing the authority of parliament, the ceremonial mace is a staff made of gold metal. It's carried into the house each sitting by the sergeant-at-arms and quietly sits on a pedestal on a table in the centre aisle while the Commons is in session. The original mace was used as a weapon. Interfering with it (e.g. touching it) is a breach of the privileges of the House—indeed, it is contempt of parliament, only a little short of high treason, as I was to find out. On returning to my Confederation Building office I got a call from one of the acting whips, Jesse Flis, who solemnly warned me that he would officially complain. I thought nothing of it, believing that the House had disrespected *me* by having the quick vote.

When I got back to my Sandy Hill apartment, I stretched out on my little green leather couch and turned on the CBC national news. There were three lead items: an airplane crash in the Arctic, fighting between Palestinian youth and the Israeli Defence Force, and an MP to be disciplined for grabbing the mace. The latter made me sit up. My ever-loyal secretary Naomi Harrison used to rib me about the time I spent helping journalism students and other student activists at Carleton University in Ottawa and elsewhere with political questions. That's how I met people like Carole Mills, Greg Younging, Bill Clay, John Horgan, Peter Bleyer and Rob Sutherland. My first loyalty was of course to my constituents, but the CBC reporter who I had encouraged as a student may have saved my bacon.

His story said there had been only three MPs who were brought before the bar of the House. The first was Sir John A. Macdonald (story accompanied by a picture of Macdonald's statute on Parliament Hill with a seagull sitting on top). Sir John was drunk so he sent Sir John Abbott in his place. (I'm not sure where the reporter got this detail, but it sounded good.) The second was Louis Riel, then an MP from Provencher (with a segment from Pierre Berton's *National Dream* TV series showing the actor playing Riel hiding behind the curtains of the House). Riel fled, led a rebellion in what is now Saskatchewan, and was eventually hunted down by the Canadian government and hanged. The third was me. Maybe this was a bigger deal than I thought.

The next day I was asked to come to the speaker's office, where Speaker John Fraser (it is a small world) told me he was very reluctant to do this, but would require me to appear before the bar of the House after question period. He said he would instruct the TV cameras to focus only on him and not me, so as not to humiliate me even more.

When the House met that morning, I rose as soon as possible and apologized for my actions. We then carried on with regular business (which, ironically, included me bringing forward a motion to amend the *Young Offenders Act*). After lunch, QP proceeded as normal. But when it concluded, no members left the House. The sergeant-at-arms led me to the middle of the aisle between the two sides of the House (in the original British parliament, the distance between the sides was supposed to be two sword lengths). There I stood just outside the bar of the House and faced the speaker. The MPs were completely silent. Speaker Fraser rose and gave me what my dad would have called a good talking-to. He reprimanded me formally for the record.

After he finished, most of the members left the House, including the prime minister and the speaker. I returned to my seat way down near the end of the House in the opposition benches. The deputy speaker returned to the chair and called on the house in a loud voice to resume debate on the amendment to the *Young Offenders Act* that we had been debating that morning before lunch. I had moved the amendment, so after a few members spoke on it, the deputy speaker recognized me to summarize. I couldn't resist. I began with "I am pleased to agree with these government amendments. I also want to tell my mother I still have my head on here so that I can speak." A few Conservative and Liberal MPs quietly supported me, including Chuck Cook from North Vancouver and Warren Allmand from Montreal. Speaker Fraser sent me a note regretting the incident, saying he felt "utterly dismal" and adding that I conducted myself "with dignity and grace." That is the kind of man he is.

When I left the House later that day, members of the press gallery were outside, waiting to surround me for the infamous scrum. It so happened that during the previous few weeks in the House, Tory MP Bill Kempling had called Sheila Copps "a slut." Kempling's colleague Jack Shields had referred to NDP MP Howard McCurdy, the only black member of the House, as "Sambo." As a number of MPs, including Dawn Black, Mary Clancy and Mary Collins had pointed out, my action was

I'm a macist, not a racist.

much less serious than hurling racist or sexist slurs. McCurdy later said, "This place—you can attack a race but you can't attack a mace."

So I explained to the media throng that, if anything, "I was a macist, not a racist." It was not the first time a little humour got me out of a jam. Subsequently, a political cartoon appeared showing me at a blackboard wearing a dunce cap and writing over and over again, *I will not touch the mace.* The caption read: "You were a naughty, naughty man Mr. Waddell… and in the future you will confine your outbursts to sexist and racist slurs, in keeping with the traditions of this House." I suppose I'm lucky. If I grabbed the mace today, I might get shot.

Each provincial legislature has a mace. Someone once took the Yukon mace on a bar tour—and lost it. When it was returned to the legislature, there was a nick on it. God knows what it was used for! In 2016, when Prime Minister Justin Trudeau elbowed an NDP MP, there were calls to drag him before the bar of the House. Veteran journalist Peter O'Neil asked my opinion. I felt like saying that Trudeau would be joining good company, but I realized maybe I had grown up a bit. So I said the whole thing was much ado about nothing.

CHAPTER 10

On the International Stage

Most MPs want to "make the world a better place." A lot of them are idealists at heart. But they spend most of their time on domestic matters—that is, when they are not in airplanes going back and forth between their constituencies and Ottawa. By the way those flights can be pretty long and boring. One exception was a flight in 1989 from Vancouver when I stood up to stretch and found a fellow passenger doing the same thing. I noticed she had a young boy asleep next to her, who turned out to be her thirteen-year-old son Angus. I recognized her as a BC judge and asked her why she was going to Ottawa. "I have just been appointed to the Supreme Court of Canada," Judge Beverly McLachlin replied. She of course went on to be one our greatest chief justices of Canada and I might add a fellow mystery novelist!

In Canada we call foreign issues, matters outside our borders, "external affairs." Sounds sort of erotic but it is a bureaucratic term. The old name for the ministry was actually the Department of External Affairs. That was in the glory days of Canada's influence in the wider world, when one minister of external affairs, Lester Pearson, won the Nobel Peace Prize for inventing UN peacekeeping. Harper called the ministry "Foreign Affairs and International Trade Canada," in keeping with our emphasis on international trade and business interests generally. Justin Trudeau changed it to global affairs.

It's difficult for an individual MP to get involved in foreign matters because the executive arm of government, meaning the foreign minister and his or her department, handles them. Each opposition party in the House has a "critic" in the portfolio who attends committee meetings. If the critics are lucky, the government of the day may invite them to join the odd Canadian delegation or sit in the UN General Assembly, as I once did. The international system itself makes things difficult for individual MPs because it is a system of sovereign states. The UN General Assembly is made up of 193 of them, and the government of each state is the official spokesperson for that state. This means the Canadian government of the day speaks for Canada, period.

So how does an MP who wants to change the world get involved in external affairs? Where there's a will, there's a way! MPs of all parties can join a myriad of international parliamentary organizations—the Inter-Parliamentary Union (IPU); various Canada–US, Canada–France, Canada–Taiwan, Canada–Israel, Canada–Europe, et cetera organizations; the Commonwealth Parliamentary Association (CPA) and others. Most of these provide members with nice junkets, paid for by the Canadian taxpayer or foreign interests. Most don't provide much opportunity for real action, with the possible exception of Canada–US groups, where MPs come face to face with real US senators (elected) or members of Congress who have some influence on matters affecting Canada.

Another exception is an organization called Parliamentarians for Global Action (PGA). It used to be called Parliamentarians for World Order, but "world order" sounded a little fascistic, so the name was changed. The Canadian branch was founded by some progressive MPs (Doug Roche, Warren Allmand, David MacDonald, Mark MacGuigan, Pauline Jewett) and from the beginning was determined to tackle some real international issues and get some results. Nuclear disarmament was one; gender equality and abolition of the death penalty were others. I joined and was taken under the wing of Tory MPs Doug Roche and Walter McLean, and Liberal Warren Allmand. For one of the few times in my life, I actually listened. These guys were relentless in their push for world peace and for creating the tools to bring it about.

PGA had a small office in New York and a small staff headed by two tireless New Zealanders, first Nick Dunlop and then Kennedy Graham, who was later an MP himself. The members, from a number of parliaments around the globe, were men and women who really wanted to change the world—people like Keith Best from the UK, and a number of politicians from South America and Mexico. We would occasionally gather in New York at the UN Headquarters and run two- or three-day seminars with experts on various international issues. These took place when parliament was on break and we paid our own way.

One time in 1984, I took as an observer my friend Bill Clay, a Canadian student at University of Massachusetts Amherst, who covered the session for National Public Radio in the United States. Our PGA speaker was John Kenneth Galbraith, the distinguished economist who was born in Canada. Warren and Walter were busy with an executive meeting and asked Bill and me to have lunch with Galbraith in the UN dining room until they could join us. We were pretty awed by Galbraith with his six-foot-nine frame and his towering intellect. After a bit of awkward silence, I hesitantly brought up the lead story in that morning's *New York Times* about a summit meeting between Gorbachev and Reagan in Reykjavik, Iceland. I asked Galbraith if he had ever been to a summit or whether he thought they mattered.

This actually got him talking, telling us about the time he was in Germany in 1945, and he and his friend George Ball (who later became a high-ranking US civil servant) decided to take their jeep down to Potsdam to crash the summit meeting between US president Harry Truman, UK prime minister Winston Churchill and Soviet general secretary Joseph Stalin. "We hadn't been invited to Potsdam, but we didn't want to compound the mistake by not showing up," Galbraith wryly mused. A US soldier at the gate just waved them through and they sat down to watch the proceedings as observers.

President Truman spotted them, came over and asked, "What are you guys doing here?" Galbraith replied, "We were nearby, so we came to observe." Truman looked hard at them and said, "Well, boys, you better join the delegation and get to work." I thought, *Wow, how things have changed today.* Warren Allmand arrived as Galbraith told us about his job controlling prices in the United States during the war. At the end of the war, however, he had the job of interrogating the surviving Nazi high command before the Nuremberg trials. He told us he was amazed at how many had become drug addicts and alcoholics, and how many had come from a fairly low-level small-business background.

The International Criminal Court

A meeting of PGA that took place in Washington, DC in September 1991 unexpectedly changed my life. We were meeting in a senate office building near the magnificent domed Capitol. I was asked to go down the hall to another room where Senator Arlen Specter was speaking on the idea of an international criminal court. My job was to take notes and report back to the other PGA meeting. With Specter and Congressman Jim Leach was a remarkable man, Cherif Bassiouni from DePaul University in Chicago, a professor unlike any I had ever known. He was a suave, well dressed Egyptian-American who spoke five or six languages and had a perfect American accent.

The idea of an international criminal court was quite revolutionary. Unlike the International Court of Justice (ICJ) set up by the UN, which dealt with crimes committed by nation states, the court they were proposing would charge and prosecute individuals who committed crimes of international character such as genocide, war crimes and crimes against humanity. Except for the Nuremberg trials and the trials of the Japanese leaders after the Second World War, there had been no apparatus to do this before. I recall Bassiouni and Specter asking questions like "After the Gulf War, should we have captured Saddam Hussein and put him on trial internationally?" and "What could be done with the people who blew up the Pan Am jet over Lockerbie, Scotland?" Domestic courts trying such cases would appear biased, which was why they proposed an international court.

Bassiouni told us how the world had missed the opportunity to set up an international legal commission after the First Word War. He especially emphasized our collective failure to respond to the Turks exterminating 800,000 Armenians. He explained that the Nuremberg judges had to look hard to find precedents for the concept of crimes against humanity. Now Nuremberg itself was a precedent, and there was lots of international law—some twenty-two crimes spelled out and 315 international instruments—that could be used in the court they were proposing. He also described discussions about prosecuting international drug traffickers that had led to a UN resolution in 1989 asking the International Law Commission to look into establishing an international criminal court to prosecute drug traffickers.

Bassiouni said this was not the same as crimes against humanity, but in any case, the International Law Commission had dropped the ball. The Cold War had also frozen a lot of initiatives, but now the time for an international criminal court had come. The one thing missing was political will on the part of governments to move the idea forward. I was mesmerized by Bassiouni, but the issue was so new to me that I wasn't sure what to do. I duly reported to the PGA meeting in the other room. Little did I know that from then on I was designated the PGA's "expert" on the international criminal court.

After I returned to Ottawa, I received a note from the PGA office in New York telling me our strategy was to get the UN General Assembly to ask the International Law Commission to draw up a draft statute for an international criminal court. We got the small country of Trinidad and Tobago to be our chief proponent at the UN. We also had one of our PGA members, UK MP William Powell, speak about the court in the British House of Commons. In October 1991 German foreign minister Hans-Dietrich Genscher called for a UN Court of Justice where crimes against humanity and peace, war crimes, crimes against the environment and genocide could be prosecuted and punished. This was one year after unification of Germany, and it showed how things might start to change with the end of the Cold War.

In November, a working group of the International Law Commission recommended that the Law Commission itself, and the sixth committee of the UN General Assembly which considers legal issues, look at the court proposals. By early 1992 we had the foreign minister of Zimbabwe and president of Venezuela each advocate at the Security Council for the criminal court to address terrorism and drugs. On March 2, 1992, the *New York Times* reported that King Hassan II of Morocco had proposed the establishment of an international court for terrorism cases. Regarding the two Libyans accused of blowing up the Pan Am airliner, the king said, "If the accused were judged in Libya, that would not be credible. If they were judged by an American or English court, that too might not seem credible." The answer was to turn them over to an international criminal court.

Then my phone rang in Ottawa. Professor Bassiouni was calling and he wanted the proposals for a court to be fleshed out in more detail. He was setting up a working session of academics in Courmayeur, Italy and wanted me to attend. I looked at an atlas, and after seeing that the village of Courmayeur was right beside the Alps and Mount Blanc, I glanced at my skis and promptly accepted. Why me? Maybe Bassiouni couldn't find another politician to go.

As it turned out, I was the only politician in a room of academics. The village was picture-perfect Italian Alps. We started working early in the morning, took long lunches, and then resumed in the early evening. I got two hours of skiing each day between sessions, and I felt like a million dollars. Drafting the details of the court was not easy, and I soon tangled with the American guy—a plant from the State Department. I realized early on that one of the hardest tasks would be to get the Americans to join a world criminal court. One afternoon I was on a difficult downhill run when I saw a skier stuck in a small crevice. It was the American. I pulled him out and suggested that he now owed me a favour, like maybe agreeing with our international criminal court initiative. Fat chance!

After a fascinating few days, the working group ended, so I decided I would try to ski up in Mount Blanc. Now, I talk a good ski game, but the truth is I learned to ski at Whistler when I was twenty-eight years old, unlike most kids in Vancouver who learn as toddlers. After I took a steep gondola up to the top of the mountain from the Italian side, I saw a white expanse of trails. It looked like skiing across a glacier. The magnificent peak of Mount Blanc shone in a sunny glow above me. There was a group of about eight skiers in front of me, just off the gondola. They were beautifully dressed in the latest Italian skiwear. I looked pretty shabby beside them. Perhaps that's why one of them signalled for me to join them, yelling to me in Italian. At least, that was what I thought he said! They put me in the middle of the group, and we took off. What seemed like two hours later, our group crossed from Italy into Chamonix, France. I could hardly walk that night.

Like other members of PGA around the world, I got periodic updates from our coordinator Robert Dickson. We were asked to raise the matter in our respective parliamentary and congressional chambers. I gave a statement in April calling on the government to support the proposal at the UN for an international criminal court, "whose time has come." That same theme was raised in Costa Rica, New Zealand, the United States (by Jim Leach) and the United Kingdom (by William Powell again). On September 24, 1992, external affairs minister Barbara McDougall, to her great credit, called on the International Law Commission to establish an international criminal court.

Professor Bassiouni's vision was picking up speed. In early December I was invited back to Italy, this time to Syracuse in the far south, for a Criminal Law Institute with parliamentarians from all over the world. Over a hundred political leaders, legal experts and UN officials looked at the creation of a court from the "political dimension," the "legal dimension" and the "regional perspective." I represented Canada on a panel on the political dimension, which included the incomparable Italian politician Emma Bonino (early in her political career she dressed up as a nun and sneaked onto the Italian national news to advocate for starving refugees), William Powell and others. We determined that there was a broad consensus on a list of twenty-two crimes that could be tried at an international court, as well as a number of treaties from the conventions on slavery and drugs to documents on genocide, using explosives in the mail, crimes against diplomats and airline hijackings.

My final involvement was on St. Patrick's Day weekend in 1993 when a delegation of MPs from around the world, including me, met with UN Secretary-General Boutros Boutros-Ghali. I recall we went on to the lobby of the General Assembly to meet with and literally lobby various delegations so they would not block the concept. When it was my turn to speak to the Chinese, I mentioned that I was a "friend of China," which seemed to prompt a change of attitude. A senior Chinese diplomat took me aside. I told him the continued research into the idea of a court was no threat to his country and they shouldn't block it. I don't know why, of course, but they didn't veto the court, probably because China had not yet begun to flex its muscle internationally. But I'd like to say thank god, again, for barbecued meat!

With the UN Secretary General and the MPs from around the world.

On June 15, 1998, five thousand representatives from 160 countries gathered in Rome for the conference that, to many people's astonishment, brought about an international criminal court. The impossible became possible on July 17, 1998 when the Rome Statute, the treaty establishing the court, was adopted by a vote of 120 to 7. Canadian diplomat Philippe Kirsch chaired the Rome conference and enacted a brilliant strategy of forcing a straight up-and-down vote after five long weeks of meetings. The ICC came into being formally in 2002 as a permanent transnational tribunal to prosecute crimes against humanity and war crimes in a world of sovereign states. Canadian diplomats like Ambassador Alan Beasley, who chaired the final Law of the Sea Treaty conference; Lester Pearson, with his idea for UN peacekeeping; and Kirsch show you what Canada can do if we want to.

An Argo Moment

I had been involved in another kind of international matter earlier, sometime in the 1980s, on a Sunday afternoon if my memory is correct.

With Ambassador Ken Taylor.

It was one of the few weekends I didn't take the long flight back to my constituency in British Columbia. I was snuggled into my couch with a good mystery novel when the phone rang in my apartment not far from Parliament Hill. A Conservative MP from Alberta was on the line, and he was inviting me for dinner!

Apparently that night, as chair of the House of Commons energy committee, he had to entertain two American congressmen. He told me they were important decision-makers for the future of western Canadian energy exports. His pitch: "I need some members of the committee." He was asking for a favour. In those days in parliament, a favour would be returned. He was also offering a big free meal and being a Scotsman, I couldn't say no. A few hours later I showed up at a good restaurant in downtown Ottawa. A Liberal MP was there, together with our committee clerk, our researcher and of course the Tory chair.

The two congressmen, Republicans from Iowa and Michigan, were fairly young and completely full of themselves. "Obnoxious" was a charitable description; on and on they went about America's exceptional role in this world. I just listened and ate, unusual for me—the listening, that is. When nature called I excused myself and went up to the second floor of the restaurant where the washroom was located. Upstairs, I saw two diners finishing up their meal. One was Ken Taylor, the former Canadian ambassador to Iran. With the frizzy hair and the glasses, you couldn't miss him. I interrupted them, introducing myself. "Yes, I know of you, Mr. Waddell." The ambassador smiled.

I asked him if he could stop downstairs on his way out. With a sense of relief, I went back down to our awful guests and another course of American exceptionalism and how the good congressman from Iowa was planning to run in the next senate primary. Suddenly there was a hand on my shoulder. "How's it going, Ian?" Ever the smooth diplomat, it was no longer "Mr. Waddell" from Ambassador Taylor. The Iowa congressman looked up angrily, as if to say, "How dare you interrupt me?" I immediately apologized to the congressman and took the opportunity to introduce "Ken Taylor—you know, our former ambassador to Iran."

This was long before the movie *Argo*, when there was a greater recognition of the role that Canadians, Ken Taylor in particular, played in helping six American diplomats first hide and then flee from Iran after Ayatollah Khomeini overthrew the Shah. The two congressmen stood bolt upright. Our boastful friend from Iowa, with his hand on his chest as if saluting the flag, said, "On behalf of the people of the United States of America, I would like to thank you." I looked down the table at my fellow MPs, and the chair gave me a discreet thumbs-up. American humble pie was served for dessert.

My Moment with Mubarak

In the early 1990s I was the only anglophone and the lone NDPer on a delegation of French-speaking Canadian MPs in Egypt. Apparently many of the Egyptian upper classes speak French as a second language. Anyway, that was our excuse for coming to Egypt on a fact-finding mission. I got to go along because I could speak some French and the delegation needed at least one NDPer. We were to have a full day visiting the awesome Egyptian Museum in the heart of Cairo. I had been looking forward to it. But as the visit started, our guide, the chief curator, arrived looking very flustered. President Hosni Mubarak wanted to meet the delegation, and he wanted us to come to his palace. Right now!

The chief curator wanted to show the delegation something for our visit. He quickly opened a side door, leading us into a dusty storage area that seemed to be full of old coffins. He opened one. Before us was Ramses II, the greatest, most celebrated and most powerful pharaoh, who ruled from 1279 to 1213 BC. Then we had to leave and travel by bus across the vast city to the suburb of Heliopolis to meet the modern (and now last) pharaoh. I remember being offered sweet mint tea in the red-carpeted waiting room of the palace and then being ushered into a large office.

Two men were inside. The one who came toward us and greeted our delegation leader in French was Boutros Boutros-Ghali, the Egyptian foreign minister and later secretary-general of the UN. Then the larger, well-dressed man came forward briskly, hand outstretched and greeted us in English, apologizing that he couldn't speak French. "So the meeting will be in English," he said. There was no doubt who was the boss here. At this point our delegation leader Louis Plamondon, who spoke English hesitantly, informed President Mubarak that he was turning the chair of the delegation over to me.

I had been hiding behind the other MPs. Now I reluctantly took the chair near the president and put aside the trivial thought that had popped into my head: *Has a New Democrat ever chaired a Canadian government delegation before?* Mubarak welcomed us with a big smile and said he would take questions. As I recall, the questions were fairly easy—about agriculture, tourism and a few other topics. I helped shape the questions from my colleagues into clearer sentences and better English. Finally when no more questions came, I couldn't resist. "Mr. President," I stammered, "I have a question. I'm a member of Amnesty International, and they tell me Egypt has a reputation for locking up a lot of political prisoners, banning some groups and not allowing really free elections."

Mubarak looked at me directly and scowled. With a raised voice he told me that we in the West didn't understand the dangers of Muslim extremism, and he warned that terrorism could come someday to our land, too. (He was right on that point.) He said that he had to take measures to protect Egypt from extremism. At the time I thought President Mubarak actually liked my question as it got him engaged and allowed him to give us a message. The Canadian diplomats in attendance were not so happy. When I got back to Ottawa, I called the Canadian head of Amnesty International and told him of our moment with Mubarak. He said, "You're lucky you're not in jail."

Peace Mission to the Middle East

In early 1990, before Iraq's invasion of Kuwait and the first Gulf War, I had an opportunity to be the lone Canadian MP to join an American "peace mission" to the Middle East. Somehow my friend Patrick Esmonde-White got me into this group, which was sponsored by American churches and led by former senator Charles Percy, who had been head of the Senate Foreign Affairs Committee. The group contained such notables as John Anderson, who had been an independent candidate for US president, and Mike Farrell of the TV series *M*A*S*H*. I took my friend Bill Clay along to keep me on track.

The delegation met with President Assad in Damascus, Syria; King Hussein in Amman, Jordan; Palestinian leader Faisal Husseini in East Jerusalem; the mayors of Jerusalem and Bethlehem; and Israeli defence minister Moshe Arens, finance minister Yitzik Moda'i, and leader of the Opposition Shimon Peres in Tel Aviv. In the middle of the trip I chose to fly back to Ottawa to vote on the Conservative government's abortion bill, since I thought it was a crucial issue. The bill—which I voted against because it gave doctors, not women, the final say in abortions—passed in the House but was defeated in a tie vote in the senate, thanks in part to senators with real courage like Pat Carney. I thought the bill would have been a nightmare in practice, causing a lot of problems for doctors, and I believed it was written as a sop to the Reform Party.

When I returned to the Middle East I was exhausted but was able to participate in a press conference in Jerusalem with Senator Percy and

John Anderson. Later Bill and I took our Arab translator out for a drink. I insisted we go to the King David Hotel because I had heard that one of my old political supporters was involved somehow when the British army staff were blown up there by the Israel independence movement. This was a bit crazy on my part. When we arrived at a darkened bar in the hotel with our reluctant Arab friend, we saw a guy sitting alone and asked to join him. It was Izzy Asper, the Canadian media mogul from Winnipeg. What a small world! We had a friendly conversation.

Later at a cocktail reception in Amman, Jordan, a young woman came up to Bill and me and offered to arrange a meeting with Yasser Arafat for the delegation. I didn't really believe she could do this, and besides most members of our group were returning home in a few days. After they left, Bill and I planned to rent a car and drive down to see Petra and go diving in the Red Sea. We had it all arranged when the phone rang in the morning in our hotel room. The woman from the reception told us Arafat had a message for the delegation and would meet me in Baghdad the next day.

After the call ended, I phoned the Canadian Embassy. The staff there told me that we were unlikely to get a visa for Iraq, and even if we did, Arafat was famous for keeping people waiting or cancelling meetings. I was still pretty jet-lagged, so I settled back to sleep. The phone rang again. The young woman gave us a number at the Iraq Embassy and told us to get going. Bill and I discussed the situation and finally agreed we had never turned down an interesting opportunity in our lives. Within an hour we had a visa and a reservation on that night's late flight to Baghdad.

A man in a crumpled suit with no tie met us and ushered us over to an old Mercedes. On the drive to the Al Rashid hotel, I felt a bit scared. Was this really a good idea? Could we be held for ransom or (thinking of the King David Hotel) blown up? On the surface, everything appeared normal in Baghdad in those days (pre-Gulf War, pre-ISIS), but who knew what was under the surface. Two rooms were reserved for us at the Al Rashid. I took one double for both of us and insisted on paying for it. The next day we were poolside in scorching heat—Bill was swimming—when I was paged. The voice on the line told me to be ready for a pickup in one hour. We were going to have lunch with Yasser Arafat. I put on my suit; Bill wore jeans and a Palestinian scarf.

The house we were taken to was a guarded bungalow. Arafat looked like he did in photographs, except that his green army suit was immaculate. I discovered that he had very little facial hair, which was the reason his beard appeared so scruffy on television. In accented English he apologized for missing the delegation and asked me to take a message to the Americans. There had been some recent attacks by boat on Israel, and he had been blamed for authorizing them. He said this was not true. The Americans should understand that there were radical elements in his movement that he couldn't always control.

After the short meeting he invited us for lunch. It was a big table and there were a small number of guests, including two women. I sat across from Arafat and Bill was down at the end of the table with one of the young women. I had a Canadian flag pin on my lapel that I was about to take off to give to Arafat when I looked at Bill. He was scowling. A few days earlier he had told me that if I gave away "any more of those silly flag pins to people who need food and other aid," he would leave me there on the spot. But it was too late; Arafat had noticed that I was offering him the pin. He glanced at an aide and then accepted the pin. A few minutes later the aide produced two red boxes. I opened one and found a gorgeous mother-of-pearl depiction of the Christian nativity scene. I noted that Bill accepted the other box.

After about four hours we were taken back to our hotel. That afternoon we went to the small Canadian embassy, which was staffed by a junior diplomat who told us things were fairly quiet under President Saddam Hussein. We asked where we could go for a beer that night in Baghdad to watch a World Cup soccer game on TV. He told us to go to the student district, which we did. We walked around until we found an actual small pub in an Arab city. No one bothered us, although we got a few curious looks. I don't think we could do that today.

When I got back to Canada I phoned External Affairs to tell them about the meeting with Arafat. They were completely uninterested. I then phoned a contact in the American Embassy, a big guy from Wisconsin who had been assigned to the NDP caucus and told us he would

Bill Clay and I meet Yasser Arafat in Baghdad.

vote NDP if he were a Canadian. Of course we guessed his real job, but he was a nice guy. He asked if he could come over to my office, and within the hour he arrived with another guy even bigger than him. I was impressed the CIA was on the job. I also wrote a letter to the minister of external affairs, Joe Clark, detailing my meeting with Arafat. He sent me back a very serious and thoughtful reply.

I didn't truly appreciate it then, but both the Israelis (through Peres) and Palestinians (through Arafat) basically said they were tired of killing each other and they wanted to talk, really talk. Later, President Clinton got Arafat and Israeli prime minister Yitzhak Rabin together. Who knows what might have happened if a Jewish extremist had not assassinated Rabin, or if Arafat had been more courageous about keeping the deal. Sometime after the trip, Charles Percy invited me to Washington and even took me onto the senate floor when it was in session. Then he took me to a closed-door coffee get-together with the powerful Senate Foreign Relations Committee, whose members greeted him warmly.

As I recall, there were a small number of older male senators and one woman, all white. One of the senators was John Kerry, later foreign secretary. Like the leading character in the movie *The Butler*, a black man in a white uniform jacket with white gloves served the coffee. The senators talked to Percy about the situation in the Middle East, and more than one of them complained openly about the intransigence of prime minister Yitzhak Shamir. One of the senators asked me what I thought. I was a bit stunned but managed to stammer that I was politically more like a member of the Israeli Labour Party and Mr. Shamir was a right-wing Likud member, but they had to deal with him since he was the elected prime minister. That's pretty damn obvious. When some of the senators started nodding their heads in agreement, I felt like Peter Sellers in his role as Chance the Gardener in one of my favourite films, *Being There*.

Time to Come Home

After our great day of March 17, 1993, lobbying at the UN for the international criminal court, the visiting MPs scattered. Five of us ended up that night in a jazz bar in Manhattan—four guys and one woman. The woman, Helen, was an MP from New Zealand. The guys were Arthur Robinson from Trinidad and Tobago, Ólafur Ragnar Grímsson from Iceland, Paddy Ashdown from Britain and me from Canada. Helen said she was going home to quit politics. After a few drinks and practically on bended knees, we urged her to continue in politics for "the cause of mankind" or something like that. Arthur became president of Trinidad; Ólafur, president of Iceland; and Paddy was head of the Liberal Democrats in the UK until 1999. Helen Clark became prime minister of New Zealand. And little Ian? The Reform Party candidate defeated me in Port Moody–Coquitlam later that year.

CHAPTER 11

Back to BC

Politics is a lot of fun when your tide is going in, but it is devastating if you almost drown when the tide sweeps you out. On election night in 1993, Preston Manning's Reform Party swept to victory across western Canada. Jean Chrétien's Liberals won the East and formed the national government. The NDP got squeezed. In British Columbia we went from nineteen seats to two. I lost mine. As I drove into the parking spot at my condo on Pinetree Way in Coquitlam, I crashed my rental car into a support beam. It was a fitting end to a horrible night.

About a year earlier, NDP MP Simon De Jong had returned from a Reform Party convention in Vancouver and warned our federal caucus of the Reform threat. We didn't think it was possible. Clearly we underestimated Manning, the strange-sounding little man, and his Fraser Institute and gun-lobby backers. We should have minded our history. They were the new prairie radicals, as we had originally been, and they took our working-class vote.

I was stunned, thinking I had been a high-profile MP at the top of my game. I had delivered tons of federal money to my riding and had fought hard for my constituents. I had really enjoyed my five years in Coquitlam and had learned first-hand the struggles suburban families go through to live the good Canadian life. I loved it when my assistant Ann Cardus took me and her coffee cart to Saturday morning kids' soccer games, and I despaired to see parents leave at an ungodly early hour on their car commutes to work. I sold my condo (at a loss, if you can believe it) and left the suburbs.

Luckily I had kept my share in a house in Kitsilano, eight minutes to downtown Vancouver, a different world. I was only fifty-one and my political career was over, or so I thought. I decided to get away, putting my backpack on and trekking around Asia for a few months. I learned to scuba dive. On my return I used some retraining money to learn how to work a computer. What did Professor Porter tell us when I was seventeen? There will be computers, and you will change your career many times over your life!

Fraser Basin Board

An article appeared in the *TriCity News* about me and "life after politics." There was a picture of me in a gym, and I talked about my travels. In truth I was a bit lost until—thank you, Lady Luck!—on a downtown Vancouver street I literally ran into my old friend Murray Rankin. He was with David Marshall, a go-getter and networker who is always moving and smiling and brimming with ideas. Marshall was executive director of the Fraser Basin Management Board, which was made up of representatives of the federal and provincial governments, municipalities and First Nations—"the four levels of government" as Marshall would say.

The mandate of this unique organization was to work to sustain the Fraser River Basin, which of course is part of the greatest salmon river in the world. It turned out the chair of their board Tony Dorcey was returning to teach at UBC. Murray looked at me, then turned to David and said, "There's your man." Thanks to federal government representative Earl Anthony and later to Moe Sihota and Sheila Copps, the environment ministers of British Columbia and Canada respectively, I got the position as the new chair of the board. Although it was only part-time, I loved the job and it was a good outlet for my energy, probably to the chagrin of the staff.

I had the idea of putting out a "report card" on the present state of the Fraser Basin. Most of us got report cards at school, so we knew the public would understand the concept and take notice, and we figured that by grading a number of issues (population growth, water, salmon, forest, economy, Aboriginal relations, planning, decision-making) we could advance the overall sustainability of the basin. I drove our poor staff, led by Malcolm Smith, relentlessly until they produced a hard-hitting document.

We released the report card at an event for the media at a Richmond dock. I showed up with a bottle of pure water from the Fraser's source, and scooped another bottle of water from the river as it entered the ocean. I drank the pure water and theatrically threw out the water from the mouth of the river as undrinkable. The reporter for the local French TV station asked me to repeat the stunt, but I got the bottles mixed up and drank from the wrong one. That night I wondered if I might come down with some strange disease. But we did succeed in getting TV coverage and a story on the front page of the *Vancouver Sun*.

David Marshall and I worked well together. He ran the board, and I came up with punchy ways to highlight our issues. He did think I was a bit over the top when one of our news brochures led with "Waddell asks, 'Who's speaking for the fish?'" The irrepressible Ray McAllister, the Council's communications man, wrote that. I thought it was a good example of how a little imagination and humour can highlight important public issues.

We sponsored a long-distance swimmer from Coquitlam (and later an MP), Fin Donnelly, who swam the whole length of the Fraser, 1,375 kilometres, from a frigid morning start at Tête Jaune Cache near the river's source in the Rockies, to Richmond in the delta. I swam with him for a few minutes near Prince George and in a promo earlier at the mouth of the Fraser. Marshall said the newspaper photo reminded him of the famous photo of Chairman Mao in the Yangtze River, as my hair was not even wet. The report card and the swim were two ways we "bit a dog": highlighting big issues like urban sprawl, poor water quality and fish protection in the basin with humour and events that caught people's attention.

At one intense board meeting I was giving the federal and provincial reps a tough time for not putting their cash where their mouths were. When Jon O'Riordan, the very cool and well-informed BC government member, who was also a fellow Scot, shot back at me, "I told him to be careful: I might be his boss someday." Who knew?

The New MLA

In early 1996, Bernie Simpson, the NDP MLA for Vancouver Fraserview and an old friend of mine, called me to say he was not seeking re-election. He asked if I was interested in running in that riding on the team of the new premier, my old assistant Glen Clark. Looking back, I can't believe I left a great job to take a big chance, but I'm glad I did. (I was happy to see Iona Campagnolo follow me at the Fraser Basin Management Board, now renamed Fraser Basin Council. She did a great job until she left to become BC's lieutenant governor in 2001.)

Elected in 1991, Premier Mike Harcourt had given British Columbia generally good government for over four years, but along the way the party had lost contact with the people who got us elected, our base. To win as a social democrat, you have to improve the life of the people you represent. So Premier Glen Clark was determined to reconnect with our supporters by announcing a few bold policies. He froze hydro rates, ICBC rates and tuition fees. He seized on Liberal leader Gordon Campbell's indication in the leaders debate that he might cut back on education funding; Clark said Campbell might want to cut taxes for the rich, but Clark would raise them and spend the money on educating working people's children with smaller class sizes. Glen's slogan was "On Your Side."

The members of the Fraserview NDP riding association welcomed me, led by Cathy Morrow and Tom Holmes. Sharon Olsen came back as an organizer, bringing with her dedicated campaign workers like John and Brenda Bray, originally from Prince Edward Island, and we began to put together a team. I got back some of my old team people like Al Warner and Duc Tran, the best sign guys ever, Jeannie Kamins (best artist ever), Cheryl Hewitt and Kim Pollock, and new people like Kerry Jang, Derrick Harder, Ros Keller, Vince Gogolek, James and Bill Duvall, and many others. Bernie "Singh" Simpson really helped me with the Indo-Canadian community. My close friend Rob Sutherland, a superb organizer, came to British Columbia from Ottawa to run my campaign in Fraserview. Harry Bains, Paul Gill, Hardev Bal and other friends in the South Asian community arranged a debate at the

Vancouver Sikh Temple and brought in a ringer, Moe Sihota. Moe and I crushed the opposition—at least, we thought we did.

At about 9:20 p.m. on election night, Rob told me I could lose by around eight hundred votes. Then we began to creep up and went ahead by four hundred. The last poll to come in was a single big apartment building near Fraserview golf course, not our strongest neighbourhood. Crying volunteer Karen Jacobson called Sharon Olsen to say that we had lost that poll by two hundred votes. Which meant we won! I was now a member of the legislative assembly. We all went crazy, then hurried down to the Hyatt Hotel, where I was carried in to the party on the shoulders of my Indo-Canadian committee. We were the last riding to come in and had helped Glen Clark pull off a come-from-behind victory. The NDP won the most seats (thirty-nine to the Liberals' thirty-three) but not the popular vote (39.45 percent to 41.82 percent), and our majority was thin.

I assumed Glen would put me into his cabinet. He didn't. I didn't think so at the time, but he was right. Provincial politics is very different from federal. He did name me chair of a committee to study Aboriginal Affairs and the upcoming Nisga'a treaty. That appointment came with a budget to hire some staff and hold hearings. Recalling my experience with the Berger Commission, we scheduled public hearings in twenty-seven communities around the province and listened to 560 oral presentations. At the hearing in Burns Lake, the middle-aged chief who came to speak before us was Emma Palmantier, my young witness in the Josephine Alec murder trial so long ago.

Using the Ottawa model, which was unlike the ultra-partisan BC practice, I made a place for the opposition on our steering committee and let them write a minority report. I think Geoff Plant, Mike de Jong and Jack Weisgerber were surprised at first, but it led to their very useful contributions to the hearings, where we actually enjoyed working together. I tried not to forget my own NDP members, one of whom, Tim Stevenson (later minister for employment and investment, and even later a Vancouver city councillor), was ahead of his time when he insisted we put an apology for our treatment of First Nations people in our report. As well-respected former MLA David Mitchell wrote in the

Vancouver Sun, our provincial committee benefited from some of the Ottawa procedures. Ironically, I was mocked in our own caucus and in the legislature for being "too Ottawa."

After a year as a backbencher, I heard that I might get into the cabinet. Bill Clay and I went skiing at Whistler, and I took along a cell phone. Today's kids won't believe this, but the phone was about six inches long and two inches wide (or should I say fifteen by five centimetres?). It was so heavy I feared it might injure me if I fell. Anyway, halfway down the red chair run, it rang. Bill told me to stop, take a deep breath and answer. It was the premier, telling me I would be sworn in as the new minister of small business, tourism and culture the next Wednesday. Tourism minister in British Columbia? Are you

The Arts Club comes to Ottawa.

kidding! Within ten minutes I was at the Longhorn Pub at the base of the gondola, having a beer with a group of German tourists, talking about Beautiful British Columbia.

A Highway Sign

Soon after I became a minister, one of our interior MLAs came to me to point out that we did not have a *Welcome to British Columbia* sign at the actual BC–Alberta border on the Trans-Canada Highway. I asked the transportation minister, my friend Harry Lali, to send me his deputy minister so I could ask him to put one there. A bit sheepishly the deputy said, "Minister, there could be a political problem." It turned out former premier Bill Vander Zalm had put a sign several kilometres into BC because a sign on the border would be in a national park and thus would have to be bilingual. I told him to put up a new sign at the border. Several months passed and no sign. When I called to follow up, they brought up a sketch of the sign. The French words were spelled wrong! Welcome to BC politics.

The Arts Club and the Stanley

Being a minister of the Crown does give you some power. One of my first acts as minister concluded a project I had been working on for some time. This project was related to something I loved as much as politics, maybe more: live theatre. My mother took me to the theatre in Glasgow when I was an infant; then I performed as a little kid in talent shows at the local cinema in Toronto and as a teen in a comedy skit at my high school's variety night. But it was in Vancouver that I found my best theatre experience. I was an articling law student living in a rented room at the Barr residence on McNicoll Avenue in Vancouver's Kits Point. New to the town and wanting to meet some people, I was told to go to the small bar downstairs at an old wooden building, the original Arts Club Theatre on Seymour Street.

After a few nights I began to drink with some of the performers after the show. I even got to buy a glass of wine (the first of many, I might add) for the new young artistic director Bill Millerd. Bill was the new energy in the theatre, taking over from founder Yvonne Firkins, a visionary woman. He asked me to serve on the board of directors. At my first Arts Club board meeting, our treasurer reported that our books would be in the black. Next item was a report from the bar manager who said that one actor was acting out of control after too much drink. I moved that he be banned from the bar. Then our treasurer asked to amend her report. Without that actor's drink tab, she reported, our books would go into the red. I then moved to reinstate the actor's bar privileges. Such was the precarious state of the Arts Club in its early days.

The board wanted to build a second theatre. At the time, the federal government's Canada Mortgage and Housing Corporation (CMHC) was redeveloping an industrial area on False Creek that it wanted to turn into a mixed-use "urban park" with light industry, retail, restaurants, arts group... The Arts Club board thought this would be a perfect place for a second theatre and chose two directors to negotiate a lease with CMHC. I was one and Ray Casson was the other. We could not have been more different. I was a young socialist storefront lawyer. Ray was an older man from West Vancouver, an accountant and a rabid Socred—that is, a strong Conservative—but boy was he good with numbers. And like me, he loved theatre.

Ray and I decided that CMHC, for all the power it had as owner of the land, really needed the lowly Arts Club. We would be one of the first major tenants in the new Granville Island and we were a sexy one. We represented the arts, in stark contrast to the industrial tenants who were already there. Bill Millerd will recall all the details of our first lease, but I believe we got a fabulous deal. It was a big gamble at the time. Would you go to a theatre that was literally under a bridge? Surrounded by warehouses, machine shops and other industrial concerns? We now know the answer. It depends how good the theatre is. Led by Bill and a generation of Vancouver actors, we were very good. And Granville Island, the urban park, became a huge success because of the imaginative mix of shops and amenities it offered. Former Liberal MP for Vancouver Centre Ron Basford played a pivotal role in making the Island happen.

The Arts Club always had a touring company. One of the most successful plays, *Talking Dirty*, played to over 100,000 patrons at home in Vancouver and 40,000 on tour in Toronto. The troupe came to Ottawa to perform at the National Arts Centre when I was an MP. I recall taking actors Jackson Davies, Norman Browning and Alex Willows, and stage manager Louis-Marie Bournival in one of Parliament's green buses up from my office to the members' entrance to the House of Commons. They were instructed to be good boys. Halfway there they had the other MPs in stitches, referring to the bus trip as, among other things, "just like a ride in the paddy wagon." I put them safely into the members' gallery, but when I looked up during question period, they were gone. Finally I spotted them in the press gallery sitting beside Mike Duffy (then a journalist) and making themselves at home.

After thirty-five seasons at the old wooden theatre on Seymour Street and on Granville Island, the Arts Club was ready to expand once again, especially after the sad closing of the Seymour Street stage in 1991. The old Stanley movie theatre on Granville Street had been closed by Paramount Pictures and was for sale. We wanted to buy it. Could it be done? The board formed a subcommittee to make a plan. Bruce Millie was the volunteer chair. Millie, an accountant, shared the sort of "double head" that Bill Millerd has; that is, a sound business sense and a love of the arts. It's not so common. People usually have one or the other.

Lawyer Harley Harris, the ever-energetic Marlie Oden and the hardworking John Sutherland were among the others who volunteered for the subcommittee, along with Jay Ono, executive director of the Vancouver TheatreSports League. Our original idea was to build two theatres in the Stanley Building: Arts Club below and TheatreSports above. We soon discovered the space was too small for two but magnificent for one. TheatreSports, whose original project it was, honourably backed off. Over many hot summer days, our group met in shirtsleeves in the Green Room of the Granville Island stage, sweating to come up with a plan. The key became selling a "density transfer" to Peter Wall for his One Wall Centre on Burrard. He gave us a chunk of money, and the City let him build a couple of extra condo floors. We had a down payment. Next we needed a mortgage. A campaign committee worked on the financing and Ann Mortifee, Jackson Davies and I were to host a fundraiser in the empty shell of the old theatre.

One of the jobs given to me as a member of the Arts Club board was to lobby the provincial culture ministry for a $400,000 "Go Grant," which had been promised to the Arts Club but not delivered. I think the ministry was no longer budgeting for the program, so my job was to remind the ministry of its promise and try to get the grant. The board, recognizing my passion for the Arts Club, let me stay on as a director even after I was elected to the BC legislature, and I kept on pressing the bureaucracy for grants, though I didn't have any more success as a backbencher than I did as a civilian.

After Glen appointed me to cabinet on that sunny Sunday afternoon at Whistler, I had a problem. I had an Arts Club board meeting on the Monday, two days before the new cabinet was announced. I gave Bill Millerd a heads-up in exchange for his vow of secrecy, and I announced my resignation at the board meeting. The only explanation I could give was that it was "for personal reasons." One of the Board members asked, "What about your work on the Go Grant?" Somewhat lamely I replied that I thought it would eventually come.

Three days later, on Thursday, I phoned the civil servant responsible for culture ministry grants. She said, "Yes, Minister, I expected your call. I'm pleased to tell you we will be sending the Arts Club a cheque tomorrow." This was after four months of mostly unreturned phone calls. I hope I didn't do anything unethical. Though if I did, I know it was for a good cause!

As minister, I got to help snip the ribbon on the night in 1998 that we reopened the Stanley. Senator Ray Perrault, representing the federal government, stole the show with a funny speech. I remember Jackson Davies and Ann Mortifee being there, and a young Michael Bublé in the first show. Since I had been so busy as a new minister, I hadn't actually seen the finished theatre until I went in to my seat. I don't cry much, but when I looked around that night, I did.

The 2010 Winter Olympics

The minister of small business, tourism and culture had a big office looking out to Victoria's Inner Harbour. My new assistant Maria Ciarniello, an Italian dynamo who probably was put there by the premier's office to keep me in line, led me to the pile of files on my big desk. Cheery young Maya Russell was there to assist Maria and me. My deputy minister Lynn Tait was prepared to back up my initiatives. The four of us made a good team. Looking at the files, I wondered what the piles for the ministers of health or education looked like. They must be huge!

I pulled out two files and put them on top: *2010 Olympic Bid* and *Film*. British Columbia was putting forward a proposal to be the Canadian bid for the 2010 Winter Olympic Games, and my ministry included the responsibility for sport. We were up against competing bids from Calgary and Quebec City, and we had to convince the Canadian Olympic Committee that we were the best. I didn't think that would be so difficult. Unlike Calgary, which had hosted the Winter Games in 1988, we had never had the Olympics in BC. And unlike Quebec City, we actually had big mountains. Whistler had been the top ski resort in North America for the last seven years.

As my officials enthusiastically briefed me, one face looked sad and out of place. It belonged to my director of sport Charles Parkinson, an Olympic-level volleyball athlete and later a CBC-TV commentator at the Sydney Olympics. "It's ours to lose, Minister," he said, "and we are losing it." He told me to talk to John Furlong, a friend of his who worked at the Arbutus Club, a private sports club in Vancouver. Like most people, I had never heard of Furlong, but Charles told me the guy really knew the Olympic scene. Over a coffee, Furlong confirmed Parkinson's view that our bid was in trouble. His advice echoed Parkinson's, which was to revamp our bid from the ground up, making it athlete-centred, youthful and connected to BC's communities. (Furlong ultimately became the CEO of BC's successful Olympic bid and of the 2010 Games.)

Bid chair Arthur Griffiths was not the best-organized guy, but he was enthusiastic, had a down-to-earth personality, and was recognized and well-liked by the public. I shared Arthur's enthusiasm, and I wanted to give the bid our government's priority. I brought my friend D'Arcy Thorpe, an external affairs diplomat from Ottawa, to help us as a volunteer and revamp the bid office. Then we got money for the Legacies Now program, which was created to put real cash into coaching and sports programs now, not after the Games. I went to open the BC Games in Quesnel and said that by accessing Legacies Now funds, some of the local kids might make it to the Olympic podium in twelve years. Later the federal Own the Podium program helped bring us medals.

I phoned Squamish Chief Joe Mathias and asked him to suggest a Squamish person who might join our Olympic Committee. He said, "How about me?" Yes! Now we were getting somewhere. I put lawyer Don Rosenbloom on the committee as well. His buoyant sense of humour belied a very sharp mind. I sat down with mayors Philip Owen of Vancouver and Hugh O'Reilly of Whistler, because in Olympic law the host city actually makes the bid. Mike Harcourt suggested we emphasize BC's incredible all-party environmental record. Former Olympic swimmer Marion Lay reminded us we should make the bid athlete-centred because we had some great world-class athletes. I got skiers Steve Podborski and Nancy Greene Raine to join us.

Then I thought, what can I bring to this effort? Rick Antonson, CEO of Tourism Vancouver, suggested it was my fifteen years in Ottawa. So I got Bruce MacMillan from Tourism Vancouver and Arthur Griffiths to go back with me to Ottawa. We got a room in the Parliament Buildings and invited all BC MPs and senators to a breakfast meeting. Every one of them showed up! We pitched for a united BC political voice. Pat Carney, who was then a senator, got up and gave a rousing speech, saying this was an all-party first. With a big cheer, our BC bid got a huge boost as we were seen working together.

Our Olympic bid team had to go to Toronto to present our case on a Saturday. We got all our speakers together the Monday before and rehearsed at Canada Place in Vancouver. We had good graphics and video designed brilliantly by David Clark. Our themes were good. We had great mountains and great athletes but our delivery at the rehearsal was weak. One of the worst was the rower Silken Laumann. That's when I got an insight into the training of an Olympian. For the rest of the week she practised her short presentation over and over again, and by Saturday she was the best. The format in Toronto was that Quebec City, Calgary and Vancouver/Whistler each got only half an hour to make a presentation. We were good, but we needed a cleanup hitter. Calgary was bringing Alberta premier Ralph Klein, a good speaker. We needed our premier.

Glen Clark said he couldn't come because his son Reid had a hockey game the Saturday of the presentation, and Glen had missed too many of his games. He told us the bad news at a meeting early that week in the premier's office. We were downcast. Clark's assistant Adrian Dix silently went to his computer and returned a minute later. He said Maple Leaf Gardens was going to be closed soon, but there was a game there on the night of our presentation. Why not take Reid along with us? And, Adrian said, "Ian can get us tickets." I thought, *What?* but didn't say anything. Clark, usually an ultra-decisive guy, never at a loss for words, hesitated and then said, "We'll have to ask Reid's coach."

The coach's reply was "Are you guys kidding? One of the last games at Maple Leaf Gardens? Go." So Glen Clark came, and his speech knocked it out of the park. My friend Ian Morrison, long-time head of

Glen Clark, son Reid and I meet Ken Dryden and Pat Quinn.

Friends of Canadian Broadcasting, got us hockey tickets. That weekend there was a series of cocktail receptions put on by the potential hosting cities. As usual, the Quebeckers put on the best party. Premier Clark and Reid attended with me. The mayor of Quebec City graciously introduced us to a short, curly-haired man. "Premier, Reid, Minister, permit me to introduce you to one of our greatest hockey players, Henri 'the Pocket Rocket' Richard."

He smiled, we smiled, and both Glen and I started talking to him at the same time. He politely cut us short, wheeled around and pointed to the man behind him. I had noticed the guy, a bit bigger than Henri, greying, older, but still with sharp piercing blue eyes. "Let me introduce you to my brother Maurice," Henri said. We were face to face with Rocket Richard, arguably the best hockey player of all time. For once, Glen and I were speechless. You would be too if you had just met God.

I'll never forget the performance of our team that Saturday morning in Toronto. We were young, energetic, athlete-led, united, happy and representative of all segments of BC society. It was November 21, 1998, my fifty-sixth birthday. We later found out that in the first round of voting, Vancouver/Whistler had twenty-six votes, Quebec City had twenty-five and Calgary had twenty-one. On December 3, 1998, the second round of voting occurred between the two leading contenders, which saw Vancouver win the Canadian bid with forty votes compared to Quebec City's thirty-two votes.

Grey Cup 1998

As minister of small business, tourism and culture, I was responsible for the government's involvement in sport. When the Canadian Football League's Grey Cup championship game was played at Vancouver's BC Place in 1998, Maria Ciarniello told me that the sitting minister was always invited to kick the first football, but she warned me that the minister usually didn't accept the invitation. The reason: the crowd would boo me! *Well*, I thought, *they won't boo this "tiny perfect minister"* (the tribute my staff had printed on my coffee cup). I wanted to do the ceremonial kick-off; I thought it would be a lot of fun. I also thought I was smart enough to avoid the boos. My brilliant plan was to get four balls to kick: one by a small boy, another by a young girl, the third by legendary BC Lions kicker Lui Passaglia and the last one by me, the minister.

The noise at ground level in BC Place during a normal game is deafening; at the Grey Cup it's almost overwhelming. My plan seemed to work as the boy and girl were introduced (small applause), then Lui (huge applause), then me. That's when I heard the boos. To top it off as we all kicked, the boy and girl did exceptionally well. Passaglia boomed the ball about fifty yards, and my kick dripped off my foot. (It had worked well at practice that morning, but I stupidly changed my shoes.) "Never mind," I later told Maria. "It doesn't hurt to get on national television with that huge audience."

"Sorry to disappoint you, Minister," she said. "The networks broke to commercial just before they introduced you."

Hollywood North

British Columbia is a little over two hours by plane from Los Angeles and Hollywood. When I took over the culture portfolio in 1997, we had great film crews, varied film locations and emerging production studios. BC was known as "Hollywood North." One of my first press conferences as minister was at Lionsgate Studios in North Vancouver, where I talked glowingly about a $630 million industry. What I didn't say was that there was competition from other places for the work and we depended on a low Canadian dollar for our success. A year later the Ontario finance minister went to Los Angeles and announced a labour tax credit of 11 percent on films made in Ontario. The BC industry went into a panic.

Premier Clark went to LA himself and talked to executives at MGM. Then he called an industry meeting in the premier's office with unions, studio people and producers. Some thought we didn't need to match Ontario's tax credit; others thought 8 percent would be enough given "our superiority." Glen listened patiently. He then informed them that the BC tax credit would be II percent and that he would announce it right away. He opened the door and thanked them for coming. Clark was a lot of things but never indecisive. Maybe that's why, after a rough departure from the premier's office, he eventually became president of the Jimmy Pattison empire.

Our film figures went through the roof. A year later BC had a billion-dollar film industry. We were third in the world after Hollywood and New York! Hollywood North indeed. I was dispatched to Vancouver to make an announcement about our success. Maria, Maya and our ministry's communications chief went along. They told me to be a good boy and take the night off, go to a movie or something light so I would be in fine form for the announcement the next day. "We know you, Minister," one of them said. So I followed their instructions. The problem is I went to see Canadian comedian Mike Myers playing the character of Austin Powers in *The Spy Who Shagged Me.*

Next day on a movie set, when I slapped down the stick on the clapperboard for the cameras as part of the press event, I said, "It's a billion *'bybee,'*" in my attempt at an Austin Powers accent. My staff was aghast. On the car back to the Victoria ferry they berated me. The radio news was full of commentators laughing at my accent. I lamely pointed out that the story did headline the newscasts.

The next day I quietly slid into our NDP caucus meeting and sat at the back. It so happened my ministry was on the agenda, so my staff was in attendance. The premier was late, and as soon as he got to speak he talked about the difficult economy we were facing, which meant it was hard to get good news stories. "But it can be done," he said. "Look at this minister." With that he held up the front page of that day's *Vancouver Sun,* which I had not seen, with my picture "above the fold," as the premier said. Of course the writer had to make fun of my accent, but the headline read, *It's a billion.*

Postscript: As I write this the industry is now $3 billion and growing but still vulnerable to Hollywood going elsewhere. In our original plan we included money for BC producers and directors. This has been lost and we are not producing local shows like we did with *Da Vinci's Inquest* and others. We are also not getting our share of federal money.

Arts and Business

What we achieved in film, we couldn't achieve in other areas of "the arts." SFU professor Malcolm Page, a tireless advocate for the arts, reminded me that the arts are an essential facet of society, not a frill. The arts are about imagination, creativity and emotions. They promote non-linear thinking, pushing the envelope. But governments of all stripes seem

"It's a billion, baby."

to cut the arts budgets first when they need to reduce expenditures, in spite of the fact that the arts are a huge provider of jobs, something that Canadians generally seem to ignore or are simply unaware of. Glen promised me he would at least stop the cutbacks, but I didn't have a lot to work with.

I tried to figure out how we could strengthen the ability of the arts community to organize and fight for its cause. Artists in Quebec are much stronger advocates for the arts generally and for themselves than their counterparts anywhere else in Canada. So I went on my own to Quebec City and met with government officials there to see what they were doing. Quebec has "status of the artist" legislation, which gives artists tools to organize and allows certain tax breaks for artists. Could we do the same in British Columbia? To put the issue on the public radar, I appointed lawyer Sandy Banister to write a report on the status of artists in BC. She produced an excellent summary of the issue, but BC artists were slow to take it up. In fact, at the release of the report, one prominent BC arts advocate showed up and dismissively asked, "What's this all about?" I didn't have the grassroots support to pursue the issue. It made me despair for English Canadian artists, who lack the political savvy of their Quebec cousins.

Another part of my ministry was small business. Left-wing governments should not ignore the people of this sector because they really are the "little guys." Strong small businesses are the motors of a good economy. They want fair taxes, less red tape and access to credit. In 1998 some of Canada's big banks were talking about merging with each other, which set off alarm bells for me. I knew that a small business could sometimes pry a loan out of one big bank by threatening to take its business to another bank. Mergers would reduce this competition and could harm small businesses. I decided to set up a three-person Task Force on Bank Mergers that would hold hearings and report back to me. It was composed of SFU economist Marjorie Griffin Cohen, Dawson Creek mayor Blair Lekstrom and lawyer David Rosenberg, the chair. David and I took the report to Ottawa and met with federal finance minister Paul Martin. We were pleased to see he later nixed the merger talk.

One story from my time as minister of small business, tourism and culture reflects a marriage of art and business. I had the honour of representing the province at the celebration of life for the great artist Bill Reid. There were probably forty speakers at the full-day event at UBC's magnificent Museum of Anthropology. After the speeches I met the very enterprising architect and businessman Herbert Auerbach. Herb recalls that I suggested to him that we needed a special museum for Indigenous art in downtown Vancouver that tourists, like the Americans who take cruise ships to Alaska, would consider a "must-see" during their stopovers in the city, sort of like the J. Paul Getty Museum in LA. When I ran into Herb a few months later, he asked what had happened to this idea. I said nothing had happened, so Herb decided to run with it himself as a volunteer. The result, the Bill Reid Gallery of Northwest Coast Art in downtown Vancouver on Hornby Street, is a real gem. Herb also told me he did finally end up getting some money from the provincial government, but the gallery is an example of what one committed volunteer with a good idea can do.

Sumo

If you want to feel small, just stand next to Akebono Taro, at six foot eight and 512 pounds the first non-Japanese-born wrestler ever to reach the highest rank in sumo. I welcomed him to Victoria, where he and his fellow wrestlers performed the traditional ring ceremony outside the Legislature Buildings. I invited him inside to wrestle our opposition, but he had to go to Vancouver to appear in the first (and last) *sumo basho* in Canada.

I next saw the great Akebono at the PNE Coliseum in Vancouver. The actual matches last about twenty seconds, but there is a huge ritual around them and lots of time to drink sake between matches. Sitting for hours next to the Japanese ambassador, I began to see why Japan's national sport is so tied to business. Normally you meet somebody at a reception for a minute or so. Here you really get to know the other

With Akebono.

guests as you drink and bet with them. Next time you see them, you are like brothers! You also need to arrange for a drive home.

The next day I arrived late and hungry at Judd Buchanan's Canadian Tourism Commission dinner for the wrestlers at Vancouver's Convention Centre. They sat me next to Akebono and plunked a huge piece of roast beef on my plate. I gobbled it up and then looked at the huge figure beside me, his plate untouched. "*Yokozuna* [the title given to the top guy]," I said, "are you not hungry?" In Victoria and at the *basho* he had not spoken a word. Now, in a strong American accent, he replied, "They've been trying to feed me all day. I'm not hungry." I later shamelessly put a photo of me posing with the *yokozuna* on my re-election poster proclaiming, *No matter how LARGE the opponent, Ian Waddell will fight for you.* It didn't help.

CHAPTER 12

The Tide Goes Out Again

Glen Resigns

Like the rest of our caucus, I was shocked when Glen Clark was accused of accepting favours in return for approving an application for a casino. I was close to Glen and his wife Dale, and had been emcee at their wedding. One night when I was at their small cottage near Penticton, I met their Vancouver neighbour Dimitrios Pilarinos, whose kids were good friends of Glen's kids. Pilarinos was working with Glen to construct a wooden deck for the cabin. (Glen was always good with his hands. As a young man he had constructed my constituency office in the old Rio Hall on Kingsway.) As I would learn later, apparently the same neighbour worked on a deck for Clark in Vancouver and bragged to his friends that he could influence Glen on gaming licences. The resulting investigation forced Glen to resign as premier, and he was ultimately charged with criminal breach of trust and accepting a benefit.

The *Vancouver Sun* reported that on the first day of Glen's trial, labour leader Jack Munro and I were the only NDPers who showed up to support him. After that was published, I got four messages on my telephone answering machine. The first three, all from friends, told me I should distance myself from Clark for my own good. The fourth was from my mother. She and I had had a slight argument the week before, something we almost never did. To this day I remember her sweet Scottish voice saying, "I'm proud of you son [for attending]. Just think how Glen's poor mother must feel."

Glen once bragged in caucus that he took on the Canadian and American governments by trying to close the submarine testing facility

Glen and Ian get crushed by Olympic wrestler.

at Nanoose Bay near Nanaimo. "Those guys have deposed a few South American politicians for doing similar things," he said with a laugh. I remember not being so amused by his remarks. I don't believe in conspiracy theories, but...

With the help of lawyer David Gibbons, Glen was acquitted of the charges. He told me later he wasn't worried because he knew he was innocent. The accusations did, however, end his political career. He has since resurrected himself as head of Jimmy Pattison's companies, a remarkable transition.

New Leaders and New Ministry

The NDP caucus chose Dan Miller as our interim leader and premier. Everybody liked Dan because he had been a real working man, and he brought the unique attribute of common sense to everything he tackled. He had a bright chief of staff, a fellow named John Horgan whom I had once helped get his first political job, then in Ottawa. The NDP leadership convention on February 20, 2000 chose Ujjal Dosanjh as the new leader and premier. Ujjal had worked on my campaigns and was respected by most parts of the Indo-Canadian community except for the Khalistani separatists, who had tried to kill him. A man of immense courage, Dosanjh survived a brutal attack at his old law office across from my constituency office on Victoria Drive.

As an MP I had raised the matter in the House of Commons. No one seemed to care. Four months later, Air India Flight 182 was blown up over the Atlantic. The Canadian government was guilty of ignoring threats before the bombing and Canadian intelligence bungled the investigation after the fact. Dosanjh says in his memoir *Journey After Midnight* that this may have been because the victims and perpetrators were brown Canadians. He also revealed, to my shock, that he and his family had been booked on the flight but changed their vacation plans.

As premier, Ujjal appointed me minister of environment, lands and parks, with clear instructions to move on a number of issues, in part so we could blunt the Green Party vote in the upcoming provincial election. I was soon meeting with my new assistant deputy minister Jon O'Riordan (remember him from the Fraser Basin Board?) to discuss the problem of the old copper mine at Britannia Beach, fifty-two kilometres north of Vancouver on the road to Squamish and Whistler. The mine had produced more than fifty million tons of copper between 1904 and 1974; by 2000 it had become the largest point of pollution on the west coast of North America due to acid rock drainage. Polluted runoff was also carrying hundreds of pounds of copper into Howe Sound each day. The BC government was pursuing a lawsuit for $300 million to clean up the site, but we were trying to get the money from some bankrupt American companies so the suit was going nowhere.

With the help of Murray Rankin, O'Riordan had persuaded the companies to give us $30 million. We would drop the lawsuit and use this money to clean the site up, then we would sell the cleaned-up land around the mine to recoup the cost of the cleanup. It was a brilliant plan, but it could be a huge political risk if environmentalists accused us of "selling out cheap." O'Riordan had shrewdly invited a couple of activists who concentrated on mining activities to be involved in the negotiations. Their inclusion worked. They wouldn't endorse the plan, but they wouldn't oppose it either.

I decided to accept the deal. There would be no big press conference to announce it. I had learned my lesson in my previous ministry when I described a plan to move the Pacific National Exhibition to Surrey, near Burns Bog, as a win-win. I got creamed and had to retreat. For the Britannia Beach announcement we simply invited a few journalists including Vaughn Palmer and Keith Baldrey to my ministerial office. And we let O'Riordan make the case. The next day a small article appeared buried in the middle of the *Vancouver Sun*. I complained to my friend Bill Clay that surely I was entitled to applause for this politically difficult decision. He replied I was lucky to get out of the matter with no criticism!

According to Bruce Ramsey's book *Britannia: The Story of a Mine*, the limewater treatment plan is now operational, a new suburb is growing fast in the area, barnacles are growing at the mouth of the creek, shorebirds are returning, "and we even had an orca 'killer whale' visit Howe Sound." I recently took my Australian cousin Bev and her husband Gary Wyfon to Squamish. We ran into a woman on the gondola who happily told us she lived in the new "clean community" of Britannia Beach. I told her they should dedicate a park to Jon O'Riordan as thanks for what a dedicated public servant can do. Of course, if you visit the site today, you will read that the mining industry claims credit for cleaning up its mess on its own!

Another issue that came up when I was the minister of environment involved a developer, Texada Land Corp., that was going to cut a large swath of trees on Saltspring Island. This spawned demonstrations, including a Lady Godiva ride by one activist, and a star-studded media-savvy campaign involving the likes of Randy Bachman and Robert Bateman, both Saltspring residents. That's when I got a call from John Crosbie, who was working as a lobbyist for Texada. We had sat together in parliament when we were both MPs. Crosbie had created an image of himself as a simple guy with a big "Newfie" accent, when in fact he was a gold medallist at law school and attended the London School of Economics.

After the defeat of his "short-term pain for long-term gain" budget in the short-lived Joe Clark government, Crosbie came back to be an effective opposition member and later minister in the Mulroney years. (When Pierre Trudeau went to Saudi Arabia and visited the desert tent of Sheik Yamani, being a Trudeau he put on an Arab robe and danced in the tent. When the prime minister returned to the House, Crosbie rose and asked in his thick accent if Trudeau had danced with Yamani "sheik to sheik." Even Trudeau broke up.) On another occasion Sheila Copps, a member of the Liberal opposition "rat pack" and one of the most effective and energetic MPs, was heckling Minister Crosbie when he was answering one of my questions. He turned to her and famously said, "Just quiet down, baby." Sheila was of course outraged, though not too outraged to call her memoirs *Nobody's Baby*. You either loved or hated Copps. Same with Crosbie. I have to admit, I loved to hear the both of them spar.

When Crosbie called me years later to ask me to meet him in Victoria where his son lived, he still called me "son." I jokingly accused him of acting for some crooked developer, then invited him for dinner. When Barry Penner and a couple of Liberal MLAs saw us late at night in the legislature dining room, I'm not sure they believed their eyes. The next day we quietly made a deal to buy out the developer at a reasonable price and turn the area into a park. The "we" were me as BC's minister of environment, Crosbie for the owner, and the minister of Canadian heritage, one Sheila Copps! It's a strange world.

Another accomplishment I'm particularly proud of involved grizzly bears. A number of environmental groups wanted us to stop the trophy hunt for BC grizzly bears. Grizzlies inhabit approximately half the area of their historic range in Canada and the United States, so I called in my officials and asked them how many bears we actually had in the province and whether they were a threatened species. I was given a number, but after some close questioning it appeared this figure was extrapolated from a study of bears in one small part of the province. On even closer questioning, even our best people couldn't give an accurate number or definitively answer the question of whether the bears were in danger.

So I put a three-year moratorium on the hunting of grizzlies in British Columbia to give researchers time to answer the question. All hell broke loose. I was summarily disinvited from giving the minister's annual address to hunters at the BC Wildlife Federation convention. I had the public onside (over 90 percent in the polls), but we lost the battle. The hunter/guide/outfitter lobby was strong, and the next Liberal government dropped the ban. There is a lesson here: I should have done a lot of ground work to get the public and environmental groups more involved. (Only recently has a subsequent NDP government brought in an outright ban on the hunt.)

But Dosanjh and I also set up the first group to protect the white "spirit bear" in the "Great Bear Rainforest" on the central coast of BC. It took another fifteen years and some incredible work by a lot of dedicated people to reach a deal between industry, environment groups, First Nations and government to protect this amazing part of our world. It can be done. Note the brilliant use of language to aid your cause— "spirit bear" (invented by a North Vancouver student) and "Great Bear Rainforest."

The Tide Goes Out Again

By early 2001 the NDP had designated ten million acres of the province as protected parks or reserves, thus meeting the United Nations' 12 percent target. Just six weeks before the election, I joined Premier Dosanjh and federal environment minister David Anderson to announce that a joint federal-provincial agreement had been formalized to establish a national park in the southern Gulf Islands and to provide joint funding with the Greater Vancouver Regional District to acquire and protect Burns Bog. Bob Peart, director of the Canadian Parks and Wilderness Society, called it "the most significant conservation initiative on private land that has ever happened in Canada."

It didn't help us electorally. We got creamed in the 2001 provincial election, losing all but the two seats belonging to Joy MacPhail and Jenny Kwan. I was out of work again, defeated by Liberal Ken Johnston.

But at least in our losing effort we had recruited smart, enthusiastic, university-aged workers who would help to rebuild the party. Rob Nagai, who later worked for the party; Megan Cassidy, who later became a lawyer; and Jonathan Silveira, who ran for us in the 2015 federal election and the 2017 provincial election, were part of my young team in Fraserview. I returned to law. I had to repass the bar exams and managed to do so on the second try. Larry Myers gave me a place in his law office, but I couldn't get politics out of my system.

I fought for and won the federal NDP nomination for Vancouver-Kingsway (which had been revived in 1996 by another electoral boundaries redistribution). We had a long way to go to increase the 15.82% NDP vote of 2000, but in the 2004 federal election we thought we had done it. On Friday campaign manager Neil Monckton told me I'd be going back to the House of Commons. On Saturday I was told the Liberal phone banks called our sign locations and urged them to vote Liberal to stop the impending victory by the Conservative candidate even though, historically, Conservatives ran miserably in Kingsway. The strategy worked and on Monday, election day, I narrowly lost to Liberal David Emerson, who became minister of industry in prime minister Paul Martin's cabinet.

I had a chance for a rematch two years later. On election night 2006, Emerson said he would be Conservative leader Stephen Harper's "worst nightmare." A week later, having been re-elected as a Liberal, Emerson was sworn in as a Stephen Harper cabinet minister. For all his reputed smarts, Emerson didn't get it. He was blind to the basic ethics of electoral democracy, feeling himself indispensable and unable to sit in opposition. His constituents on all sides were outraged and felt betrayed. As one of his Liberal supporters wrote to me, "It is because of people like David Emerson whose actions show loyalty to a party, to a political philosophy, or to any cause other than themselves that Canadians have lost faith in government and become disenchanted with politicians." Those sentiments were echoed by Bill Graham, speaking in the House of Commons, who said Emerson's actions diminish "the faith of citizens in a system under which we have to govern."

Later I saw Emerson, by then Harper's foreign affairs minister, attend the opening of an Olympic facility in the riding. He needed police protection as constituents screamed at him. I thought he looked pathetic. As Canadian foreign minister he could go anywhere in the world without protection except perhaps North Korea, Iraq or Vancouver-Kingsway. In the end, will Emerson be remembered as an accomplished government bureaucrat or lumber businessman? No. He will be the guy who was called a turncoat and hypocrite by his own electors! I knew if I ran a third time I could easily win Kingsway, but for me it was over. Don Davies did run for the NDP and won big. He has been a very effective member of parliament.

International Bid

While I was the provincial minister responsible for the 2010 Olympics bid, I had quietly kept opposition leader Gordon Campbell informed of its progress. When he became premier, he got Jack Poole to put together another great team to take the bid to the international level. On July 2, 2003 I huddled next to my buddy D'Arcy Thorpe at GM Place (now Rogers Arena) with ten thousand silent Vancouverites until International Olympic Committee president Jacques Rogge announced that Vancouver/Whistler had won. The place exploded! We had won the Twenty-First Winter Olympiad by only three votes, fifty-six to fifty-three over Pyeongchang, South Korea.

The road to opening day was still rocky. I wrote an op-ed that was critical of the new committee, VANOC, for being too corporate, not a community bid but rather "all suits and numbers." In retrospect, this may have been a bit unfair, as it was essentially a private sector bid and they had to raise money. However, new mayor of Vancouver Larry Campbell shocked VANOC by calling a municipal referendum on the bid. This turned out to be a stroke of genius, as it forced the committee to explain what it was doing and to reach out to people. Vancouverites supported the Olympics, big time, which had the effect of silencing the critics. These were no longer the elite games; we had a popular mandate.

The rest is history.

Premier Campbell was gracious enough to invite me to the opening ceremony. I was proud of the inclusion of so much Indigenous culture and Canadian music. The Games got off to a bad start with the death of a Georgian athlete Nodar Kumaritashvili in a training accident on the luge track hours before the opening. Furlong handled it well with a moment of silence and a tribute to the luger at the opening ceremonies. The mood picked up when Canada won a gold medal. Up to that time, we were the only country never to win a gold medal when we hosted the Games (in Montreal in 1976 and Calgary in 1988). Then there was a lack of snow, which wasn't surprising for a city that spends most of its winters laughing at the rest of Canada and gloating over its moderate weather. Now we *wanted* cold and snow. Again, that problem faded when we won more gold.

Every Canadian sports fan remembers where they were when Sidney Crosby scored the gold medal–winning goal in the men's final ice hockey game. I was with Blaine Culling and Bill Degrazio of Granville Entertainment Group in their Irish House, a pub set up in a big tent on a parking lot in downtown Vancouver. (Earlier that week the comedian Stephen Colbert had wandered into the tent and ended up on stage. At that very moment a fight broke out in the crowd, prompting Colbert to exclaim, "I think I have breaking news. There is a fight in an Irish bar.") After Crosby's goal, people streamed into downtown Vancouver to celebrate but I had to leave with my guests, Jonathan and Chris Andersen, because they had a small child. A friendly police officer and his squad escorted my car as we made our way out of downtown against the throng coming over the Granville Street bridge. The officer was yelling, "Don't run over my men, Ian." It was pure bliss.

There were still critics of the Olympics, but consider this: British Columbia got a ton of money from central Canada—read "the feds"— that we wouldn't normally have received. We now have a superb transit line from the airport to downtown, a much safer highway to Whistler, new sport facilities in Richmond and East Van that are used by tons of families, and other improvements. VANOC reported a balanced budget of $1.8 billion. We ran a clean Olympics. We also got Legacies Now and Own the Podium to train future athletes. The world saw a city and country that was really cool, beautiful, peaceful and, for once, happy!

Life After Politics

I got a golden retriever, Frankie; a hot car; an office courtesy of the irrepressible Art Vertlieb QC and the Dosanjh Brothers, Aseem and Pavel; and time to travel, read and do a little law. Now that I was finally out of it, I was able to look at politics a little differently. I thought that most Canadians didn't know what actually happened on the ground during an election, so I wanted to show them the inside workings of a campaign—for example, how phone banks worked to raise money, the role of the campaign manager, the demands on a candidate, et cetera. Given my background, I figured the best way to do this was with a short documentary film.

I had produced a couple of other films: *Picaro*, which I made with Iain Ewing when we were both at university, and the introduction to the Berger inquiry shown at our southern hearings. After being defeated provincially in 2001, I produced a short documentary with Peter Chrzanowski on Golden, BC showing the transition from railway town to skiing town. Then I produced *Edythe*, which was the story of my friends Blaine and Laurel's mother, a gritty woman from Saskatchewan who helped her kids start the famous Roxy Bar on Granville Street. The director of *Edythe*, Kyle McCachen, really impressed me. So I gave him a little money to direct my new film on elections.

We decided to film during the 2013 BC provincial election, and chose the riding of Point Grey, where the NDP challenger David Eby, a charismatic young lawyer, was up against premier Christy Clark. (He eventually won, and the premier had to find another riding.) Kyle hired young actor Dylan Playfair, the son of a prominent hockey family from Fort St. James, BC. Dylan's dad Jim was a coach with the NHL's Arizona Coyotes and his uncle Larry played for the Buffalo Sabres and LA Kings. Dylan told us that a lot of people his age (the millennials, aged eighteen to twenty-four) were not even voting. As I talked to Dylan, I began to see how serious this problem of young people not voting might be for the future of our democracy.

BC's Election Commissioner Keith Archer told us that only 38 percent of young people voted in the 2011 federal election, versus 75 percent of those over sixty-five. What's more, the percentage was dropping steadily from one election to the next, so I went out and tried to raise money for a bigger film. It wasn't easy. BC's Knowledge Network turned me down even though I had some of the best young film talent in the province. I did get money from CPAC (the parliamentary channel), TVO (TV Ontario), Rogers and the Canadian Media Fund, as well as contributions from personal friends.

I inked the deal for the new documentary with TVO at Massey College where the head of the college John Fraser had given me a "visiting fellow" designation and thus a place to hang my hat. I talked to filmmakers Peter Raymont and Michael McMillan in Toronto, and they reminded me that above everything else, a film has to tell a story. So our documentary told the story of Dylan Playfair's journey from the BC provincial election to the House of Commons in Ottawa in search of answers to the question of why young people don't vote.

He talked to NDP leader Tom Mulcair and Liberal leader Justin Trudeau. (We tried in vain to get PM Harper to participate.) In the film, Dylan scrums Justin Trudeau, whose party was then in third place and looking like it would stay there. In his conversation with Dylan, Trudeau was remarkably insightful when he talked about why young people don't vote and what he intended to do about it. It was a glimpse into what became his successful campaign. After Ottawa, Dylan went to Burning Man in the Nevada desert for some incredible pictures and interviews with young people, returned to Ontario to cover the 2014 civic election in Toronto, travelled to North Carolina to watch how Republicans suppressed the youth vote, and then went to Ferguson, Missouri, to observe the efforts of young black activists to increase youth involvement in the political process.

In the course of producing the film (with the help of award-winning Toronto producer Robert Lang) I got a look at this new generation and I liked what I saw. We finished *The Drop: Why Young People Don't*

Vote in 2015 and released it nationally a few months before the federal election. It ran on CPAC and TVO, and we showed it to students in Vancouver, Victoria and Ottawa. We got support from Vancity Credit Union, unions, BC teachers and, I'm pleased to say, some former parliamentarians.

The film was a big success as "the drop" stopped. In the 2015 federal election the millennial vote increased by twelve percentage points. Our film was only a small part of that turnaround, as many organizations around the country had been working to get youth involved. Under chief electoral officer Mark Mayrand, Elections Canada worked with these groups, and all those involved should be applauded for their efforts. So it wasn't by chance that more young voters came out to the polls. The mainstream media missed this "behind the scenes" story of new young voters literally changing the government of Canada. For once they used their political power.

The Drop was presented at the Beverly Hills Film Festival in Los Angeles in April 2016. We were thrilled to be there and thought we were lucky to be included in the screenings. Then we went to the gala

The Drop film team: Morgan Baskin, Maalik Shakoor, Levi McCachen, Kyle McCachen, Dylan Playfair and Ian.

dinner where awards were announced, just like the Oscars. I almost choked when the emcee announced, "Award for Best Producer [pause] *The Drop...*" We even beat Morgan Freeman!

Accepting the shiny glass trophy on behalf of Bob and Dylan and Kyle, I mentioned that they had just given the award to the former BC minister of culture who had implemented the tax credits that sucked up their industry from LA to Vancouver. That got a big laugh and applause, and one producer of the hundreds there yelled, "Thanks! I made three movies there." I then told them that there was an obvious message for the upcoming American election, and added, "A film can make a difference." There is nothing better than young people speaking to young people, as is done in the film, and then adding the experience of my generation of politicians. It's a winning formula. It's also the future of a healthy democracy.

CHAPTER 13

Take the Torch

To you, from failing hands, we throw the torch: be yours to
hold it high.

— John McCrae, "In Flanders Fields"

In the early 1970s I was flying from Vancouver to Toronto with Judge Berger. My grandmother, who was in her eighties, happened to be travelling on the same Air Canada 747, and a friendly flight attendant let me take her up to the lounge on the upper deck. Grandma Dickie ordered a scotch. We toasted each other and looked down on the Saskatchewan prairies passing below us. In her very thick accent she described her youth in Scotland in her father's blacksmith shop—"Gardiner's Smitty" it was called. Then she casually mentioned that as a little girl she heard about those "brothers in the States" who first flew an airplane!

During her lifetime we progressed from the horse and buggy through the car to the jet airplane. She even saw men land on the moon. I've lived through the introduction of credit cards and computers, the landing of rovers on Mars and, 112 years after the Wright Brothers got their shaky airplane to fly, the voyage of a small machine, *New Horizons*, from Earth to the dwarf planet Pluto three billion miles away. Clearly we are creatures of change. And change is accelerating.

In 1964 when I was in my early twenties, we had a rebellious cry: "Don't trust anyone over thirty." It illustrated the divide between my parents' generation and my own generation, which took part in the women's liberation movement, the civil rights movement, the peace movement, the beginnings of the environmental movement and the gay and lesbian movement, among others. Many of those movements are still active, still trying to achieve their objectives, but they have been joined by new movements focused on Indigenous rights and reconciliation, climate change and economic justice.

Activists are rarely able to say, "We've achieved our goals. We can all go home now and relax." We may make some advances, but there are always setbacks, and even when rights are won or objectives realized, we must ensure they aren't eroded quietly over the years. In 2008, for example, Barack Obama was elected the first black president of the United States; many thought it was a sign the civil rights movement had triumphed. But only four years later, Black Lives Matter was formed to address the ways black people are marginalized and deprived of their basic human rights. To me, these activist movements are like a relay. People of my generation, who have been involved in them for years, are now ready to pass the baton, or the torch, on to younger people.

You've read about some of the things I and others like me did, our activism, the changes we made, and I'm proud of that. But the race is unfinished. If I were a young person today, I would work for Indigenous rights, the environment, peace and the prevention of climate change and nuclear war. It's good to see that young people are taking on these issues—it feels like I'm passing the torch to them.

Canada's Indigenous People: Their Time Has Come

In early 1991 a federal constitutional committee of which I was a member came to Victoria from Ottawa for a hearing. Our first witness was Moe Sihota, the first Indo-Canadian elected to a provincial or federal government in Canada. (Later that year he became the first Indo-Canadian provincial cabinet minister after the NDP formed government in British Columbia.) Moe was young, charismatic, confident and articulate. My fellow MPs and senators, and the media, were all impressed by him, and they should have been.

Moe was followed by a delegation of three First Nations chiefs led by Chief George Watts. They were all but ignored. More importantly, and sadly, politicians and media ignored their message, which was basically *We've been here forever and we're not going away.* In spite of colonialism, residential schools and our efforts to eradicate their culture, Canada's Indigenous people are still here. And now as I write, I believe Canada is in the midst of an Indigenous revolution that's long overdue. From the Truth and Reconciliation Commission to the Inquiry into Murdered and Missing Aboriginal Women to Indigenous writers, lawyers, scientists, skilled workers and radical youth who are coming to the fore, it's happening. Canada's First Nations, Inuit and Métis people will no longer be ignored.

Section 35, the Aboriginal rights clause of the Canadian Constitution, is playing a huge role in this movement, and my involvement in its drafting, along with Jack Woodward, Ed Broadbent and others, is the act in my political career that I am proudest of. We used our political leverage—Pierre Trudeau's need for NDP support—to the maximum to ensure Section 35 was included. Indigenous people also lobbied governments in Ottawa and London, England, and took their challenge to court to support the clause. We worded the section broadly, hoping the courts and later governments would define terms and provide meaning that would give Indigenous peoples some real power over their lives, particularly when it came to dealing with resource development on their ancestral lands.

The courts are doing their part. The Supreme Court has ruled on Section 35 at least fifty times in the last twenty-five years. In over two hundred decisions since 1980, the court has consistently affirmed the rights of Indigenous people. In Delgamuukw (1997) and Tsilhqot'in (2014), Aboriginal title itself was recognized as one of the rights noted in Section 35. So we are now seeing resource companies consulting with Indigenous communities not just because they want to but because they have to. The Canadian courts have done their part but governments have generally failed the cause. Get going! It's up to the federal and provincial governments to complete the move to recognition and equality. The Justin Trudeau government has pledged to do just that, but we'll see.

An example of this recognition is the historic Nisga'a treaty, the first modern treaty signed in British Columbia, which set out the Nisga'a

Nation's right to self-government and the Nation's authority to manage its own lands and resources. This treaty was signed while I was a member of the provincial government, and I remember standing with Tom Berger and Jack Nichol in my ministerial office, watching the Nisga'a people chant and dance in the rotunda of the legislature to honour all their negotiators of the past one hundred years.

The "two solitudes" in Canada used to be French and English. Today they are Indigenous and non-Indigenous people. In his book *Canada's Odyssey: A Country Based on Incomplete Conquest*, Professor Peter Russell points out that from the beginning of Canada's history there has been no agreement between Indigenous nations and Britain, or its successor state Canada, on sovereignty. In 1992 the Royal Commission on Aboriginal Peoples, chaired by Georges Erasmus and René Dussault, called for a First Nations Parliament to replace Indian Affairs, transfer payments to a centralized First Nations administration and seats reserved in parliament for Aboriginal leaders, but nothing was done.

In 2015 the Truth and Reconciliation Commission, chaired by Justice Murray Sinclair, released a report that called for Canada to implement the UN Declaration on the Rights of Indigenous Peoples as the model for reconciliation. That declaration includes the right of Indigenous

With Jack Layton.

peoples to self-determination and their right to use and benefit from the resources on the territories they traditionally occupied. Are we ready for this?

I believe change is coming. Recognition of Indigenous rights and reconciliation with Indigenous peoples is Canada's greatest unfinished business. I challenge you to be a part of the revolution that will ensure Indigenous people have a recognized and equal place in Canada's future. Bear in mind the comment of Grand Chief Stewart Philip of the Union of BC Indian Chiefs: "We are in this together." It won't be easy, but at least now we are on the right road.

Environment, Climate Change and Water

My knowledge of the condition of First Nations and Inuit people, and my concern for their future, was inspired by my work with Judge Thomas Berger, which had an incalculable impact on my life and career. Tom Berger was my mentor in so many ways, and I was lucky to have been part of his pipeline inquiry, which taught me so much about the North and about activism. Berger was one of the first to struggle with the competing claims of economic development, environmental protection and in the case of First Nations, the traditional way of life. Sound familiar? These same issues resonate today in discussions about oil and gas, pipelines, trees, bears, fish and more. We can still learn lessons from the Berger Inquiry. Judge Berger taught us how to conduct an open inquiry by listening to people in their own communities and using the power of the media. He showed that if environmental groups get together and are properly funded, they can fully participate and broadcast their message. His work saw the development of a whole generation of Indigenous leaders.

Berger's model can be applied to today's commissions of inquiry and even to institutions like the National Energy Board, whose recent hearings on pipelines failed to include all interests. The Berger style, if I can call it that—community-based, inclusive, media savvy—can be adopted to shape a new national energy policy that would include a rational transition from oil and gas to alternative, renewable energy sources. This isn't going to be easy. It will likely set Canadian regions against each other, just as Pierre Trudeau's National Energy Program did. But if we are to tackle climate change, clearly the biggest challenge of this generation, we have to come up with an energy strategy that a majority of Canadians will embrace.

How do we do this? Here we might learn from the BC experience with the Great Bear Rainforest. In the 1970s and 1980s there was a war in the British Columbia woods with protests against logging old-growth timber on what were then called the Queen Charlotte Islands (now Haida Gwaii) and in Clayoquot Sound. Environmental groups learned how to put pressure on the industry by lobbying consumers of wood products in the United States and Europe, but there was animosity between loggers and environmentalists, with threats of violence. When premier Ujjal Dosanjh and BC's environment minister—me!—announced support for a group that wanted to save the Great Bear Rainforest from clear-cuts and mining, we didn't anticipate the birth of a new process.

The Great Bear Rainforest is a 6.4-million-hectare area along British Columbia's north and central coast, a temperate rainforest that attracted logging and mining companies because of its wealth of trees and minerals. Environmentalists saw it as a potential gold mine for tourism that was more valuable with the trees standing and the wildlife undisturbed. As minister of environment, lands and parks, I obviously agreed with them and urged the government to explore this possibility.

When the NDP lost power, Gordon Campbell's Liberals took over the fight, naming the white "spirit bear" of the Great Bear Rainforest a provincial symbol. After a series of blockades, and pressure in the European market, environmentalists, forestry corporations and loggers realized they could work together and reached a deal to preserve a portion of the forest. They took it to the BC provincial government, which signed on. Then, and this is crucial, the BC government took the deal to First Nations "government to government." In 2016, more than 80 percent of that great chunk of rainforest on the BC coast was protected.

The remaining portion will be logged, with First Nations involved in decision-making, sustainable logging and sharing in the economic benefits.

Can a similar process be used in the Fort McMurray tar sands (or if you prefer, oil sands)? Premier Rachel Notley of Alberta is to be commended for creating a major climate plan that includes a carbon tax that rises to $30 per tonne in 2018, a 100-megaton-a-year cap on emissions for the tar sands, and a phasing out of coal by 2030. That took some political courage. However, the struggle over the extraction and use of oil and gas is going to be child's play in comparison to the coming fight over "blue gold": water.

Fifteen years ago I wrote a mystery novel, *A Thirst to Die For*, about a plot to export Canadian water to a drought-ravaged, fire-stricken California. You will forgive me if I say I may have been a bit ahead of my time. Canadians think Canada is awash with fresh water, and they are right. Canada has about 25 percent of the earth's fresh water (the Great Lakes alone contain 18 percent of the planet's surface fresh water), and less than 1 percent of the world's population. We have taken this abundance for granted, and sometimes we have abused it. Look at Walkerton, Ontario where the drinking water supply was polluted by agricultural runoff. Look at how fracking in the pursuit of oil and natural gas reserves pollutes the drinking water of farmers and others, and look at the many First Nations without useable water.

And make no mistake: other people are eyeing our water. Fresh water will soon be the major resource issue on the North American continent. There have already been many proposals to export bulk water, from damming and diverting James Bay to digging a Rocky Mountain trench that would collect water to be shipped south. As climate change causes longer and more serious droughts in the southern United States, the demand for Canadian fresh water will only grow. Activists like Maude Barlow have been calling for the Canadian government to draft a clear policy that would treat access to water as a right, not a commodity to be sold and exported.

The water issue goes further than exports. We humans have altered the global water cycle, and a 2015 report from the United Nations, *Water in the World We Want*, noted that hydro-climatic destabilization is now a major threat to advancing global development. We see this in extreme weather events, like the hurricanes in late 2017 that devastated Puerto Rico, Cuba and other Caribbean islands, as well as some US states.

Water security and climate security are inseparable. Tackling our water security is a crucial part of dealing with the warming planet, and it calls for environmental action. The form that action takes is up to today's young people. Remember, though, that phrases like "global warming" or "climate action" are too general. People's eyes glaze over when they hear them. But if you talk about floods, boil-water advisories and devastating forest fires that burn all summer, people begin to get it. They take action, and they push their politicians to act.

Nuclear War and the Peace Movement

Of course the big "change" we're facing now is a literal one, climate change, and young people understand that. But I believe the threat of a nuclear exchange, whether it happens by accident as a result of terrorism, or through stupidity on the part of world leaders, is a real threat that today's youth may not be so aware of. After a nuclear exchange, the world would face a nuclear winter—a different kind of climate change. The firestorms produced by nuclear bombs would send smoke and soot into the air, cooling the Earth's climate, devastating agricultural production around the world and possibly breaking down the ozone layer of the atmosphere. Radioactive fallout from the bombs would circulate far beyond the blast zone, bringing radiation sickness and killing millions of people not killed by the initial blast. This is what people feared during the Cold War from the 1950s to the late 1980s when the United States and the Soviet Union faced off against each other on the world stage, in diplomacy and in the small regional wars that happened in Korea, Vietnam, southern Africa and elsewhere.

But when the moment is right, things can happen. In the early 1980s at the height of the Cold War, young Vancouverite Joseph Roberts held up a poster outside a Pete Seeger concert at the Queen Elizabeth

Marching for peace.

Theatre inviting people to walk for peace. His plan was to assemble at Kitsilano Beach and walk across the Burrard Street Bridge to Sunset Beach. That year, thirty-five thousand people showed up.

The next year, on April 23, 1983, I marched over the bridge along with sixty thousand others to Sunset Beach with my friend Jim Wilson and his golden retriever Luke. When not chanting "Give Peace a Chance," a group of us would sing "Don't nuke Luke!" It was joyous but serious (and healthy). We had a cause. We had a river of people. We also had music, which really helped bring out young people. The next year the march drew a hundred thousand. (I was proud to see BC attorney general David Eby has a photo of the 1983 march over his desk).

I marched with Rob Sutherland, Shane Simpson, Danielle Page and a million people through the streets of New York City to call for an end to the nuclear arms race. The march was followed by a huge concert in Central Park with musicians like Jackson Browne, James Taylor, Bruce Springsteen, Carly Simon and Joan Baez. At the time it was the biggest public protest in US history and reflected the growing power of the anti-nuke movement. I believe this show of public opinion was noticed and may have been a factor in nuclear disarmament discussions by Reagan and Gorbachev that ultimately led to the end of the Cold War.

But when the Cold War ended, so did the public's anxiety about nuclear weapons. The anti-nuke movement evaporated in most parts of the world—even though the risk of a nuclear catastrophe is higher than ever. New weapons are still being made to replace old ones, and there are regular reports of radioactive material being stolen, possibly by terrorists. I wrote earlier about meeting a woman who had survived the atomic bomb dropped on Hiroshima in 1945. Speaking in Hiroshima seventy-one years later, former US president Barack Obama said, "Science allows us to communicate across the seas and fly above the clouds, to cure disease and understand the cosmos, but those same discoveries can be turned into ever more efficient killing machines... Technological progress without an equivalent progress in human institutions can doom us."

One such institution that is in trouble and crying for reform is the United Nations. Dag Hammarskjöld, the second and probably best secretary-general of the United Nations, once said that "the UN was not created to take mankind to heaven, but to save humanity from hell." Now with 193 members, nearly four times the number at its founding after the Second World War, the UN is dysfunctional, paralyzed by the five permanent Security Council members (US, Russia, France, the UK and China) with their individual vetoes on any proposed resolution or action. We haven't had another world war but neither have we had the end of war. Thousands, millions of people have died in regional wars, and $1.7 trillion is spent annually on military budgets and armaments, many of which find their way into the hands of terrorists.

Think big. We need the end of vetoes in the Security Council, and we need a standing UN emergency police force. This goes beyond traditional peacekeeping, as it allows the international force to go into an otherwise-sovereign country that is killing its own people. This idea is not without controversy, as exemplified by Iraq and Libya, where international intervention turned into chaos. As we now truly do live in a "global village," we need to realize there is more to international law than the supremacy of the nation state. We need a parallel UN assembly of individual parliamentarians (that is, a world parliament).

Today the UN General Assembly struggles to choose the secretary-general. How about a direct worldwide election of the secretary-general? Ultimately we need, in addition to national governments, a world government representing all the people of the planet. This would be a step to end war and provide the security and resources that will be required to combat climate change—or to survive the devastating impact if it is too late to prevent the rise in global temperature that has been forecast. As Emery Reves wrote in *The Anatomy of Peace*, "There is no first step to world government. World government *is* the first step." And we need peace. The distinguished Canadian scholar and activist Ursula Franklin once said, "Peace is not the absence of war but the absence of fear, which is the presence of justice." Will it take a nuclear war to bring us to our senses (if we survive), or will that happen the day we make the first contact with life in other galaxies?

When as a nineteen-year-old history student I drove Lester Pearson, soon to be prime minister, around southern Ontario, I got a glimpse of a man who was as comfortable with diplomats from the world's superpowers as he was with a Canadian student. He had seen the death, destruction and evil of the First World War, and along with other Canadian diplomats he'd had a huge role in creating the post-Second World War international security system, including NATO and the UN. He made Canada relevant in international affairs. Perhaps we can aspire to that again.

Today's Generation

Is today's generation up to facing these new challenges? My answer is a resounding yes. I found this out through my work on *The Drop: Why Young People Don't Vote*, where I discovered that today's teenagers and twenty-somethings may be the smartest generation in history. They are certainly committed to social change. As we filmed and did interviews, I could see many young people were political but not in the conventional sense. They were not bound to a political party, and they were open to a variety of new ideas from both the "left" and the "right."

Think tanks like the Fraser Institute and politicians like Ronald Reagan and Margaret Thatcher preach that government is not the solution for anything. My friend Charlie Smith, long-time editor of the *Georgia Straight* newspaper, points out that millennials came of age in an era when corporations were more powerful and marketing was far more ubiquitous than ever before. Whereas my generation grew up when people were largely seen as citizens, now people are seen as consumers and taxpayers. This has discouraged people from voting, and it is what makes it a challenge to get young people to become involved when they reach voting age. This has consequences. In the United States, Hilary Clinton didn't draw as many young people to vote as Barack Obama did; this is probably one of the reasons she lost the 2016 election. In the UK Brexit referendum, only 36 percent of young people, who tended to support staying in the European Union, voted versus 80 percent of those over sixty-five.

In the 2015 federal election, Canada reversed "the drop" in the percentage of young people voting: it rose from 38 percent to 50 percent and helped change the government. In Hong Kong, youthful activists from the "umbrella movement" got young people to vote in local elections, to the surprise of Beijing, and elected some of their leaders. I like the attitude of Micah White, one of the founders of the Occupy Movement, who has written, "Now we are realizing, *No, actually sovereignty can only be achieved through winning wars and winning elections.* So social movements need to figure out how to win elections because I don't think the war route is very productive." Not only is this guy smart; he's also got a sense of humour, which will take him a long way.

I like the fact that the younger generation brooks no criticism of LGBTQ+ people, unlike my generation, and understands the importance of the environment. Many are prepared to take on the establishment of the day, and they do not see "socialism" as a dirty word, especially if it means a stronger social safety net, higher education accessible to all without incurring a huge debt, good childcare for families, and better protection of the environment.

Now a short word to my generation: Yes, we have left the new generation a lot of challenges, but most of us have tried to make our country and our world better. We should draw on our experiences to mentor the young—this will give us a new purpose in retirement. Try not to be crabby. Keep your sense of humour and listen more (I can't believe I actually said that!). And remember that we benefited from post-Second World War prosperity and government programs that allowed our parents to raise us in comfortable suburban homes and send us to decent public schools. This social situation, as much as our intelligence and skill, allowed us to attend college in record numbers at reasonable costs, and even to attend grad school at the world's greatest universities. When we completed all that schooling, there were jobs available.

One caveat (lawyer language for an exception): in that post-war generation, "we" didn't include Indigenous Canadians, many of whom, from age five to seventeen, were raised not by their parents but by residential schools, where they were mentally, physically and culturally abused. Because most of the rest of us were lucky enough to come of age in an ideal situation, people of my generation should not condemn today's youth for living in a time that's not quite so prosperous. In the 2000s, full-time jobs are hard to find, and student debts are huge.

Modern capitalism has left the unskilled and semi-skilled workers in Canada and the United States behind. My generation lost the fight against the big trade deals, and it is small comfort to see they turned out as we feared: vehicles to extend corporate property rights internationally, not to help workers or the environment. The good news, and the challenge for the younger generation, is that future jobs will be in the green economy as opposed to the fossil economy. They will be based on education, creativity and imagination. Trump may try to take America back to the old economy, but it's finished.

Taking the Torch

How can we in Canada tackle such huge issues? We can begin with small steps and learn from and build on our successes. That's what my story has been about. In my prologue I said I wanted to show how it is possible to make social change; to provide an insider's view, so to speak.

In my stories about Canada's first class-action suit, the Berger Inquiry, the National Energy Program, Section 35 of the Canadian constitution, the creation of the international criminal court, and even the development of the Vancouver Olympics and the BC movie industry, you saw, I hope, how what seemed impossible became possible with some vision, some idealism and a lot of creative thinking.

My message to young activists is that you can make a difference. But you have to rock the boat a bit, bite a few dogs. Embrace a cause and create a vision, the bigger the better. Based on that vision, use your imagination as well as effective tools—the law, politics, communications, education, even music—to achieve the goal. Don't forget a sense of humour, and never lose your passion.

I showed how I and others used the law as a tool to achieve social justice. I'm proud that the first class-action suit in Canada was one that benefited students, the unemployed and poor people against the arrogance of BC Hydro. Now class actions are everywhere in our legal system. That story also shows what a ragtag group of community lawyers could achieve when they tackled established power. The "rule of law" in Canada faces many current challenges, including delays and poor funding for legal aid. One goal for activists would be to make the legal system work for ordinary people again, giving them access to justice.

Farther afield, I wrote about my small role in the birth of the international criminal court. After surviving the Bush administration's early attempt to destroy it, the international criminal court remains a work-in-progress, but the political lessons in its creation are universal. First, you need a champion with a vision—in this case, Professor Cherif Bassiouni. Second, you need a game plan. A few MPs get involved and informed; a small staff and a group like Parliamentarians for Global Action coordinate them. They raise the issue in speeches in parliament and write op-ed pieces, as I did in the *Globe and Mail*. Third, you receive some editorial endorsements (the *Times*, the *Globe*, the *Economist*) and start a discussion in the public sphere. Fourth, key government officials speak out in support (Barbara McDougall, Canada's external affairs minister, the German foreign minister) and others are lobbied. Fifth, history is cited (the Nuremberg trials) and current questions are offered answers (like Saddam Hussein, the Lockerbie bombing, international narcotics problems, Bosnia and ethnic cleansing, terrorism—all of which could be dealt with by an international court). Finally, there is an opening, however brief, for new international institutions—in this case, the opening came as the Cold War ended. All this can be used again as a roadmap for achieving change.

You don't have to reinvent the wheel. I hope this book has set out some universal tools that can be used to make change. As well, I tried to provide an inside look at events that actually changed Canadian history. You can add this information to your amazing new tools: the Internet and social media. These tools allow you to brand your cause and reach millions of people, including politicians at all levels of government and activists in every country in an instant. But be cautious: technology is advancing and changing rapidly, and you want to be sure it doesn't end up controlling you.

As for me, the small and bewildered boy in a kilt who arrived in a new country on that snowy Toronto night, I'll keep going as long as I can. We are still building this country and we are not finished yet. But for you, the new generation, take the torch!

Acknowledgements

I'd like to acknowledge the following people in helping me create the book:

Rick Antonson, Audrey McClellan, Chris Gainor, Sharon Olsen, David Mossop, Jack Woodword, Howard White, Silas White, Zoe Grams, Ustin Vaskin, Joshua Berson, Steve Goudge, Diana Crosby, Colin Edmundson, Roger Larry, Blaine Culling and Leonard Schein.